THE TRAMWAYS OF SOUTH LONDON AND CROYDON

by K.G. HARVIE

PART ONE: SOUTH EAST LONDON TRAMW

The London County Council became a tramway operator on January 1st, 1899 and five years later the first electric tramway service in South East London commenced operation. Since that time the electric tramcar has proved a faithful friend to this district and has played a vital part in the life of the community.

This survey seeks to tell, in chronological order, the story of the tramways during the years 1899 to 1949.

HORSE TRAMWAYS

On January 1st, 1899 the London County Council acquired the horse tramways of the London Tramways Company, which had been formed in 1873 by the amalgamation of two smaller companies. The first stretch of horse tramway in S.E. London was opened between Blackheath Hill and New Cross Gate on December 13th, 1870.

Further sections were opened as follows:-

Deptford Bridge - Christ Church, East Greenwich (March 4th, 1871);
New Cross Gate - Old Kent Road at Peckham Park Road (May 1st, 1871), extended to Bricklayers' Arms (July 2nd, 1871);
Bricklayers' Arms - Blackfriars Road at Stamford Street (September 6th 1871);
St. George's Circus, Southwark - Westminster Bridge Road, and
Elephant & Castle - Camberwell Green (September 25th, 1871);
Camberwell Green - New Cross Gate (January 29th, 1872);
Camberwell Green - Vauxhall Station (L. & S.W.R.) (April 15th, 1872);
Elephant & Castle - St. George's Church, Borough (August 1874);
Great Dover Street (December 28th, 1874).

The London Tramways Company operated double-track routes from East Greenwich through New Cross to Westminster Bridge Road (white cars), Blackfriars Road (brown cars), and St. George's Church, Borough (yellow cars) via both Old Kent Road and Walworth Road, and from Victoria Station to Vauxhall Bridge (red cars); also a single-track route with passing loops from Vauxhall Station to Camberwell Green (green cars).

Depots were situated at Walworth Road (opposite East Street), Camberwell Green, Peckham (Bellenden Road (X) and Queen's Road Station), Great Dover Street, Old Kent Road (Bowles Road (X) and Leo Street), Greenwich Road (X) and Old Woolwich Road.

(X) - these yards are still used for permanent way work, stores and supplies, etc. by London Transport Tramways). The siding off Greenwich Road leads to Deptford Wharf on Deptford Creek, where supplies and materials for the tramways can be unloaded from Thames barges and conveyed thence by L.C.C. works cars. Camberwell Depot was rebuilt by the L.C.C. to house electric tramcars, while Leo Street Depot was converted into the L.C.C.T. Central Stores Department in 1905, but the premises were sold in 1928, after the new Central Stores Department was opened at Charlton Works.

The London Tramways Company also operated routes from London to Tooting and Streatham, the latter being worked by cable traction between Kennington and Streatham from December 19th, 1892.

On becoming a tramway operator in 1899 the London County Council introduced better pay and working conditions for the tramwaymen with a shorter working week of 60 hours, while the travelling public benefited from cheaper fares. The L.C.C. started all-night services between Blackfriars Road and New Cross Gate (via both Old Kent Road and Walworth Road) on February 12th, 1899.

Four smaller horse tramways also served South East London. These were the companies:-

The Southwark and Deptford Company

First section opened on November 28th, 1880. Routes: Tooley Street - High Street, Deptford (via Rotherhithe); Bricklayers' Arms - Grange Road - Blue Anchor Road (Southwark Park Road) - Raymouth Road - Rotherhithe New Road; also along Spa Road, St. James's Road, Rotherhithe New Road (all single track with passing loops). The depot - in Evelyn Street, Deptford - was later used by the L.C.C.T. to house trailer cars. This system was taken over by the L.C.C. on July 7th, 1904.

The London, Camberwell and Dulwich Company

Single line with passing loops, opened about 1885, from Peckham via Brayard's Road, Choumert Road, Adys Road, Crystal Palace Road to the 'Plough', Dulwich, with a branch to Peckham Rye. The depot was in East Dulwich Road by the 'King's Arms'. The service worked only spasmodically for some years. The system was acquired by the L.C.C. on August 15th, 1904, but the tracks were abandoned in 1906, apart from the sections in East Dulwich Road and Lordship Lane which were reconstructed for electric traction.

The South Eastern Metropolitan Company

Single line with passing loops, opened on October 11th, 1890, from Greenwich Station (S.E.R.) to Lewisham Obelisk, extended to

St. Laurence's Church, Catford. 'Chain Horses' ('Cock Horses') assisted the tram horses up Lewisham Road. The car livery was white. The depot - in Rushey Green, Catford - is used as a motor coach station today. The through fare on the horse trams was 2d. single.

The Woolwich and South East London Company

Narrow gauge route (3ft. 6ins.), mainly single track and loops, opened on June 4th, 1881, from St. Nicholas's Church, Plumstead to Christ Church, Trafalgar Road, East Greenwich, where it met the route of the London Tramways Company. Through running to London was impossible owing to the narrower gauge made necessary by the width of the Woolwich streets. 'Chain Horses' (Cock Horses) were used on Church Street hill, Woolwich. Another line traversed Powis Street. The depot - in Lakedale Road, Plumstead - remains intact today. A special feature was the 'Dinner Hour' cheap return fare available between 1.0 p.m. and 2.0 p.m. which benefited the workers at Woolwich Arsenal.

When the L.C.C. wished to purchase this horse tramway the Woolwich company demanded an exorbitant sum, which the L.C.C. rightly refused to pay. After getting the purchase price reduced to a reasonable amount by successful legal action, the L.C.C. took over the system on June 1st, 1905.

THE LONDON COUNTY COUNCIL AND THE CONDUIT SYSTEM

The London County Council decided to acquire all the tramways in the County and electrify them wherever possible. The overhead system of current collection was the cheapest and most reliable, but opposition from certain metropolitan boroughs on so-called "aesthetic" grounds compelled the L.C.C. to largely adopt the underground conduit system, despite the greater expenditure and road excavation involved. Water and gas mains had to be diverted; some roads had to be closed until work was completed. Main roads were far narrower fifty years ago, and their present widths result from the construction of the L.C.C. Tramways. Pavements were cut back and, in some cases, gardens - as in the High Road, Lee.

Double track tramways were reconstructed for electric traction as follows: First the down line was converted. The horse trams were diverted to the up line, along which temporary passing places were installed at intervals. Afterwards the horse trams used the new down line while the up line was converted. Interruption of the horse tramway services was thereby avoided.

(The conduit system employs a slot conduit between the running rails within which parallel conductor rails of T-section are carried on porcelain insulators. The tramcar collects electric current from these conductors by copper brushes (or cast-iron shoes) on a wood and aluminium plough (which slides laterally on the tramcar's carrier frame), through which it is transmitted to the tramcar's electric motors).

THE INAUGURATION OF ELECTRIC TRACTION

During 1900 conduit track was laid in Camberwell Depot yard and the following year an electric tramcar was demonstrated to an august assembly of London municipal dignitaries. The L.C.C. Chief Officer (Tramways) from 1899 to 1903 was Alfred Baker Esq., who left to become the General Manager of Birmingham Corporation Tramways. He was succeeded by A.L.C. Fell Esq., who superintended the electrification of the tramways and served the L.C.C.T. until 1924, his position being redesignated Tramways Manager, then General Manager from 1922.

On May 15th, 1903 the L.C.C.'s first electric tramway was opened from Westminster Bridge Road to Tooting by H.R.H. the Prince of Wales (afterwards King George V), who drove a decorated white tramcar from Belvedere Road. Princess May and their sons, Prince Edward and Prince Albert, were among the distinguished passengers.

The Kennington - Camberwell route was doubled and reopened for electric traction on June 25th; the Kennington - Vauxhall route on August 2nd. A temporary power station was provided at Loughborough Junction until a permanent power station was completed near Grosvenor Road, Pimlico.

South East London's first electric tramway services commenced in 1904 with routes from Westminster Bridge, Waterloo Station and Blackfriars Road to New Cross Gate and Trafalgar Road, East Greenwich via Old Kent Road on January 17th and via Walworth Road on January 24th. From Bricklayers' Arms routes were opened to Southwark Bridge on August 1st and Tower Bridge on September 19th.

The tramcars, which were painted chocolate and cream, had open tops and reversed staircases. Class A (Nos. 1-100) were bogie cars mainly operating in S.W. London. Cars on local routes were mostly four-wheelers of Class B (Nos. 102-201) and Class C (Nos. 202-301) temporarily housed at Rye Lane Depot, Peckham until New Cross Depot, the largest in London, housing 326 tramcars, was completed in 1906. At the former horse depot at Rye Lane the tramcars were moved by means of an over-running trolley on overhead wires connected to the car by a long lead. New Cross Depot, however, was equipped for conduit operation from the first. Another hundred bogie tramcars, Class D (Nos. 302-401), were built during 1904/1905.

On June 17th, 1905 the L.C.C. steamboat service on the River Thames was inaugurated by H.R.H. The Prince of Wales, who travelled from Westminster Pier by special steamer to Greenwich Pier, accompanied by the two young Princes. His return journey to London was made in the special decorated white tramcar, which he drove from King William Street, Greenwich. Special tickets were issued on the steamboats, available for return by tramcar. Unfortunately the steamers, unlike the trams, were not a financial success, partly due to foggy winters and a wet summer, and they were withdrawn after the Summer of 1907.

A new electric tram route from New Cross down Loampit Hill to Lewisham Obelisk was opened on January 30th, 1906 and extended along Rushey Green to St. Laurence's Church, Catford on June 10th. The Greenwich route was extended along Woolwich Road as far as the corner of Tunnel Avenue and Horn Lane on the same day, while a branch along Blackwall Lane to Blackwall Tunnel was opened on June 18th. The new L.C.C. Tramways Power Station had been opened with much ceremony on May 26th, 1906, at Old Woolwich Road, Greenwich.

At this time there was a dispute in the Council whether Lee Green or Rotherhithe should be the next district to be served by electric tramways. The Lee Green party won the day and reconstruction of the High Road, Lee commenced, a new sewer being laid and horse 'buses diverted meanwhile from Lee Green via Burnt Ash Road, Southbrook Road, Leahurst Road, Eastdown Park and Gilmore Road to Lewisham. (Rotherhithe had to wait until 1911 for electric trams). A new route from New Cross via Brockley was also approved.

Several incidents concerning the new Lewisham electric tram route may be of interest. At Greenwich Police Court on April 17th, 1906 a motor car driver was fined 40/- for obstructing a tramcar in Lewisham High Road for seven minutes, while two men were fined 2/- each for spitting in a tramcar in New Cross Road. On March 15th, 1907 a tramcar ran off the end of the line at Catford terminus about 6.30 p.m. leaving its plough in the conduit slot. The disabled car was towed back to New Cross Depot. On April Fools' Day the tram service in Rushey Green, Catford was held up while a boy's iron hoop was removed from the conduit slot. It was a favourite prank of mischievous boys in those days to drop their hoops down the slot.

CROSSING THE BRIDGES

At this period a great tramway controversy raged in Parliament. The L.C.C. sought powers to extend the tramways over the Thames bridges to give South London direct access to the City and West End. They received the wholehearted support of the Liberal Government, but were fanatically opposed by the Tories, as transport became the victim of political wrangling on this, as on many subsequent, occasions. Sir Edward Coates, Conservative M.P. for Lewisham, alone voted against his own party, rightly putting the welfare of his constituents before party loyalties.

The L.C.C. bill was successful and on August 5th, 1906 electric trams were extended across Vauxhall Bridge to Victoria Station and on December 15th over Westminster Bridge and along Victoria Embankment to John Carpenter Street, Blackfriars.

Top covers with end balconies were being fitted to many tramcars at this time. This work began in 1905 and lasted until 1910, after which Classes A to D were fitted with fully-enclosed top decks at the Works. During this interim period the suffix 1 was added to the class letter of balcony cars, the suffix 2 to that of enclosed cars with reversed staircases, and the suffix 3 to that of enclosed cars with direct stairs. Open-top cars with trolley poles received the suffix 4, any remaining open-top cars being known by the class letter only. (e.g. A/2, B/4, C/1, D/3, etc.) At this time some cars were still running with reversed staircases, but gradually all were fitted with normal quarter-turn stairs.

Kingsway Tramway Subway, the underground link with North London, (opened between Bloomsbury and Aldwych on February 24th, 1906) was completed in 1908 and the first trams between Bloomsbury and Victoria Embankment ran on April 10th. Two tramway stations were provided in the Subway at High Holborn and Aldwych and there was a triangular junction at Victoria Embankment, the eastern curve of which was rarely used and was removed in 1930. Owing to a Board of Trade regulation, only tramcars of steel construction were allowed to operate passenger services through Kingsway Subway, in order to obviate risk of fire. The dimensions of the Subway were smaller than now, and for the next twenty years single-deck bogie tramcars of Classes F & G (Nos. 552-601) worked mostly between Highbury and Westminster or Elephant and Castle, though there were several experimental changes of route and southern termini over the years.

On September 14th, 1909 the Lord Mayor of London drove the first tramcar (E/1 Class No.1032) (suitably decorated) over Blackfriars Bridge amid scenes of pageantry. This new line was the property of the City Corporation, but was leased to the L.C.C. Tramways and worked by them. Tramway services (including all-night cars) previously terminating at Stamford Street were extended over Blackfriars Bridge to John Carpenter Street - some as far as Waterloo Bridge.

HILLY ROUTES

A new L.C.C.T. conduit route, operated by Camberwell Depot, opened up a fresh approach to Dulwich. On November 19th, 1906 electric trams were extended from Camberwell Green via Denmark Hill, Dog Kennel Hill (previously a narrow country lane) and Lordship Lane to Dulwich Library. A branch from Goose Green via East Dulwich Road to Peckham Rye (Stuart Road) was opened on November 28th, 1907. An extension from Dulwich Library brought the trams to Forest Hill Station (London Road) on December 19th, 1908.

All tramcars of the B & C Classes operating these routes were fitted with special track brakes so that they might negotiate the steep hills between Camberwell Green and Forest Hill in safety. However, there were a few cases of C Class tramcars ascending Dog Kennel Hill which ran back and hit tramcars waiting at the bottom, the first being in 1907.

The Board of Trade ruled that only one tramcar should ascend and one descend Dog Kennel Hill at a time. This caused delays during rush hours and the L.C.C. obtained powers to lay two additional tracks to speed up traffic. These were constructed in 1912, opening on May 6th, and so the unique four-track layout came into being, two ascending and two descending trams now being permitted on the hill together.

KENTISH DEVELOPMENTS

New Cross tramcars commenced electric operation on the Lewisham -Greenwich route on April 4th, 1908 and opened new extensions from Lewisham Clock Tower to Lee Green on May 4th, 1907 and along Woolwich Road to Rainton Road on July 22nd, 1909. At this spot the L.C.C. erected the Central Repair Depot to service all their tramcars; the first buildings were opened in August 1908, other premises being added subsequently. Here major overhauls were carried out and new tramcars assembled. A siding from the S.E. & C.R. Angerstein Wharf branch brought materials direct to the Works by rail. Tramcars were shunted around the works yard by a L.C.C. 0-4-0 steam tank locomotive, obtained secondhand from Beckton Gas Works, but in later years tractors were employed to do this job.

Electric trams could not reach Woolwich at first because of narrow streets. Beyond Woolwich, Bexley Urban District Council's electric tramways, which used the overhead system, were opened on October 3rd, 1903. Their brown and cream four-wheel tramcars ran from Bexley Heath to the 'Plume of Feathers', Plumstead and to Northumberland Heath. Dartford U.D.C's maroon tramcars from Bexley Heath to Horns Cross started running on February 14th, 1906. They also worked a branch from Wilmington to Dartford Station (S.E. & C.R.), crossing the main route and continuing to the depot. Erith U.D.C. opened its overhead route from Abbey Wood via Belvedere and Erith to Northumberland Heath on August 22nd, 1905. By agreement with Bexley, Erith's green and cream tramcars were permitted to work through to Bexley Heath Market Place.

The L.C.C. acquired the line between the 'Plume of Feathers' and Wickham Lane, Plumstead from Bexley U.D.C. and opened an overhead electric route from Beresford Square, Woolwich on April 17th, 1908 (replacing the horse trams). Owing to the narrow streets there were numerous sections of single track. Twelve open-top B/4 Class tramcars fitted with trolley poles operated temporarily from Lakedale Road Depot, Plumstead; later they were joined by four open-top D/4 Class cars also fitted with trolley poles. Bexley U.D.C's tramcars were granted through running powers over the L.C.C.T. to Beresford Square, Woolwich.

On July 26th, 1908 the L.C.C. trams were extended to Abbey Wood, where a new depot was being erected - this was opened in April 1910. Nearby was the terminus of the Erith Council trams, but no connection existed and the L.C.C. never allowed them on its Woolwich route. The horse trams from Beresford Square to Woolwich Free Ferry were replaced by electric trams on November 30th, 1909. The overhead standards from Woolwich to Abbey Wood were elaborately decorated with scrollwork on their crossbars and with cast-iron bases.

NEW TRAMCARS

In 1906 the L.C.C. introduced Class E, a fine new design of double-deck tramcar, supplied by Hurst Nelson & Co. Ltd., of Motherwell. The top deck was totally enclosed and normal quarter-turn stairs were provided. At first, no doors were fitted on the top deck, but the resulting draughts soon brought the provision of glass screens and doors upstairs. Three hundred E Class tramcars (Nos.402-551; 602-751) were built before an improved design known as Class E/1 was evolved.

Class E/1 proved so successful that a thousand tramcars of this design were built between 1907 and 1922, forming the backbone of the L.C.C. tramcar fleet. Hurst Nelson received an order for 250 E/1 Class tramcars (Nos. 752-1001) in 1907 and delivered parts for fifty more in 1908 (Nos. 1002-1051), which the L.C.C.T. assembled. Subsequently they supplied Nos. 1052-1206 during 1908/9, Nos. 1477-1676 in 1910 and Nos. 1727-1801 in 1922. The Brush Electrical and Engineering Co. Ltd., of Loughborough supplied Nos. 1207-1426 in 1910 and Nos. 1802-1851 in 1922. At first, the E/1s were equipped with two 42 h.p. motors and seated 78 passengers on two longitudinal wooden seats in the lower saloon and transverse wooden slatted seats upstairs, but Nos. 1727-1851 were supplied new with two 60 h.p. motors in 1922.

The fact that many E/1s have seen over 35 years' continuous service (1949) witnesses to their sound construction. Their popularity led the L.C.C. to introduce all these improvements to the rest of the tramcar fleet. Top decks were enclosed and normal stairs with doors and draught screens were fitted to all tramcars as they passed through the Works for customary overhaul. Whenever the L.C.C.T. introduced an innovation which proved a success it became standard for all tramcars.

It should be mentioned that several municipal tramways began fitting glass windscreens to the driving platforms of their tramcars during the years 1910-1914, but unfortunately the Metropolitan Police refused to allow windscreens to be fitted to London tramcars and omnibuses and remained adamant on this subject until 1930, when relaxation of this rule allowed the L.C.C.T. to begin fitting windscreens to its tramcars.

L.C.C. TRAMWAY SERVICES IN 1909

The following tramway services were operated by the L.C.C. in S.E. London during the Summer of 1909. The services were grouped into routes for administrative purposes, but no route numbers were carried on tramcars, though the services were denoted by a three-colour light code shown above the destination boxes at night.

Route 15:	(RGR)	Highbury Station - Tower Bridge via Kingsway Subway.
16:	(-B-)	Woolwich Road (Rainton Road), Charlton - Waterloo Bridge (Savoy Street) via Kennington.
17:	(WWW)	Woolwich Road, Charlton - Blackfriars Road) via
	(W-W)	New Cross Gate - Waterloo Station) Old Kent
		'Marquis of Granby' - Blackfriars Road) Road (all-night service).
18:	(-W-)	Blackwall Tunnel - Savoy Street via Old Kent Road & Westminster.
19:	(B-B)	Lee Green - Waterloo Station) via Walworth Road.
	(BBB)	New Cross Gate - Blackfriars Road)
20:	(-R-)	St. Laurence's Church, Catford - Southwark Bridge via Old Kent Road (rush hours and Saturdays only).
	(-R-)	New Cross Gate - Southwark Bridge (daily service).
	(RRG)	Catford - South Street, Greenwich.
		Catford - Elephant & Castle (Sundays only).
21:	(WWB)	St. Laurence's Church, Catford - Victoria Station via Lewisham.
	(WWB)	Rye Lane, Peckham - Victoria (rush hours only).
22:	(GRR)	Peckham Rye - John Carpenter Street via Westminster.
	(WRG)	Dulwich Library - Victoria Embankment (weekdays).
	(BWR)	Dulwich Library - Southwark Bridge (rush hours only).
23:	(W-W)	Forest Hill Station - Victoria Station via Dulwich.
31:		Deptford (High Street) - Tooley Street;
		St. James's Church - Bricklayers' Arms via Spa Road;
(horse services)		Rotherhithe ('Red Lion') - Bricklayers' Arms via Southwark Park Road;
		Canal Bridge, Old Kent Road - Rotherhithe New Road.
32:		Rainton Road, Charlton - Beresford Square, Woolwich (horse traction);
	(W-W)	Beresford Square - Abbey Wood (overhead electric traction).

(Colour-code reference:-
B - blue; G - green; R - red; W - white;

blank or black shown thus - e.g. (---).

The white code sometimes appeared as yellow and the blue as purple, depending upon the state of the electric light bulbs and the glass shades used in the destination boxes.

A UNIQUE SYSTEM

Another overhead electric route was opened on July 23rd, 1910 from Beresford Square, Woolwich to Eltham Church. Unlike the usual overhead trolley system, two wires (positive and negative) were provided for each track, as Greenwich Observatory was afraid of electrical interference with its delicate magnetic instruments, had the tram rails been used as a return for the current. The overhead standards were of the same decorated style used on the main line to Abbey Wood.

The Eltham route was of a rural character, and one fare stage was known simply by the number painted on the appropriate overhead standard, which stood in open heathland! At the Woolwich end there is a one-way system passing Woolwich Barracks (in via Grand Depot Road, out via New Road), followed by a loop via Thomas Street, Green's End, through Beresford Square, then round into New Road again. At Beresford Square the line passes through the market and there is a connection with the Abbey Wood route. At first, the double-trolley system extended round the Beresford Square loop, but after 1914 the double-trolley system from Eltham Church ended at Anglesea Road crossover and the trams used only one trolley pole round the loop, the other pole being hooked down out of use.

Abbey Wood Depot worked the service with four-wheel tramcars of Class M, equipped with two trolley poles. Class M was the improved version of the four-wheel tramcar and one hundred were built: No.1427, the prototype car, was built by the L.C.C. but Hurst Nelson supplied Nos. 1428-1476; some worked in the Woolwich district, others on the Highgate Hill route in North London. The Brush Company supplied Nos. 1677-1726, some of which also worked on the Dulwich routes.

A new conduit route from Lewisham High Road to Brockley Cross was opened on February 26th, 1910, the up line running along Shardeloes Road while the down line uses Malpas Road. This was extended on February 25th, 1911 to Forest Hill Station (L.B. & S.C.R.) at Perry Vale terminus. The basic service operated between Forest Hill and John Carpenter Street, Blackfriars via Walworth Road (colour-code: (BBB), with rush-hour workings to Southwark Bridge.

POLICE OPPOSITION AND TRAMWAYMEN'S WELFARE

The L.C.C. Tramways encountered much opposition from the Metropolitan Police, who unfortunately seem to have been very obstructive. They objected to regular stopping places (as these would cause crowds to gather), passenger shelters and loading islands; they disliked supervised queueing, also the provision of used ticket boxes, route maps and advertisements inside tramcars.

Tramwaymen were persecuted by the Police, who lurked about with stop-watches waiting to catch speeding tram drivers (legal tramcar speeds were ridiculously low). In April 1905 two tram drivers were fined £1 each with costs for exceeding 10 m.p.h. in Greenwich Road, at a time when wages were about 30/- for a 60-hour week. At Greenwich Police Court on May 24th, 1907 a tram driver was fined for bringing his car too close to the rear of another tram, while on May 31st another tram driver was fined £1 with 2/- costs for 'excessive speed' in Woolwich Road.

Magistrates were usually 'carriage folk' who preferred horses; they were often hostile to electric trams as well as to motor cars and omnibuses, whose drivers were frequently summoned for speeding, dangerous driving and noise. (Early motor 'buses were unreliable and in 1913, for instance, there were several local cases when the steering gear failed and omnibuses mounted the pavement, as in Old Kent Road, or hit other vehicles). The London County Council treated its tramway staff with more consideration than many transport operators, especially the omnibus companies.

Despite police opposition, the L.C.C. did obtain powers to erect shelters for tramway passengers and on local routes these were provided at Westminster Bridge, Blackfriars Bridge, Camberwell Green and New Cross Gate during 1911, and later at Goose Green (East Dulwich) and Eltham Church (1912) and Abbey Wood (1913).

During 1904 the Vicar of St. Mark's Church, Kennington founded a Tramwaymen's Brotherhood at his church. Besides catering for the men's spiritual needs and holding special services, the Brotherhood arranged social functions, with outings to Brighton and other seaside resorts and to beauty spots in the Home Counties for tramwaymen and their families. Later, membership was broadened to include busmen and taxi-drivers; unfortunately the Brotherhood declined in London Transport days and seems to have petered out during the 1939-1945 War. An annual service for tram-men and busmen is still held, however, at Upper Holloway Baptist Church on Route 35 (1949).

The L.C.C. Tramways Employees' Mutual Loan and Investment Society was founded on December 6th, 1911, with its registered office in New Cross Road.

'BLACK SPOTS'

Two tramcars from New Cross Depot were involved in serious accidents during 1911. On May 16th a tramcar nearing Lee Green terminus left the rails at Quaggy Bridge corner and crashed into a toyshop. Traffic was held up for nearly an hour until the Police had completed their investigations. As a result of this accident, the row of shops was demolished and the Imperial Picture House - now called the Savoy Cinema - was built on the site, opening in 1913.

On September 2nd, 1911 B Class Tramcar No.110 on the Forest Hill - Southwark Bridge service, in charge of a learner driver and instructor, ran down the slope in Shardeloes Road, Brockley and, after derailment, shot across Lewisham High Road and turned over on its side. One passenger was fatally injured of the 42 on board. Another accident occurred at the same corner on October 31st, 1912, when the conductor and 19 passengers were injured. As a result, property was acquired to widen Shardeloes Road corner and a curve of greater radius was laid into Lewisham High Road. Tramcars were ordered by the Board of Trade to stop twice before taking the junction, hence the two signs "ALL CARS STOP HERE" placed close together at this point along the route.

During the morning rush-hour on February 4th, 1913 traffic was delayed for twenty minutes when two tramcars from Lee Green bound for Waterloo Station collided in Loampit Vale, Lewisham, the front car being badly damaged. Another collision between two tramcars occurred in Loampit Vale on June 20th, 1914.

Just before 5 o'clock on Saturday afternoon, June 28th, 1913 a tramcar going towards Greenwich ran off the line at Blackheath Road/ Greenwich Road corner and the New Cross breakdown gang was called out to rerail it. 1913 seems to have been rather an unlucky year for the Lee Green route as a down car was derailed at the Clock Tower, Lewisham on September 18th, causing an hour delay, while on October 10th another tramcar bound for Lee Green terminus was derailed further along the High Road, Lee, where the P.W. gang was working on the track.

A temporary breakdown at Greenwich Power Station on March 21st, 1913 brought 119 tramcars in South London to a standstill, but this fault was soon rectified. Another breakdown on April 18th lasted two hours from 9.0 a.m. until 11.0 a.m. The L.C.C. burnt a certain amount of imported foreign coal, which sometimes was cheaper than British coal, but at times the quality was inferior and caused trouble in the boilers. During coal strikes the workers objected to the use of imported fuel and in May 1921 they refused to handle Belgian coal and 200 men walked out. The L.C.C. had to use oil fuel and employ naval ratings to keep the trams moving.

RIVERSIDE DEVELOPMENTS

Electric trams replaced horse trams between Tooley Street (Bermondsey Street) and Surrey Docks Station (E.L.R.) on February 25th, 1911. They were extended to Greenwich Church (St. Alfege's or St. Alphege's) on August 5th, but passengers had to alight on either side of Deptford Creek and walk across, as Creek Bridge was under reconstruction. (The service on the east side operated to Chapel Street, Woolwich). Trams first carried passengers across the new Creek Bridge on October 30th, 1912.

In Tooley Street the route was extended to London Bridge Station on December 9th on the understanding that this section was only to be used during weekday rush hours and evenings and on Saturdays and Sundays. During the day trams terminated at Bermondsey Street, owing to congestion from heavy dock traffic in Tooley Street to and from the wharves.

In 1913 the Tooley Street service (by then No.70) was extended from Greenwich Church to Chapel Street, Woolwich on Saturdays and Sundays, but was soon curtailed, as the cars frequently derailed on the sharp curve at Greenwich from Church Street into Nelson Street.

During 1914 three petrol-electric cars ran on the Tooley Street route experimentally for about three months; they operated from Evelyn Street Depot, Deptford. (The electric tramcars for this route have always operated from New Cross Depot).

All L.C.C. tramway services were reduced temporarily from March 25th, 1912, owing to the month-old Coal Strike, which lasted until April 6th.

The Woolwich Road route was extended on April 1st, 1911 from Rainton Road, Charlton to Chapel Street, Woolwich. Horse trams worked a shuttle service between Chapel Street and Woolwich Free Ferry, whence electric trams ran to Abbey Wood. A standard-gauge wagon fitted with narrow-gauge track and a lifting ramp was used to transport the horse tramcars between Lakedale Road Depot, Plumstead and the remaining stretch of horse tramway in Woolwich.

Considerable road widening had been necessary for the electric extension, especially alongside Woolwich Dockyard, and near Charlton Lane a house and garden lay right in the way of the down line. As the lease was running out, the L.C.C. bided their time. Meanwhile, the trams came nearly up to the garden fence, reversed on to the up line, passed by the house and regained the down line beyond! Double track was opened here on November 5th, 1911.

Three years elapsed before the gap at Woolwich was eliminated, owing to the widening involved in Church Street and High Street. The last horse tram in Woolwich ran on November 24th, 1913 and eventually through electric tramway services between Victoria Embankment and Abbey Wood commenced on April 5th, 1914, cars changing from conduit to overhead trolley operation at Woolwich Free Ferry: E/1 Class tramcars were used. Abbey Wood Depot had been enlarged in November 1913 to house the new services. A lay-by was installed at St. Nicholas's Church, Plumstead during 1914, being ready for use on August 9th. The 1914-1919 War delayed the fitting of trolley poles on

Classes A, D & E until 1920, after which these tramcars joined the E/1s on the Abbey Wood route.

Dr. John Wilson, the Scottish minister of Woolwich Baptist Tabernacle from 1877 to 1938, was so well-loved and respected in Woolwich that the tram drivers always slowed down on Sundays during service times when passing his church in Beresford Street. (The L.C.C.T. paved the tracks outside churches and hospitals with wood blocks instead of granite setts to reduce the noise).

Once he befriended a repentant drunk and saw him to a tramcar. But when the conductor refused to allow the man on his car Dr. Wilson said that he would be his surety and travelled the three miles to the man's home.

For fifty years Dr. Wilson and his family lived in an old double-fronted house (Montague House) on Woolwich Road, set in a beautiful secluded garden full of trees with a view across to the River Thames. He became a familiar figure on the trams as he travelled regularly between his home and his church and spoke many a good word to his fellow passengers and the crews.

When he returned to the Tabernacle after a serious illness in the 1920s the tram drivers always waited for him outside his gate - between two stopping places - until he was quite strong again.

At his Diamond Jubilee in 1937 Dr. Wilson was made a Freeman of the Borough of Woolwich as a tribute to his social work among its people.

CATFORD EXTENSIONS

From St. Laurence's Church, Catford a new conduit tramway was opened via Stanstead Road to Brockley Rise corner on May 29th, 1913. On opening day passengers were carried free, but the trams were so popular that many people were unable to board them.

The main Catford route was extended from St. Laurence's Church along Bromley Road to Southend Village on April 5th, 1914, terminating by the Pond at the corner of Beckenham Lane. Only a limited service was run beyond Bellingham Station at first, as track paving was not yet completed, but the full service began to operate to Southend Pond terminus from April 9th, 1914.

ATTRACTING THE PUBLIC

The L.C.C. policy - "Travel by Tramway for Cheapness and Comfort - for Business and Pleasure" - was a boon to Londoners. Cheap Workmen's fares enabled many people to move from inner London to the suburbs; local people could travel to London for business more easily. Cheap fares induced working people to relax in the Kent and Surrey countryside.

At public holidays and weekends, crowds alighted from trams at Bostall Hill, Eltham, Lee Green and Southend Village, eagerly anticipating pleasant walks in the surrounding fields and woods and by the peaceful waters of the Kid Brook and the Quaggy and Ravensbourne Rivers. Other folk preferred the sylvan charm of tranquil Dulwich.

The 1914 fare from London to suburban termini was 3d. single, 5d. return. Transfer facilities were generous; e.g. Lee Green to Lewisham Library 1d.; to Catford 1½d; to Southend Pond or Forest Hill Station 3d. return. The London General Omnibus Company and Thomas Tilling's motor 'buses offered violent competition, but they were unable to undercut the cheap L.C.C. tram fares (with the halfpenny minimum). A check of tram and bus passengers taken at New Cross Gate and the 'Marquis of Granby' during October 1913 showed that the proportion of tram passengers to bus passengers was five to one.

In 1909 and 1911 the L.C.C. published a 144-page tramways guide, price 1d. Unfortunately this was not a financial success, so they decided instead to publish a free route map with a list of tramway services. Route numbers were introduced in September 1912 to help the public. At first they were shown on metal plates hung from the canopies of the tramcars (in the centre until tall drivers complained, then moved to one side). Several experimental schemes were tried - Mr. A.W. Morant remembers seeing a No.56 crossing Westminster Bridge in 1913 with large stencils (similar to those introduced about 1929 on the new HR/2 and E/3 Class Tramcars). By 1914 the L.C.C.T. adopted black oblong stencils of the 'Venner' type, perforated with small holes in the shape of the route number, placed in front of a white oblong metal plate fixed in the rear and front upper-deck end windows and illuminated at night. (These are still used on original E/1 Class tramcars today (1949). Narrow route boards were carried outside the lower saloon windows, in addition to the roller blinds fitted in the end destination boxes. The first issue of the L.C.C. TRAMWAYS map was published in January 1913.

<u>L.C.C. TRAMWAY SERVICES IN 1914</u>

During the Summer of 1914 local electric tramway services were as follows:-

Route 33 : Highbury Station - Tower Bridge) via Kingsway
35 : 'Angel', Islington - Westminster Station) Subway
36 : Blackwall Lane (or Tunnel) - Victoria Embankment via Old Kent Road & Blackfriars; (extended to Abbey Wood on Sundays).
38 : Wickham Lane, Plumstead - Embankment via Old Kent Road & Westminster; (extended to Bexley Heath Market Place on Sundays).

Route 40 : Abbey Wood - Savoy Street via Kennington & Westminster.
42 : Abbey Wood - Woolwich Free Ferry.
44 : Eltham Church - Beresford Square, Woolwich.
46 : Lee Green - Waterloo Station via Walworth Road.
48 : Lee Green - Victoria Station (weekday rush hours, Saturdays & Sundays only).
50 : Blackwall Tunnel - Forest Hill Station via Catford.
52 : St. Laurence's Church, Catford - Southwark Bridge via Old Kent Road (rush hours only).
54 : Southend Village (Pond) - Victoria Station via Lewisham & Peckham.
56 : Peckham Rye - Savoy Street via Westminster.
58 : Forest Hill Station - Victoria via Dulwich.
60 : Dulwich Library - Southwark Bridge (rush hours only). (certain cars to Forest Hill: Mon. to Fri. afternoons).
62 : Dulwich Library - Savoy Street via Westminster; (certain cars to Forest Hill) (rush hours only).
64 : New Cross Gate - Waterloo Station (extended to Catford on Sunday afternoons & evenings).
66 : Forest Hill Station - Somerset House via Brockley & Blackfriars (weekdays); New Cross Gate - Blackfriars (Sundays only).
70 : Greenwich Church - Tooley Street, Bermondsey.
72 : Forest Hill Station - Southwark Bridge via Brockley (weekday rush hours, Saturdays and Sundays only).
84 : Rye Lane, Peckham - Embankment via Blackfriars (rush hours only).

All-night services (unnumbered) connected Victoria Embankment with New Cross via Blackfriars and Old Kent Road or Walworth Road. It was stated that all-night services did not pay but that they would be continued as they were a benefit to night workers, no alternative public transport being available.

Short workings of the main tram routes, extra workings and special cars usually displayed EX in place of a number stencil.

A lay-by was constructed in Harder's Road, Peckham during 1913 for No.84 trams; it was in regular use on August 19th, 1914.

Before 1920 many people worked much longer hours than nowadays and many shops remained open till 9 o'clock at night or even later. Consequently rush-hour travel on the tramways was spread over a longer period of time and rush-hour services operated earlier in the mornings and later in the evenings, and on Saturdays some ran for most of the day.

e.g. Service 52 : Last car (Mondays to Fridays) from Southwark Bridge:

1914	1922
11.18 p.m.	7.2 p.m.

TRAILER CARS

In order to deal with the huge crowds of workers during rush hours the L.C.C. obtained permission from the Board of Trade for open-top trailer cars to be attached to tramcars on certain busy routes in South London including Embankment - Abbey Wood; New Cross - Embankment circular services; Woolwich - Eltham; Greenwich Church - Tooley Street; and Southend Pond - Victoria Station. After successful experiments at Charlton Works, the first trailer cars commenced operation on Service 44 on March 9th, 1913 and Service 42 on June 7th, 1913. Eight horse cars had been converted into trailer cars (Nos. T1 - T8), but 150 new trailer cars were supplied by Brush during the next two years (Nos. T9 - T158). Lattice gates were fitted between the motor tram and the trailer to prevent anyone passing between the vehicles when they were coupled together.

FAREWELL TO THE HORSES

Two horse-tram routes still remained in the Rotherhithe area when the L.C.C. numbered its tramway services in September 1912. These were:-

Route 88 : 'Red Lion', Rotherhithe - Bricklayers' Arms
via Southwark Park Road.

Route 90 : 'Red Lion', Rotherhithe - Canal Bridge, Old Kent Road
via Rotherhithe New Road;
known locally as 'The Ha'penny Bumper'.

However, these were not destined to continue much longer. The Rotherhithe New Road service (90) ceased operation on July 12th, 1913. The Rotherhithe - Bricklayers' Arms service (88) kept going after the Great War broke out on August 4th, 1914 and achieved the distinction of being the last horse tramway route in London, finally closing on April 30th, 1915. Neither of these routes was ever electrified because of the War and the roads were covered by motorbus services.

THE 1914 - 1919 WAR

The L.C.C. Tramways Bills which were presented to Parliament during 1913-14 contained proposals for many routes which were never constructed, partly because of local or commercial opposition, but mainly because of the War. Routes proposed included many in the West

End and also Forest Hill - Crystal Palace via Dartmouth Road (meeting an extension from West Norwood); Herne Hill - Goose Green, East Dulwich; Catford Hill - Crystal Palace via Sydenham Road; Lee Green - Catford via Burnt Ash and Brownhill Roads; and Southend Village - Bromley. An earlier application for a tramway across Blackheath to Shooter's Hill had been unsuccessful.

The 1914-1919 War halted tramway extension, apart from a short link between London Road and Park Road, Forest Hill on August 13th, 1915. Waldram Road had to be lowered and widened under the railway bridge. Service 58 was extended to Blackwall Tunnel, No.50 becoming a rush-hour service.

During 1915 Services 42, 50 & 64 were withdrawn, also the Sunday extension of No.38 to Bexley Heath, but No.50 was reinstated later during the War as a basic service, No.58 being curtailed at St. Laurence's Church, Catford. Service 33 was also withdrawn and No.35 Highbury - Westminster became the only Subway service. Tower Bridge was served instead by a new No.68 to Waterloo Station. The Government requested the L.C.C. to suspend work on the Lee Green - Eltham and Southwark Park Road electric tramways, which had been authorised, for the duration of the War.

During the Summer of 1914 the L.C.C. had wanted to employ 'boy conductors' aged 16-21 on the Tooley Street trams, but the Union objected on behalf of its members at New Cross Depot. This scheme seems to have been dropped because of the War. However, women conductors were first employed on the L.C.C. Tramways on December 4th, 1915 and rendered yeoman service during the War.

Woolwich Borough Council decided in November 1914 to erect a weather shelter at Beresford Square costing £200, towards which the L.C.C. agreed to contribute £80.

On December 11th, 1914 there was a complete breakdown at Greenwich Power Station and L.C.C. tramway services were paralysed throughout most of South London for all of Friday evening and most of Saturday due to a switchgear fire. (The faulty equipment was due for replacement the following week). Widespread inconvenience was caused to thousands of homebound travellers, who had to find alternative means of transport. Tramcars were able to operate only between the Elephant & Castle and Lee Green and from Lewisham to Catford, as current for these routes came from Deptford Power Station. By Tuesday 1400 tramcars were operating, but full services could not be resumed until Thursday (December 17th).

Rifle ranges were installed at New Cross Depot and Charlton Works in January 1915 for military training.

During 1915 there were numerous complaints from the public about the Woolwich tram services. The War caused heavy traffic on these routes as crowds of munition workers flocked to Woolwich Arsenal. There were not enough cars operating, but the single-line sections reduced track capacity. The L.C.C.T. said in March 1915 that the Woolwich service was now 100% greater than in 1914. The Woolwich sub-station was being extended to provide more electric current.

To provide more tramcars for the Woolwich route, Service 48 (Lee Green - Victoria) was reduced in February 1915, while in June a shuttle service of two cars was put on between Lee Green and Lewisham only (Service 46) at certain hours of the day. This caused complaints by local residents, as did a subsequent reduction of the No.66 and 72 Forest Hill Services 'in the national interest'. From January 1st, 1917 all services (except Woolwich) were further reduced and fuel restrictions in 1918 caused even more reductions to tram services (except Woolwich,of course).

It seems that, during the latter part of the War Services 48 & 72 were temporarily withdrawn and that Service 46 was diverted via Old Kent Road to Southwark Bridge on weekdays, probably only at rush hours. On Sundays No.46 worked Lee Green - New Cross Gate only.

On May 14th, 1915 an unfortunate strike broke out at New Cross Depot and spread to Abbey Wood Depot. 6,437 men and over 200 tramcars were idle. Tramwaymen in the Armed Forces condemned the strike and the L.C.C. took decisive action in dismissing all strikers fit for military service. This caused the Strike to fizzle out and by June 2nd 90% of the normal tramway service was operating.

The problem of congestion on the Woolwich routes was now acute as this could adversely affect the war effort. So, at the request of the Government, the L.C.C. (with permission from the Woolwich Borough Council) doubled several sections of single line in Woolwich and Plumstead. From Beresford Square to Plumstead Station the track was doubled by September 1916 and further sections in Beresford Street and High Street, Plumstead (on either side of Lakedale Road) were doubled in July 1917. Facing crossovers were laid in Beresford Street and also between Lakedale Road and Wickham Lane, Plumstead to allow single-line working if one track was blocked by other vehicles. At many places there was not the statutory clearance between tram tracks and pavement, but this was permitted because of wartime exigency and no alteration has been made since.

Shacks were erected at Abbey Wood and on the slopes of Shooter's Hill for munition workers' families, thereby increasing traffic on Routes 36, 38, 40 and 44 respectively. On April 24th, 1915 one trolley pole of a No.44 tramcar crossing Woolwich Common stuck in the branches of a tree bordering Academy Road! The trailers helped to carry the wartime crowds, especially on Service 44 and Nos. 36 & 38, which had been combined to form a circular route between the Embankment and Abbey Wood.

Later in the War (at least from 1917), circular services using trailers were operated at rush hours between New Cross Gate and Victoria Embankment: No.64 via Old Kent Road, No.84 via Peckham & Walworth Road. In the mornings both services worked in via Blackfriars, out via Westminster; in the afternoons both services worked in via Westminster, out via Blackfriars - in order to provide direct services to and from Blackfriars for City workers. This arrangement continued until about 1920. Mr. A.W. Morant recollects a Saturday working of No.84 between Southend Pond and Elephant & Castle (via Peckham & Walworth Road) just after the War, on which trailer cars were used to move the crowds.

One day during the War a tramcar on the 36/38 route broke its coupling near the Elephant & Castle and proceeded for some distance towing a trailer several yards behind it by a pair of very extended lattice gates, before the driver became aware of the mishap! Commenting on a similar occurrence in High Street, Peckham, which held up the traffic, an angry omnibus driver shouted:
"Why don't you take that chicken-coop away and burn it?"

On August 7th, 1917 all Dartford Council's tramcars, which had carried huge Bank Holiday crowds the previous day, were destroyed in a depot fire. Henceforth Bexley Council worked their services and the L.C.C.T. supplied Bexley with some B Class four-wheel cars to keep full services running on the Woolwich - Dartford route, which also served Vickers' Works at Crayford.

At the suggestion of the Ministry of Munitions, thirty B Class tramcars, idle because of staff shortage, were sold to Southampton, Sheffield, Rotherham and Newport (Mon.) Corporation Tramways and others lent to, and later bought by, Bexley Council Tramways, making a total of 59 cars.

In 1915 Erith Council borrowed four open-top bogie tramcars from the London United Tramways, purchasing them in 1919 and reconstructing them in 1922. In 1916 Erith also bought a massive balcony bogie car from Hull Corporation Tramways, which was promptly nicknamed 'The Tank'.

The L.C.C. Tramways Department was re-organised in February 1917 into five branches: Traffic, Electrical, Rolling Stock, Permanent Way, and General Office. J.K. Bruce Esq., became Traffic Manager, while in June T.E. Thomas Esq., of the District Railway was appointed Development Superintendent of the L.C.C. Tramways.

Several L.C.C.T. technical officers were lent to the Ministry of Munitions. During the War at Charlton Works and some depots 18,300 gauges for field guns and 7,725 H.E. shells were manufactured for the Army, also 214 height measuring apparatus for aircraft work. In addition 36,039 extra shells were banded there.

There were not the same restrictions on holiday travel in the 1914-1919 War as in the 1939-1945 War. During a four-day omnibus strike at Whitsun 1917 two million more passengers travelled by L.C.C. tramcar on this sunny Bank Holiday. On Easter Monday 1915 £10,500 had been taken in fares, but the figure for Whit Monday 1917 reached £13,000. A child was born in a tramcar at Blackwall Lane, Greenwich on August 5th, 1917.

Travel facilities suffered and fares were increased because of the War. In May 1917 the 8d. through return fare to Bexley Heath from London termini was withdrawn; so were all ½d. fares and return tickets (except ½d. Child's ticket and Workmen's Returns). All transfer tickets were withdrawn in September, except on journeys where no through cars were run. In May 1918 the maximum single fare was raised to 4d., while the 2½d. fare and all children's fares were withdrawn in South London. The average distance for a penny journey was reduced from 2 miles to 1.8 miles. Canvas bags were provided on L.C.C. tramcars for used tickets from August 1918. During the same month women conductors on 'buses and trams went on strike for some days, but the men managed to keep the trams moving.

The explosion at Silvertown munitions factory on January 19th, 1917 shook up the whole of S.E. London: at first many folk thought that Woolwich Arsenal had been blown up. German air raids on London began in 1915, and to warn tramwaymen of imminent air raids the L.C.C.T. fitted blue lamps on the top of roadside feeder boxes. These were illuminated on the approach of Zeppelins or Gothas. Compensation was paid to families of staff killed or injured while on duty. The worst daylight raids over London by Gotha bombers were on Wednesday, June 13th; Friday, June 15th; and Saturday, July 7th, 1917. There were further air raids, mostly at night, in 1918, but the provision of more anti-aircraft guns, making a total of 284, and a balloon barrage helped to counter the German air menace. The air raids do not seem to have seriously disrupted tramway services in South East London, as regards actual damage, though the habit of sometimes cutting off the current during raids (on government instructions) caused considerable delays and public annoyance. Police on occasions limited the number of tramcars inside the Central London area; this led to queues of cars on the outskirts.

The author Edith Nesbit, who wrote 'The Railway Children', 'The Treasure Seekers' and many other children's books, lived at Well Hall in the Red House from 1899 to 1922. When the tramway service was suspended during air raids she would bring out cups of coffee for the crews of No.44 tramcars halted outside the gates of Well Hall. Once, watching a raid from the top deck of a tram, she saw the first Zeppelin shot down in flames.

Wartime arrears of maintenance, difficulty in obtaining new steel rails and special trackwork, and the shortage of expert staff led to an increase in tramway accidents. Unfortunately there were two serious accidents on the Abbey Wood route at this time. On July 24th, 1916 a tramcar overturned at the foot of the gradient in Basildon Road, so a compulsory stop was installed at the corner of McLeod Road. On December 8th, 1918 two tramcars were badly damaged when they collided at Abbey Wood terminus (Knee Hill).

Three times during the War trams left the rails in Church Street, Woolwich and hit the bird fancier's shop (No.43). In October 1915 trams were off the line at Kashgar Road loop, Plumstead twice within a few days; the first felled a tree, the second hit a house.

On September 16th, 1915 a lorry hit a tramcar ascending Albion Hill, Woolwich. The tram controller was smashed, the driver killed and the car ran back downhill and hit a stationary tram at the bottom. A munitions lorry sent a tram off the lines in High Street, Plumstead on October 30th.

Collisions between pairs of trams occurred on the single line in Beresford Street, Woolwich on June 7th, 1915; in Lewisham High Road (near Malpas Road) on Boxing Day 1916 in dense fog; at Rushey Green, Catford on September 9th, 1917; at Peckham in July 1918; at New Cross Gate on August 13th, 1918; at Greenwich Church on August 27th, 1918; and in Bromley Road (near Bellingham Station) on January 3rd, 1919. A New Cross - Embankment tramcar and trailer hit an Embankment - Woolwich car at St. George's Circus, Southwark on April 23rd, 1917.

At Forest Hill a No.50 tram left the lines at Sunderland Road corner on January 19th, 1918 and landed in a tree! On July 21st, a tram in McLeod Road, Abbey Wood ran off into an orchard, two passengers being injured. In this month Deptford Borough Council complained of tramlines in the borough being 'in a wicked state'. Accidents between tramcars and other vehicles were too numerous to mention, but generally the tram drivers were not to blame. On March 10th, 1919 a tram was off the line at Brockley Cross, while another jumped the points in Greenwich Road on May 26th, 1919.

In November 1918 Deptford Borough Council gave the L.C.C.T. permission to erect overhead wires at Evelyn Street Depot to obviate shunting trailer cars with horses; an over-running trolley on the over-head was now used.

On Armistice Day: November 11th, 1918, workers leaving Woolwich Arsenal at 11.0 a.m. thronged London-bound trams. This was the most crowded day on the L.C.C. Tramways to date.

On Sunday, December 12th, 1920, after a ceremony at the new Cenotaph in Whitehall, L.C.C. Tramwaymen attended a Memorial Service for their Fallen Comrades in Westminster Abbey.

A war memorial window dedicated to the memory of the L.C.C. Tramwaymen who gave their lives in the 1914-1919 War was placed in St. Mark's Church, Kennington; it depicted a driver and a conductor with a L.C.C. tramcar. Unfortunately it was badly damaged during the 1940-41 air raids and was put in the crypt.

PEACETIME PROGRESS

During April 1919 the track in South Street, Greenwich was doubled in several places. From July 1st, 1919 Children's Fares were restored (1d. minimum, 2d. maximum).

Special trams ran on Peace Day, July 19th, 1919, many carrying crowds to watch the Victory Procession of Allied Troops through London to The Mall, where they were reviewed by T.M. King George V and Queen Mary. (While the procession was passing along Westminster Bridge Road and over Westminster Bridge the trams had to turn back at the Elephant & Castle and crossovers in Kennington Road, Lambeth Palace Road and Lambeth Road).

There was a railway strike between September 27th and October 6th, 1919. Tramway traffic increased thereby and there were long queues of passengers at Blackfriars, Westminster Bridge and other important stops.

(It seems that during the War the rush-hour cars on Route 46 were diverted to Southwark Bridge and this became a regular weekday working in 1919).

Trailer cars were withdrawn on most L.C.C. tram routes in S.E. London during 1919, as they caused traffic delays, but they still ran on Route 70 for a few more years.

(On July 31st, 1919 a passenger riding in a tram in High Street, Lewisham complained of an electric shock. Two trams collided outside the New Cross Empire on August 16th, while on November 20th a New Cross - Westminster car collided with a Lewisham - St. George's Church car in Old Kent Road. During bad weather in July 1920 three trams from New Cross to Forest Hill ran into each other at Brockley Cross; another tram had been derailed there on March 8th. During P.W. works in Lewisham High Road (near Breakspears Road) a tram was derailed on May 17th, 1920 and its rear bogie was stuck in the excavation for two hours).

The public complained about the rough riding of many tramcars, especially the four-wheelers, and the infrequency of some tram services - in particular the Brockley route. However, as soon as men and supplies became available, the L.C.C. made an all-out effort to repair and relay tram tracks wherever necessary and bring up to a proper state of maintenance all tramcars needing overhaul. Many informed members of the public showed their appreciation of the L.C.C. Tramways and perhaps one may be permitted to mention in particular Mr. A.E. Southernwood of New Cross who has written scores of pro-tram letters to national and local newspapers since 1920 and is still going strong today (1949)!

The extension from Lee Green on the double-wire overhead system, which had been held up by the War, was constructed and opened on November 29th, 1920 to Lyme Farm, Eltham Hill (by Sherard Road). It was operated by E/1 Class tramcars on Service 46 using two trolley poles. A new conduit change pit was installed in Eltham Road, Lee and trolley poles were raised or lowered opposite Leyland Road. Plain overhead standards (without scrollwork) were used on this extension and on all future L.C.C. tramway extensions in South London. (About this time certain cars on Service 46 were diverted at New Cross Gate via Old Kent Road to Southwark Bridge - instead of Waterloo Station).

After the High Street outside Eltham Parish Church (St. John's) had been widened enough for a single track, Service 46 was extended to Beresford Square, Woolwich on March 22nd, 1921 over the No.44 route. (Service 44 has continued to operate as an extra service between Woolwich and Eltham on weekdays ever since; from 1923 to 1927 it was extended to Lewisham on certain journeys Mondays to Fridays, but this arrangement was short-lived). When High Street, Eltham had been further widened, after property had been acquired, double track was laid outside Eltham Church.

From September 26th, 1920 Service 48 had been diverted to run from Lee Green to Blackwall Lane (extended to Blackwall Tunnel at rush hours). Economies due to the 1921 Coal Strike led to its withdrawal in May 1921 and it was never restored.

Commencing June 26th, 1921 Service 46 worked to Southwark Bridge on Saturday afternoons and evenings and all day Sundays (instead of to Waterloo). The No.46s were diverted during the Summer of 1921 at New Cross Gate to run regularly as a daily service to Southwark Bridge via Old Kent Road. No.72 became a daily service: Forest Hill Station - Savoy Street via Walworth Road & Westminster. Waterloo Station was served by Service 68 to Tower Bridge, later extended to Greenwich Church on October 22nd, 1923, by means of a new east curve and junction at the corner of Tower Bridge Road and Tooley Street.

A water main burst in the High Road, Lee early on January 27th, 1922. Other traffic had to be diverted but the No.46 trams carried on, using single-line working until the main was repaired. A thunderstorm on July 10th, 1923, flooded the High Road and Eltham Road, Lee and uprooted wood paving blocks. Some early trams on Service 46 had to be diverted via Greenwich, but by the morning rush hour the No.46s were operating normally once more.

From February 16th, 1922 double-trolley operation was resumed round the Beresford Square loop from Anglesea Road, Woolwich. The double-wire overhead system between Woolwich and Lee Green lasted until 1927, when it was realised that the Southern Railway suburban electrification could affect Greenwich Observatory's instruments more than the trams could, so the extra negative wires were removed once the rails had been bonded, though some of the extra insulators still remain on the span wires today (1949). The No.44 & 46 trams began to use a single wire on November 13th, 1927.

During 1928 the Lee Green overhead was extended ¼ mile westwards to the Savoy Cinema and normal overhead operation was extended to Lee Road fare stage in order to remove traffic delays at Leyland Road. Also, trams from Woolwich could now reverse at Lee Green (when short-working) without taking up the plough.

About this time the L.C.C.T. stripped the older overhead standards of their elaborate scrollwork and cast-iron bases throughout South London as these adornments tended to promote corrosion; only a few standards have escaped to preserve these decorations today (1949). Elsewhere, replacement was by plain standards.

Route 64 was reinstated as a rush-hour service between New Cross Gate and Blackfriars via Walworth Road on January 10th, 1921. Its suburban terminus varied during the 1920s, sometimes fixed at Peckham or Camberwell Town Hall and at other times reverting to New Cross Gate; this route number disappeared in 1932.

On February 15th, 1921 the Ministry of Transport approved the use of trailer cars in Blackwall Lane; between Lewisham and Lee Green; in Stanstead Road; and on the Brockley route, but it is not known if any ever operated on these routes.

Many of the remaining B Class cars were converted into snowbrooms and stores vans during 1920-1922, but Nos. 107 & 158 were used as staff cars at Charlton Works until 1929.

From June 16th, 1921 certain Victoria Embankment services (including 36-38, 56-84, 66-72) which had previously terminated at Waterloo Bridge (Savoy Street) or John Carpenter Street, Blackfriars became circular routes, cars changing route numbers while running along the Embankment. At the same time Service 62 was extended from Forest Hill Station to St. Laurence's Church, Catford to satisfy the demands of Catford residents for a direct service to Westminster (this facility had been withdrawn in 1907). On December 24th, 1921 an improved lay-by came into use at Forest Hill Station (Perry Vale) for Nos. 50, 66 & 72. (The previous layout, consisting of a single-line siding off the west-bound track in Park Road which necessitated the use of the crossover in Park Road at Westbourne Road since 1915, had caused delays to up No.58 & 62 trams on the Dulwich route. The new siding branched into double track before joining Routes 58 & 62).

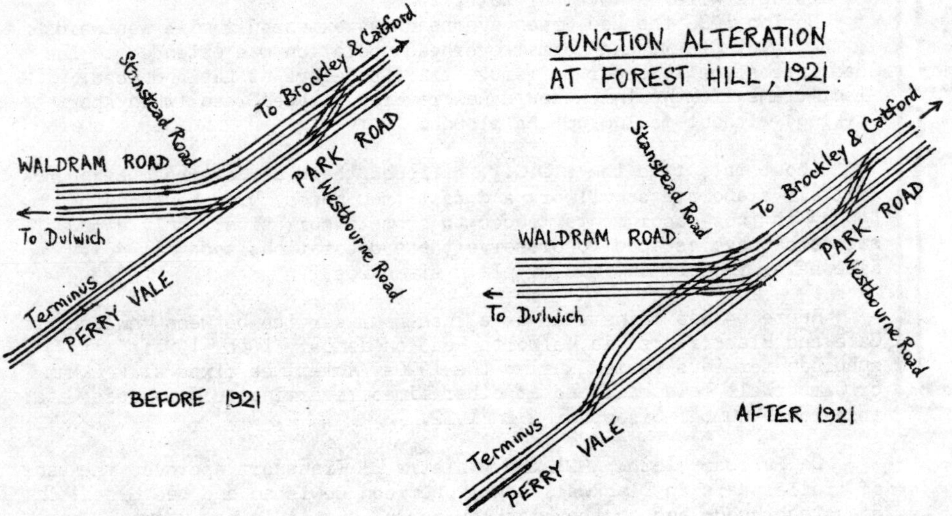

From March 30th, 1922 rush-hour Service 52 was extended from St. Laurence's Church, Catford to Southend Village terminus at the Pond. About the end of the year the all-night service via Old Kent Road was experimentally extended to St. Laurence's Church, Catford; this arrangement proved satisfactory and was continued for a further period from April 1923.

On August 14th, 1922 Service 62 commenced to run from Blackwall Tunnel to Savoy Street (via Dulwich & Westminster) on weekdays, Service 50 working only at rush hours and all day Sundays. Service 58 operated between Victoria Station and St. Laurence's Church, Catford on weekdays, but was extended to Blackwall Tunnel on Sundays (when No. 62 did not run) from September 10th, 1922. Track at the foot of South Street, Greenwich was doubled in November 1923, but the single-track section by Blackheath Hill remains to this day, together with several stretches of single line in Lewisham Road.

Trailer cars had continued to operate on Service 70 (Greenwich Church - Tooley Street), but they were withdrawn at the end of 1923. (Unfortunately a little girl of six had been knocked down and killed by an up No.70 tram and trailer in Evelyn Street, Deptford on February 12th, 1921). The extension of Route 68 from Tower Bridge to Greenwich Church on October 22nd, 1923 compensated for the withdrawal of the trailers on Route 70. On main routes previously carrying trailers more frequent and speedier services were provided as the older E/1s remotored from 42 h.p. to 60 h.p. re-entered service from the Works.

No.74 appeared as a rush-hour service from Forest Hill Station to John Carpenter Street, Blackfriars (via Brockley & Old Kent Road) on November 13th, 1922; on September 2nd, 1926 it became a weekday service.

In April 1923 the L.C.C.T. stated that 700 parties of children had been carried by tram the previous year at a rate of 7/6 per car single, 10/- return for each penny stage, the minimum cost per car being 15/- single, £1 return. On August Bank Holiday 1923 the L.C.C. Tramways carried 2½ million passengers.

On November 12th, 1923 the L.C.C. paired up the Victoria Embankment services to form circular routes. In practice, many trams had continued from Westminster to Blackfriars or vice versa, changing their numbers en route. Now the conductors did not have to change the numbers. Local routes combined were 36-38 (Abbey Wood); 56-84 (Peckham Rye); 66-72 (Forest Hill via Brockley). Nos. 38, 56 & 72 operated in via Westminster, out via Blackfriars; Nos. 36, 84 & 66 in via Blackfriars, out via Westminster.

Since the War, considerable numbers of surplus army vehicles, especially motor lorries, had been sold to private buyers. Many of these were converted into motor-buses and numerous 'pirate' omnibus companies sprang up and those that were successful were able to purchase new motor-buses from the rapidly expanding motor industry. Not only were these 'pirate' companies both a nuisance and dangerous rivals to tramways, whether municipally or company-owned, but they were an increasing embarrassment and deadly rivals of the regular omnibus companies, such as the General and Tilling's.

At Greenwich Police Court during April and May 1923 several 'pirate' omnibus drivers had their licences suspended for causing accidents to tram passengers at New Cross and Peckham when boarding or alighting from tramcars and also when the 'pirates' collided with tramcars through dangerous driving. There were numerous similar cases heard at this court and other London police courts during the next twelvemonth. The Lewisham Borough Council voiced a strong protest to the L.C.C. about dangerous driving in the 'Bus War' between the 'Red' and 'Blue' motor-buses competing between Bromley and Catford; there were frequent crashes on Bromley Hill and along Bromley Road caused by these bitter rivals.

In 1924 London tramwaymen (and busmen belonging to the regular omnibus companies) went on strike from March 22nd to March 29th - some until the 31st - in protest against indiscriminate pirate omnibus competition. As a result, legislation was introduced which curbed the 'pirates' wild excesses and from which the tramways and their staff benefited.

(On August 9th, 1921 a No.54 tram to Catford ran off the line opposite St. Mary's Church, Lewisham, while another No.54 (for Victoria) left the rails opposite Lewisham Market on February 8th,1922. At Forest Hill a tram left the track at the corner of Stanstead Road and Sunderland Road and hit a house, nobody being injured, on March 14th, 1924.

During 1923, two trams collided in Trafalgar Road, Greenwich on February 2nd, while at New Cross on August 24th a No.54 leaving the Depot for Southend Pond hit a No.66 bound for Forest Hill and knocked it on to the pavement).

On August 1st, 1924 an elderly man was robbed on a No.52 tram going to New Cross. A workman gave the alarm and the robbers were arrested by the Police.

The London correspondent of the 'Manchester Guardian' in the issue dated June 6th, 1924 praised the No.46 tram route as 'a pretty tram ride', referring to the section from Lee Green round Eltham to Woolwich.

The L.C.C. Tramways were always experimenting with various improvements to rolling stock. During 1924, an E/1 Class tramcar, No.1235, embodying all the successful innovations made since 1922, began operating from New Cross Depot in August; the L.C.C.T. publicised this as the new 'Pullman' type and during the next two years they studied the public's reaction, which was highly favourable.

Side route numbers were introduced on the trams about 1923 on the suggestion of Driver R.J. Garwood of Norwood Depot, who was to complete 41 years' service there as a motorman. Small stencils were hung on the white glass sides of the metal boxes carrying the offside platform signal lights.

Driver Garwood had noticed that passengers queueing at Victoria terminus had difficulty in seeing the end route numbers of trams standing in a long line. He received an award for this useful staff suggestion, which was of great benefit to the travelling public.

On August 31st, 1924 track widening which had been in progress in High Street, Woolwich between Powis Street and Hare Street was completed.

Tram Services terminating on the south side of Southwark Bridge (including local services 46, 52, 60) were extended over the new bridge to Queen Street (corner of Thames Street) in the City on July 14th, 1925. Destination blinds were amended to read 'CITY & SOUTHWARK'.

During the General Strike of 1926, when transport workers came out on strike in sympathy with the miners, there were few trams running between May 3rd and May 12th. Mounted police guarded tram depots. Some volunteers helped to drive trams, mostly on overhead sections as the conduit could easily be blocked and tracks obstructed. But some special cars did operate from New Cross and Camberwell Depots, guarded by police constables. At the start of the Strike, twelve trams driven by volunteers left Camberwell Depot for Westminster, but only four reached their destination. On the way they were attacked by huge mobs which forced the others to return to the depot with broken windows and injured crews.

<u>FARES AND TICKETS</u> (For illustrations of tickets see between pp.100/101.)

The 1914-1919 War caused fare increases, and rising costs made it necessary for the L.C.C.T. to shorten the distance for penny fares from 1.8 miles to 1.5 miles on April 27th, 1919, while in September 1920 the distance scale dropped to 0.6 mile for 1d., 1.2 miles for $1\frac{1}{2}$d, 1.8 miles for 2d., 3 miles for 3d., corresponding adjustments being made to higher fares, the maximum becoming 6d. single. (An average section was now only 0.6 mile). This was the most expensive fare scale for short-distance riders ever instituted by the L.C.C.T., necessitated by the serious economic situation in Britain at that time, but it was eased after fifteen months.

Longer mileages were introduced from December 1st, 1921:- Two stages for 1d., four for 2d., six for 3d., eight for 4d., ten for 5d., and over ten stages for 6d. single. (At the same time the $1\frac{1}{2}$d. fare was withdrawn from South London). Normal Workmen's scales operated from January 1st, 1923 (see below), while on July 9th, 1923 the maximum Children's fare became 2d. (1d. Child's ticket for 2d. adult fare) - it had been raised to 3d. in 1920.

On January 1st, 1924 the maximum adult single fare was reduced to 5d. and from the same date 5d., 6d. and 8d. Returns were issued. The new maximum fare of 5d. Single, 8d. Return in the County of London was very reasonable and this scale remained unaltered until June 1939. Tickets issued were:-
1d. (for 1.2 miles), 2d.(2.4), 3d.(3.6), 4d.(4.8) and 5d.(over 4.8 miles) Singles; 5d. Return for 3d. journey, 6d. Return for 4d. journey, 8d. Return for 5d. journey; 2d. Workman Return (for 4.8 miles), 4d. Workman Return (9.6) and 6d. Workman Return (for over 9.6 miles).

Tickets were coloured 1d. white, 2d. purple pink, 3d. dark blue, 4d. green, 5d. brown, 6d. primrose yellow, 7d. mauve and 8d. grey. All tickets showed geographical stages and those referring to the regular route also showed stage point numbers, on single tickets, transfer stages being unnumbered. No stage numbers were shown on return tickets. The availability of transfers was greatly increased during the years 1924 - 1928, many new facilities being made available.

The 2d. Cheap Midday Fare was introduced on April 19th, 1920 in South London as the maximum for any journey leaving London termini between 10.0 a.m. and 4.0 p.m. Mondays to Fridays and arriving at London termini between 10.30 a.m. and 4.30 p.m. From January 1st, 1923 three sections were allowed for a penny at these hours, while in July the 1d. Child's 'All the Way' Midday Ticket was introduced. From April 11th, 1927 transfers on midday fares became available, widely publicised through the slogan 'Board the First Car'. Starting on June 20th, 1927 the hours of availability for cheap midday fares were slightly extended - ever since they have been available on all trams leaving London termini between 9.30 a.m. and 4.30 p.m. Mondays to Fridays and arriving at London termini between 10.0 a.m. and 5.0 p.m., one transfer being allowed en route. Later this facility was extended to 'all day Sundays' in the summer months of 1930 and 1931, but never repeated since then.

On January 3rd, 1925 the popular 1/- (Shilling) All Day Ticket appeared, giving unlimited travel on trams in the County of London and Borough of Leyton on Saturdays and Sundays; becoming available every day from July 21st. The 'All-Day' facility was extended to cover through services to East Ham, West Ham and Walthamstow from December 1st, 1926 and also all local services in these boroughs from June 1st, 1927. Croydon Corporation joined the scheme on June 1st, 1932 and the

1/- All Day Ticket now allowed unlimited travel on trams in the County of London, Croydon, East Ham, Leyton, West Ham and Walthamstow - a boon to commercial travellers and visitors to London. The same facilities were available on the 6d. Child's All Day Ticket, which was introduced in August 1927. "Riding the Trams" became a popular holiday pastime for children, and Kingsway Subway was a special attraction. Tram riding incidentally taught them the topography of London.

TRAMWAY MANAGERS

Further mention should be made of the General Manager of the L.C.C. Tramways, Aubrey Llewellyn Coventry Fell Esq., who held this office from 1903 to 1924. He was very capable, efficient and enterprising, and many of the improvements which resulted in the high standard of the tramway services were due to him and his staff. He successfully overcame the teething troubles of the conduit system by strengthening the anchoring of the track and he planned the vast Charlton Works for building and overhauling tramcars. His name was familiar to many Londoners as it was shown in full on the rocker panels of every L.C.C. tramcar.

Joshua Kidd Bruce Esq., General Manager from January 1st, 1925 until June 30th, 1930, had to face the threat of insolvency due to intensive omnibus competition. Fortunately, by the modernising of existing tramcars under the 'Pullman' programme, the provision of new trams and the introduction of bargain fares, he was successful in restoring the fortunes of the L.C.C. Tramways.

Theodore Eastaway Thomas Esq., General Manager from July 1930 continued in the service of the London Passenger Transport Board on its formation in July 1933. New tramcars were built and planned during his term of office with the L.C.C.T., new extensions opened and further mileage planned. He continued as Tramways Manager with London Transport until 1939, but his name was no longer shown on the sides of the trams, as in L.C.C.T. days.

TRAMWAYMEN

Many tram drivers and conductors have been fond of jests and witty remarks. Some have become masters of repartee and real local characters. One of the famous ones, Mr. Robert Arnold ('Dr. Tibbles') flourished on the No.72 (Brockley) route. He was a conductor from 1891 until 1936 and a pioneer member of the Tramway and Vehicle Workers' Union and he addressed many meetings and wrote frequently to the local press on tramway and union matters.

His speciality, when on duty, was calling out nicknames at every tram stop. He called Brockley Cemetery the 'Garden of Rest', Brockley

Railway bridge 'Marble Arch', because of its white tiles, and St. Donatt's Road 'Doughnut Road'. At the junction of Shardeloes Road and Lewisham High Road he shouted: "Hold tight around Tattenham Corner!" He jumbled the names of public houses in the Old Kent Road as 'The Green Cow' and 'The Dun Man'. At Bricklayers' Arms he announced 'Jamland' - a reference to Hartley's and Pink's factories nearby.

The kindness and sympathy of many tramway staff is illustrated in this true story of a tram conductor on the 36-38 route. Two eight-year old boys boarded his tram at the Elephant and asked him for the longest tram ride for a halfpenny. Seeing that they were well-behaved boys (unlike the cheeky kids who tried to 'pinch' rides on the Embankment) he let them travel all the way to Abbey Wood and back again and refused their halfpennies.

Another story of the 1920s concerns an ancient baby motor-car whose wheels were the same gauge as the tramlines. One wet day the wheels dropped into the tram rails in Camberwell Road and the driver was unable to dislodge them. At Camberwell Green he wanted to go straight up Denmark Hill, but the points were set for Peckham and round the corner into Church Street he went!

<u>LEARNING TO DRIVE</u> by A.E. (Bert) SUMMERS of Plumstead

This is, I think, a very funny bit of a 'learner' tram driver's trials. During the '20s I was working on the inside staff of the Bexley Council Tramways. I was told to get instructions <u>in my own time</u> from a number of drivers and this was given. Amongst them was Charlie Bareham, a very good driver.

This particular run out with Charlie was to be my last as I would have done my required time (50 hours) on our way back to Bexley Heath Market Place from Horns Cross. As we reached Dartford it started to snow, so Charlie goes inside out of the cold, knowing that I could now manage a car in service all right.

When we got to Crayford I was one mass of snow all up the front, all the Bexley trams having open fronts. So, while waiting for the conductor to ring me off, I opened the door of the lower saloon and said to Charlie: "Come on; out you come!" He told me to carry on up to the Market Place, but I replied that according to my reckoning I had just finished my 50 hours. After some little banter I said: "All right, Charlie, I'll take the old car on, but I shall put in for a bonus!"

We often laughed over this whenever we met, but I was passed fit to drive a tram on service or one which was often wanted by the permanent way staff or breakdown gang. The foreman of the inside staff was pleased to have another driver whom he could call on if wanted and I was very pleased to get a licence out.

(After $3\frac{1}{2}$ years on the inside staff, Mr. Summers became a regular driver of passenger tramcars. He was awarded 29 medals for Safety First before retiring in 1950).

A DULWICH RUNAWAY

On July 31st, 1925 an up C Class tramcar ascending Dog Kennel Hill, East Dulwich ran backwards for 85 yards and crashed into a stationary M Class tramcar at the bottom of the hill. Both trams were badly damaged and the force of the impact was so great that the stationary car was forced backwards nearly 50 yards: windows, seats and woodwork being shattered. 21 injured passengers were treated at King's College Hospital for cuts, but only the driver of the M Class car was detained with cuts and bruises.

Mr. P.T. Cooke of Whateley Road, East Dulwich, the conductor of the runaway tram, who was also injured but allowed home, had shown great presence of mind in calming several panic-stricken passengers and preventing them jumping off the rear platform as his tram ran away down the hill, otherwise fatalities might have occurred.

This accident may have resulted from brake failure, but the greasy state of the rails after rain was probably a contributory factor. Until 1929 the Dulwich routes (Nos. 56, 58, 60, 62, 84) were operated solely by four-wheel tramcars of Classes C & M, fitted with track brakes.

THE DOWNHAM ESTATE

The L.C.C. was laying out a new housing estate between Southend Village and Grove Park, called the Downham Estate, and to provide the new residents with cheap travel the tramway was extended from Southend Pond as the estate progressed. Unfortunately, the tracks were laid in the roadway up Downham Way and an admirable opportunity to provide a separate tramway reservation was lost. (At this time many provincial cities were building tramway extensions through new housing schemes on reserved sleeper tracks between grass verges, bushes and trees). The Downham extension was equipped for overhead operation (like all post-war extensions), but a short length of conduit track was constructed from Southend Pond along Bromley Road and round the corner to a new change pit in Downham Way.

Service 54 was extended to Valeswood Road on September 28th, 1926; on July 28th, 1927 it reached Southover; the final extension to Grove Park Station (S.R.) was opened on November 15th, 1928. This was as far as the trams went, except for one driver who overshot the terminus and took his tram down to the railway line in 1937! Powers were obtained to continue this route along Baring Road and a new road - Westhorne Avenue - to Well Hall Road, Eltham, but unfortunately London Transport allowed them to lapse when only the Eltham section had been constructed.

On April 19th, 1928 Service 58 was routed to Blackwall Tunnel at rush hours and all day Sundays and No.62 was diverted at Catford to Downham (Bromley Road) by means of a new south curve and junctions installed in 1927 outside St. Laurence's Church; No.62 was extended to Southover on June 23rd and to Grove Park Station on November 15th, 1928. On the same day, rush-hour Service 52 was also extended to Grove Park terminus. Downham now had a direct service to Westminster as well as to Victoria, but by 1930 the 62s were reversing at Southend Village or Bellingham Station. From April 25th, 1929 Service 58 began to operate regularly to Blackwall Tunnel as a daily service and has done so ever since.

A new east curve and junctions at Brockley Rise (Cranston Road), constructed in 1926, came into regular use on April 2nd, 1930. Service 74 from Blackfriars was diverted from Forest Hill terminus to Grove Park terminus via Catford. By 1931 Service 62 had reverted to its former terminus at Blackwall Tunnel and Service 74 operated normally to Downham (Bromley Road) only, though it was extended to Grove Park Station on Saturday afternoons and evenings and all day Sundays. At the London end No.74 was extended from John Carpenter Street, Blackfriars along Victoria Embankment to Somerset House on Sundays only.

The all-night service via Blackfriars & Old Kent Road, previously extended to Catford, was now further extended to Downham (Bromley Road).

On January 6th, 1928 tram services along Victoria Embankment had to be suspended temporarily owing to the River Thames overflowing through winter floods.

During 1928 there were two accidents caused through failures of the magnetic brake. On June 27th E/1 Class Tram 1369 (Service 54) ran into the rear of C Class Tram 212 (Service 52) on the up line outside the Goldsmiths' College, New Cross. Both trams were packed with early morning workers and twenty were injured. On December 22nd a No.46 descending Eltham Hill ran into a stationary No.46 and the interlocked trams ran downhill for forty yards. Both trams carried crowds of Christmas shoppers, eleven being injured in addition to the tramwaymen.

On the credit side, it must be remembered that serious accidents were infrequent, considering the mileage run by the trams, also that the robust construction of tramcars always reduces the likelihood of injury to passengers. Safe driving awards to L.C.C. tram drivers annually from 1929 were: 349 (1929), 647 (1930), 447 (1931) and 776 (1932), when Motorman C.J. Grantham of New Cross Depot was top with a gold medal for 14 years' safe driving.

THOUSANDS ATTRACTED TO THE TRAMS

New passenger shelters had been erected at Shooter's Hill Road (1916), Peckham Rye terminus (1920), Catford (St. Laurence's Church) and Kennington Park (1924). To popularise tram travel further, commencing with E/1 Class No.1675, trams were given 'Pullman' treatment in 1926 with a new dark red and pale yellow livery, also the L.C.C. crest instead of initials. Longitudinal seats in the lower saloon were mostly replaced by transverse seating on the 2+1 pattern, except by the doors. Seats were upholstered in moquette downstairs and leather upstairs, where smoking was allowed. Broader side route boards were fitted below the lower saloon windows, sometimes accompanied by shorter boards advertising all-day and cheap fares, also certain parks and public buildings en route. E/1 Class trams now seated 73 passengers (27 inside, 46 upstairs). On the bogie cars the plough carrier had been attached to the truck frame until 1927, when a start was made on equipping all E and E/1 Class tramcars with centrally-slung plough carriers. Many E/1 Class cars previously equipped with 42 h.p. motors were being remotored at this time, receiving 60 h.p. motors.

A telephone control system introduced in 1928 reduced delays to a minimum. During the same year a new Central Stores Department was opened at Charlton Works.

The trams, which assisted the rates annually by several thousand pounds, played a major part in moving rush-hour crowds, but the L.C.C. determined to attract off-peak passengers also. Pamphlets on sporting fixtures, parks and open spaces, historic buildings, exhibitions and entertainments were issued, giving clear details of appropriate tram services and fares. Trams ran up till midnight to bring folk home from evening entertainment.

In this respect, it is interesting to compare times of last trams in 1927, 1932 and 1949:-

	From London terminus to:	L.C.C.T. 1927	L.C.C.T. 1932	L.P.T.B. 1949
	ABBEY WOOD	11.44 pm.	11.44 pm.	10.42 pm.
	WOOLWICH	12.20 am.	12.20 am.	10.42 pm.
	DOWNHAM	11.32 pm.	12.1 am.	10.45 pm.
	CATFORD (via Lewisham)	11.40 pm.	12.1 am.	10.45 pm.
58	FOREST HILL (via Dulwich)	11.34 pm.	11.46 pm.	11.35 pm.
62		11.37 pm.	11.49 pm.	11.0 pm.

FINAL PROGRESS

In 1929 two experimental trams were put into service. Nos.1852/1853 were specially tested on the Dulwich hills. As a result, the largest order in the country at that time was placed for 150 new trams of steel construction embodying the latest improvements. Class HR/2 (Nos.1854-1903), bogie trams with equal-sized wheels, four motors giving a total h.p. of 140 and special track brakes supplied by the English Electric Co. Ltd., were built for the Dulwich routes, while Class E/3 (Nos.1904-2003), on maximum traction bogies with roller-bearing axles and two motors giving a total h.p. of 115, supplied by Hurst Nelson, could operate on all other routes. Each tram bore the notice "ONE OF 150 NEW AND BETTER TRAMS FOR SOUTH LONDON" and displayed large route number stencils. The first E/3s had open platforms, but No.2002 appeared with metal-framed glass windscreens in May 1931 and from then on all new trams were so fitted. A second order comprised 60 HR/2s (Nos.101-160), supplied by Hurst Nelson, fitted for conduit operation only, but No.160 became an E/3 in 1932 when its HR/2 bogies were placed under the new No.1 'Bluebird'.

The L.C.C. provided another fifty E/3 Class tramcars for Leyton Council (Nos.161-210), supplied by the English Electric Co. Ltd. Until the 1939-1945 War these Leyton E/3s operated mainly north of the Thames and on the Kingsway Subway services, but during 1939 most were transferred to South London depots, leaving about sixteen at Holloway Depot.

These Leyton E/3s and the 101-159 series of HR/2s were supplied with aluminium-framed windscreens when built.

In October 1929 the 4d. Pupil's Ticket was introduced on the L.C.C. Tramways and in May 1932 the 6d. Evening Tourist Ticket - available in the L.C.C. Area (South of the Thames) and Croydon - was instituted. (There was a corresponding ticket for the Northern area).

On February 3rd, 1930 Kingsway Subway was closed for alterations. The tunnels were widened and deepened to take double-deck tramcars. (Meantime the L.G.O.C. ran a special omnibus service between Bloomsbury and Victoria Embankment). The bogie trucks and electrical equipment of the single-deck tramcars were fitted to new E/1 Class double-deckers with large route number stencils, but these did not normally work on the Subway routes (Nos. 552-601).

Kingsway Subway was reopened by the Chairman of the L.C.C. on January 15th, 1931 driving E/3 Class Tram No.1931 painted white with blue and gold lining. Other E/3 Class trams and also E/1 Class Tram No.1506 - the first L.C.C. tramcar to be fitted with a windscreen - took part in the ceremonies.

E/3 Class trams in a new red livery took over the new Subway Services and have operated them efficiently ever since. The journey time from Bloomsbury to Westminster is seven minutes. No.35, S.E. London's new Subway service, commenced to run from Highgate (Archway Tavern) to New Cross Gate via Kennington, extended to Brockley Rise (Cranston Road) from May 14th, 1931. During Summer 1931 Service 35 was extended from Cranston Road to Downham Estate on Saturday afternoons and evenings and all day Sundays. On March 5th, 1932 Service 35 reached Forest Hill Station - its present terminus - and it was rerouted via Walworth Road from June 30th, 1932. (Journey time from Highgate: 86 minutes; through fare 9d. single, 1/- return).

In September 1930 Mr. Wilfred Westley of Highgate set up a record by travelling 207 miles by tram in less than 22 hours on a 1/- All Day Ticket.

On October 1st, 1930 Timothy, a black and white cat, was rescued alive from the conduit in Shardeloes Road, Brockley, where he had been imprisoned for 17 days after permanent way repairs. The cat was a little thin but quite unharmed.

One Saturday about this time, when Charlton Athletic Football Club were playing at home, the track by New Cross Gate Station was under repair. A D-Class tram was derailed while passing over the P.W. works and came to rest at an alarming angle of 45 degrees. The Breakdown Crew hurriedly propped up the tram and secured it by means of a rope right across the main road tied to a tree in St. James's Church Road. Trams had to be reversed on either side of the obstruction and other traffic diverted from 12.45 p.m. until 3 o'clock.

Mention may be made here of the efficient way in which convoys of trams have always handled football crowds to and from Millwall, Charlton and Dulwich Hamlet grounds and served sporting events at New Cross and Catford Stadiums and cricket matches at Kennington Oval.

The A Class Tram No.93 was completely burnt out in Stondon Park, Brockley on the foggy evening of December 22nd, 1930, fog delaying the fire brigade. Fusing caused fires on trams in Stanstead Road and New Cross Depot, but these were soon extinguished. Fire was a risk during fog when trams had to be driven at low speeds and the resistances were apt to become overheated. Similar fires occurred on trams in London Road, Forest Hill and Loampit Vale, Lewisham during the 'Black Fog' of January 1934, but these were speedily checked.

A roundabout was installed at the junction of Well Hall Road and Rochester Way, Eltham during September 1931, the trams following the other traffic round the perimeter. A new route along Westhorne Avenue, Eltham was opened from Well Hall Road to the railway bridge on October 1st, 1931, worked by Service 44A from Woolwich. It was opened throughout to Eltham Green (Middle Park Gates) on June 30th, 1932. No.72 (whose route was now covered by the new 35) was allotted to the Westhorne Avenue service, working from Beresford Square, Woolwich to Savoy Street via Kennington & Westminster. Unfortunately this was destined to be the L.C.C.'s last tramway extension.

Films made during 1931/1932 included 'Murder on the Second Floor' with scenes in Kingsway Subway. 'London Wall (After Office Hours)' showed shots in a Pullman tram at Forest Hill.

Since 1926 L.C.C. trams had been painted dark red and pale yellow; but in 1932 their colour was changed to deep vermilion and cream, similar to the present shades. (The old brown livery disappeared in 1931 with the withdrawal of Classes A, C and D). Several C Class cars became snowbrooms and P.W. cars.

In 1932 E/1 Class Trams 835 & 1360 were fitted with bow collectors and E/1 Class Trams 844 & 1172 with pantographs, being based at New Cross Depot. Experiments were made on the overhead section in Downham Way, where the wires were specially aligned for bow and pantograph operation, and trams ran in regular service on Routes 52, 54 & 74, but no more trams were fitted and both reverted later to trolley poles.

The Dulwich routes were speeded up from March 5th, 1932, because from that date M Class cars were no longer used, not even at rush hours, the fast HR/2s being completely responsible for Services 56, 58, 60, 62 & 84 ever since. (The Ms were sent from Camberwell Depot to Leyton, Hammersmith and Wandsworth Depots).

Three M Class cars: Nos.1441, 1444 & 1446 were rebuilt as bogie cars (Class ME/3) in 1932/1933 similar to the E/1 Class, by having a new length spliced in the centre after the bodies had been cut in half; this gave an irregular window spacing because of the wider corner pillars. No.1446 was renumbered No.1370 when it appeared as a ME/3. The original E/1 No.1370 had overturned at Kennington Oval in June 1933, and from its remains another modern tramcar was constructed, entering service as No.2 about 1934.

In April 1933 the Ministry of Transport gave permission for revised (increased) speeds for L.C.C. tramcars. A general speed of 20 m.p.h. is now permitted, except at crossings, junctions, curves, single lines and special restrictions. Higher speeds are allowed on some roads in the outer suburbs, e.g. 25 m.p.h. on Bromley Road and Eltham Road, with 30 m.p.h. on Downham Way. It may be added that the trams are capable of much higher speeds and on one occasion a police car timed a speeding HR/2 doing 45 m.p.h. at Dulwich.

A short working of Service 35, numbered No.35A, commenced regular operation between Highbury Station (L.M.S.) and Elephant & Castle on June 1st, 1933, terminating at the crossover in St. George's Road, Southwark.

No.1 a streamlined version of the HR/2 Class, built by the L.C.C.T. at Charlton Works, appeared in royal blue and white livery on May 19th, 1932. It won the travelling public's admiration at once and soon became known as the 'Bluebird'. This luxury tram seats 66 passengers (28 downstairs and 38 upstairs) on comfortably upholstered transverse seats; it is fitted with air brakes, automatic doors, concealed lighting, drop windows and electric heaters. The driver has his own cabin at each end, fitted with a seat. Straight stairs connect the lower and upper saloons. No.1 worked on the Kingsway Subway services from Holloway Depot until 1938, when it moved to Telford Avenue Depot, Streatham. At least one hundred new trams of this advanced type were scheduled for construction when the blow fell.

A Government Commission on Public Transport in the Metropolis having recommended co-ordination of services in the London Area, an Act of Parliament was passed which, among other provisions, ordered the London County Council to surrender its extensive tramway undertaking (comprising 167 miles of route and 1713 tramcars, of which 261 were less than three years old) to a new London Passenger Transport Board. Thus on July 1st, 1933 a successful and progressive municipal undertaking passed into the hands of a government monopoly, which stifled all healthy competition.

The years 1931 - 1933 saw the London County Council Tramways at their zenith and this is fully emphasised in the following reminiscences kindly contributed by Mr. S.P. Harris of Dulwich, who was a schoolboy during those years and depicts the L.C.C. Tramways seen through the eyes of an intelligent and observant boy.

THE LONDON COUNTY COUNCIL TRAMWAYS 1931-1933: BOYHOOD REMINISCENCES by S.P. HARRIS

Having provided the Metropolis with an enlarged tramway subway, a fleet of new and reconditioned tramcars and a splendid public service, The London County Council set about doing something to sell these amenities to the people.

A well-organised publicity campaign, seemingly endless, sent coloured posters extolling tramway facilities to every corner of London. Pamphlets by the score gave details of sporting, theatre and other facilities of the Council, the L.C.C. Evening Institutes and public museums and art galleries were also publicised, together with tram accessibility. All this reading matter was distributed through every single channel of civic service to the public.

Beautifully printed London guides were produced (published by a well-known firm specialising in such books) and a periodical in newspaper format entitled 'The Holidaymaker' appeared at Easter, Whitsun and August Bank Holiday. (I cannot recall a Christmas number!) Issued free, like all other pamphlets, leaflets and tram maps, it was obtained from any conductor or regulator for the asking.

The free L.C.C. Tramways maps, beautifully produced, clarified travellers' problems of getting about London and, printed to a scale of one inch to the mile, showed connections and through running services with adjacent municipal and company-operated tramway systems. These maps were distributed by the million; they found their way into the L.C.C. schools and were given away regularly to the children.

It became well-nigh impossible to enter a public library, a local town hall, a government office, a labour exchange, a hospital, a police station or any public building and not find a framed L.C.C. Tramways map within one's field of vision. Like as not, there would be a pile of leaflets and maps with the invitation: "Please take one" prominently displayed.

At every terminal and tramway junction, at stage points and important tram stops were posted details of tram times and destinations, which were punctually adhered to! On the nearest wall there was always a framed map of the L.C.C. Tramways.

London children loved those L.C.C. Tramways maps as they loved the great red trams. They rode the cars on their school holidays all equipped with 6d. All-Day tickets and the free coloured maps. The new tramcars appearing from 1930 onwards amid a blaze of publicity and the reopening of Kingsway Subway brought the 'Ride-at-Will' facility more into children's ken than ever before. Trams carried hordes of excited shouting children day after day, especially through Kingsway Subway.

At first this invasion of the trams interfered with adult traffic and a compromise was reached later by restricting the kids' passports until after 10.0 a.m.

It was impossible for us schoolboys in the tramway areas not to feel a sense of London pride when seeing the brand-new trams humming along the rails bearing the legend "ONE OF 150 NEW AND BETTER TRAMS FOR SOUTH LONDON". We felt that we were taking part in a great new adventure, for at the ages of eleven and twelve (long before the onslaught of disillusionment comes and tells you that life is not a fairy story after all) you notice innovations with a keener eye than an adult four times your age.

What a thrill it was to be able to recognise at last the different types of tram without referring to the class letter painted on the lower right-hand corner of the tramcar body (E/1, E/3, HR/2).

The name THEODORE EASTAWAY THOMAS, GENERAL MANAGER at the other end conjured up in my mind a vision of a grey-haired benevolent and jovial old gentleman running his trams just for the enjoyment of boys and girls - the 'Santa Claus' of the L.C.C. Tramways!

Naturally, on boarding a tram, we usually clambered up the stairs and dashed along the top deck to the front window.. From time to time disregarding the long-winded notice: "The London County Council will NOT be RESPONSIBLE FOR ACCIDENTS caused through PASSENGERS LEANING OVER THE SIDE OF THE CAR", we leant out of the side windows to shout at other boys on the pavements who were not fortunate enough to be sharing the delights of our sixpenny magic carpet!

The lower saloon is admittedly more comfortable with its wide moquette seats, but there you have to conform to better standards of behaviour for most of the time you are under the conductor's watchful eye! Although the windows do not open, the lower deck has some advantages for we can watch the activities of the motorman through the maroon anti-dazzle glass of the bulkhead door (locked open on warm sunny days) and try to figure how the tram starts, moves and stops!

The driver notches up the brass controller handle over a symbol SERIES 1,2,3,4 with his left hand; then four more notches to another cypher PARALLEL, his right hand caressing the handbrake. Watch his feet on the sanding pedal when the wheels stall on the greasy rails; see him stamp on the gong-pedal and hear the sonorous 'boing!' which startles the errant motorist or horse and cart from the tram track ahead. The tram shoots onward to the hiss from the overhead wire, the song of the electric motors and the drumming of wheels over railjoints.

In those boyhood days, the motorman was an awesome and impressive figure in voluminous capes and huge gauntlet gloves in Winter, as many trams then had open platforms; in Summer, both driver and conductor wore a smart, neat navy-blue uniform with red piping.

What's in that mysterious red wooden cupboard under the stairs? Then one day we saw it opened and tools and equipment taken out to assist a disabled tram - a rare enough occurrence in L.C.C.T. days - and what a tale to tell our pals!

The single mystic word 'Interlock' painted in white on the controller box was like a rune and puzzled our youthful minds for a very long time and who was this mysterious 'Dick Kerr' whose name was embossed on the brazen controller top? Around the bell push was the notice: TO STOP THE CAR STRIKE ONCE: and on the lower saloon ceiling in the E/3s and HR/2s it read: STRIKE ONCE SHARPLY in a circle round the bell push, so that we could read it as SHARPLY STRIKE ONCE or ONCE SHARPLY STRIKE - Which was correct? There was plenty of reading material in the tram: painted notices, printed advertisements and transparencies pasted on the lower saloon windows, such as 'Rinso', 'Phospherine', Hayward's Military Pickle and some from the Tramcar and Omnibus Scripture Text Mission.

Route No.40 took us to Abbey Wood, with picnics in the vicinity of the mysterious ruined Lesnes Abbey and 'Cowboys and Indians' among the trees until the sound of the Trams became louder and more imperative than the call of the spurious Comanche! Then there was the long fast run from Beresford Square across Woolwich Common, over Shooter's Hill and past Well Hall to Eltham.

The drunk who swayed on the platform of the No.54 climbing Downham Way was decanted at the Downham Tavern, while the tram reeled on to Grove Park Station. From here we once walked the route of the 'authorised extension' to Middle Park shown on L.C.C.T. maps visualising the permanent way that never came, unfortunately!

Happy kids, riding out to Horniman's Museum at Forest Hill, to Peckham Rye, Dulwich Park and Brockwell Park. Croydon Corporation's comfortable No.18 tram sailed majestically on mile after mile, to Purley in Surrey, with games on the scrubby slopes of Riddlesdown.

Grubby kids, fooling around on the leather-cloth seats on the top-deck of a grinding No.34 tram from Camberwell Green to Clapham Common or on down Cedars Road and Lavender Hill, then following the hidden Falcon Brook to Battersea. Grinning kids hanging about Hungerford footbridge at Charing Cross watching the silver tram roofs slide below us and turning to the counter-attraction of the rumbling green electric trains of the Southern Railway right behind.

Then northwards once again via the exciting Kingsway Subway (a never-fading thrill) to Highgate and to the steep hill up which HR/2 trams on Route No.11 make their way to the Village. We visited all the L.C.C. northern frontier posts - Hampstead Heath, Stamford Hill, Manor House and Finsbury Park, the latter reached in the MET's new steel-girt 'Felthams'.

Glide along the shining steel tracks, rumbling over manganese crossings, to Dalston, Hackney, Victoria Park and West India Docks - the trams seemed to reach to all points of the compass, yet we longed for financial resources to take us beyond L.C.C. territory. Golder's Green, Sudbury, Canons Park, Barnet, Enfield, Waltham Cross - what lay at these outposts with strange-sounding names? Tally Ho Corner sounded like John Peel's happy hunting ground!

Then eastwards over friendly corporations' routes to Epping Forest, Ilford Broadway and Barking Broadway, meeting and sampling trams of different types and colours. We competed eagerly to guess the owners of the different trams on joint services, "spotting" them by their shapes and colours and fleet numbers on the dash. In our eyes the L.C.C. emblem of city cross and barry wavy (familiar to us at school and carried also on fire engines and ambulances) rode the rails more proudly than the crests of the other councils.

But westwards at Young's Corner, Hammersmith and 'near Willesden Junction' we watched other strange types of trams on London United and 'MET' tracks, angry and envious because our L.C.C.T. 6d. All-Day tickets did not allow travel on foreign lines! Beyond Wimbledon travelled more weird trams with open tops and strange angular staircases, but at weekends L.C.C. trams took us on L.U.T. metals across Kingston Bridge to Hampton Court Palace and Bushy Park.

What a thrill to revel in the exciting dash down the steep incline from Southampton Row, Bloomsbury to dart under Kingsway itself, gliding into the smart little stations at Holborn and Aldwych. We rumble on, snaking round mysterious pillars and winking red signal lamps, passing the very catacombs of Bush House and then suddenly we see straight ahead tugs and barges passing on the River and trams crossing the junction on the Embankment.

"Not much down this road!" - "Okay, let's get out and go back!" Our sixpenny tickets became a mass of perforations as conductors 'cancelled' them, though many were unable to do so by the time that evening came, so mangled were the little bits of coloured pasteboard.

At night, tired after a day's 'tramble', H.G. Wells's 'ships of light' were almost ships of romance and adventure to us boys. But how we wished that we could stand behind the controller and move the brass controller handle through its notches with the same nonchalant air as our driver!

Sometimes we managed to slink into the depots at Camberwell and New Cross. At slack times our tall red friends would be quietly resting in the tranquility of the interior gloom, nothing moving except perhaps the depot cat and her playful kittens. Sometimes we were lucky enough to see trams 'going sideways' on the traverser and being shunted on to storage tracks. "Look at those queer odd-looking cars over in that corner, single-deck jobs fitted with revolving brooms below their high buffers!" "They're snow sweepers for use during the winter months".

"Do you think someone will let us drive a tram - just a little way - if we ask politely?" - but unfortunately somehow we never got the opportunity, and I had to wait until maturer years before I drove a tram.

Odd lay-bys and stubs and little-used curves had a special fascination for us, such as the siding at Harder's Road, Peckham (which we wrongly imagined as the start of an extension to Nunhead; it was actually the No.84 terminus for a time); the little-used western curve at New Cross Gate (once used by the Embankment circular services) and the track in Bellenden Road, Peckham, which led to the old Rye Lane Depot and the Permanent Way Yard. Did any service ever operate round the disused curve at Goose Green from Peckham Rye towards Dulwich Library?

A neglected curve from Battersea Park Road into Queen's Road, Battersea would have suited us admirably for going home from school by tram. Then there is the circular reversing loop branching from the main line near Nightingale Lane, Clapham Common, used for training learner-motormen and once used by trailer cars. There is a proper training school for motormen at Clapham Depot.

I once heard, with envy, my Father relate that many years before, when a tram broke down in High Street, Clapham, following trams were diverted via Clapham Depot, the traverser bridge and the depot line in Clapham Park Road to Clapham Common. If only I'd been there and had the chance to travel on one of those diverted trams - oh boy! - but perhaps I might get the chance some day, I thought to myself, - one never knows!

Other curiosities which fascinated us were the railway crossings in Nine Elms Lane, where one can still see a S.R. tank locomotive hauling a string of wagons over the tramlines. In Grove Street, Deptford the Southern Railway has its own 'tramway' where goods trains serving Deptford Wharf rumble down the middle of the street for a quarter of a mile or so.

"And why don't they let the No.32 trams run over Chelsea Bridge to Sloane Square, Dad? "And why don't the No.58s and 62s go through Blackwall Tunnel to meet the No.65s and 67s at Poplar?" But poor old Dad couldn't give a satisfactory answer to my persistent questions!

No.1931, the white and gold E/3 which had opened the enlarged Kingsway Subway in January 1931, excited London kids from Hackney to Wandsworth on Route No.31 when it first appeared and was actually nicknamed 'The Ghost Tram'. There is a story that a drunk in Nine Elms Lane one winter evening was nearly frightened out of his wits when this white tramcar suddenly loomed up through the river mists! Soon after, it was repainted red and cream.

No.1931 was a disappointment, however, teaching an early lesson that 'all that glisters is not gold'; inside it was no different from the other E/3s - a real let-down, after waiting so long for it to come along! What we expected to find I don't remember, perhaps white upholstery, free ice-cream and books to read?

But next year came glorious No.1 - 'Bluebird' - to win our affection and everyone's admiration as it glided along Routes 33 & 35. Then on Route No.14 came a silver tram, No.795, running between

Battersea and London Bridge, finished in bare aluminium. With red, white, blue and silver trams to ride in, what more could a Cockney lad desire?

These wild tram trips gave me a wide knowledge of London and developed a sense of civic pride and loyalty. It may be argued that if the L.C.C. had begun its extensive publicity campaign earlier - about 1920 - and kept it up, its tramways might have escaped London Transport's clutches - but this can only be speculation. Increased revenue, however, was a practical effect of the L.C.C. Tramways publicity schemes and the number of passengers carried in the financial year 1930-1931 alone reached the astonishing high total of 713,642,686 passenger journeys.

THE LONDON PASSENGER TRANSPORT BOARD (South East London Tramways)

The L.C.C. received inadequate compensation for the loss of its tramways and within a year all progress virtually ceased when the L.P.T.B. cancelled all plans for the construction of new tramcars and started in 1934 its tram-scrapping campaign. Trolleybuses were said to be "the vehicle of the future" and the same ridiculous propaganda levelled against the trolleybuses in the 1950s was first used against the trams in the 1930s. It is said that some of the London Transport hierarchy had reservations about scrapping all trams and wished to keep major trunk tramway routes, but the London General omnibus faction gained control of the L.P.T.B. and the trams were virtually doomed from the outset.

London Transport had also taken over the other municipal and company-owned tramways in the London Area, and soon after its formation in July 1933 all the Bexley Council tramcars were gradually replaced by ex-L.C.C. M Class cars, which became entirely responsible for working the Woolwich - Dartford route. After October 1933 all the open-top Erith Council tramcars were withdrawn and replaced by further M Class cars, ex-Croydon open-top car No.349 and ex-East Ham balcony cars Nos. 53 & 58. The Erith balcony cars later received trucks and equipment from ex-Croydon cars withdrawn after the Penge route closed. (see Croydon section).

When Driver Penney was taking a M Class tram from Charlton Works to Bexley Heath Depot in 1933, he waited a long time at a red signal guarding a long stretch of single track (about ¼ mile) in Wickham Lane. Becoming impatient and thinking the signal was faulty, he started off along the single track and about halfway down he encountered a Bexley car bound for Woolwich, whose driver remonstrated angrily with him: hadn't he seen the red light? He was forced to turn his trolley pole and reverse up the line. On reaching the double track again he found two other trams bound for Dartford and there was some delay before he could regain the double track and let the grumpy Bexley driver through!

A connection was put in between the Erith and L.C.C. tracks at Abbey Wood on December 18th, 1933, but this was in order that the Erith local service could be worked from Abbey Wood Depot; no through tram service was ever worked from London to Erith. The tram depot in Walnut Tree Road, Erith was returned to Erith Urban District Council for their own use, once the trams were moved.

The Bexley Heath/Dartford and Erith local services were numbered from October 3rd, 1934 as follows:-

Route 96 : Beresford Square, Woolwich - Welling - Bexley Heath - Crayford - Dartford - Horns Cross;

98 : Abbey Wood - Belvedere - Erith - Bexley Heath Market Place.

The Wilmington branch at Dartford was withdrawn on April 17th, 1934, the route being covered by motor-buses.

In April 1935 the 4d. Pupil's Ticket was replaced by 1d. and 2d. Scholar's Returns available up to 6.0 p.m. Mondays to Fridays and 2.0 p.m. on Saturdays. Pupils aged 14-18 years were allowed to use them up to 10.0 p.m. on Mondays to Fridays. Schoolchildren had to show Identity Cards to get these concession tickets; usually the schools applied for these Cards and distributed them to the appropriate pupils.

Every year the children of L.C.C. tramwaymen had enjoyed Christmas parties and Summer outings and these continued during L.P.T.B. days, but during the 1930s tramwaymen also entertained children of the unemployed each Christmas at depots and Charlton Works. Special trams brought them from such places as Peckham, Lewisham and Downham. During the Summer of 1935 the Bexley and Erith tramwaymen organised their ninth annual outing for local blind folk.

A new roundabout was installed at Eltham Green (Middle Park Avenue) and came into use on August 25th, 1935. It is complementary to that at Well Hall Circus and the trams run round the perimeter, the points being operated automatically from the overhead wires at both roundabouts. On May 6th, 1935 King George V and Queen Mary celebrated their Silver Jubilee at St. Paul's Cathedral in a Thanksgiving Service and the processional route through the City and West End to Buckingham Palace was thronged with spectators, many of whom travelled thither by London Transport trams. The decorated streets and shops and floodlit buildings attracted large crowds of sightseers and during that month the King and Queen toured the suburbs in an open carriage pulled by the royal horses, visiting North, South, East and West London on successive Saturdays, so that many people could see them. This, together with the fact that there were many visitors in London for the Jubilee celebrations, made the trams very busy indeed.

About this time E/1 Class Trams Nos.982, 1260 & 1373 received new domed-roof top covers and were thoroughly modernised both internally and externally. (Unfortunately, No.1373 became a 'blitz' casualty during the 1939-1945 War).

An inquisitive little dog investigating the chassis of a stationary tram at Well Hall Road, Eltham one January evening in 1935 became jammed in the equipment, but he was released unharmed by the inspector after a quarter of an hour.

Trolleybuses replaced the Erith and Dartford local tram routes in the Autumn of 1935. No.98 (Erith) trams last ran on November 9th and No.96 (Bexley Heath & Dartford) a fortnight later on November 23rd. The 696 trolleybus route terminated at Dartford Market Place (instead of Horns Cross) but at the Woolwich end it was extended to the Free Ferry, as was the 698 via Erith, dual working being instituted over the section between the Free Ferry and Abbey Wood. Tram Service 40 was cut back to Beresford Square at normal hours, but it operates to Wickham Lane corner, Plumstead at weekday rush hours only.

Twice during 1936 water mains burst in the High Road by Lee Green Police Station. On March 22nd single-line working was possible on the up line (other traffic being diverted). Normal working was resumed four days later. A second burst on June 26th twisted the tramlines and through services had to be suspended for the evening. Permanent way gangs worked all through the night to restore full tram services the following morning.

In 1934 the L.P.T.B. wanted to scrap all London's trams (just over 2,500 cars) within five years, but fortunately this proved impossible. Due to a revision of this plan in 1936 certain E/1 Class tramcars were modernised with flush panel sides, inset roller blind route numbers, windscreens, modernised interiors and electric bells - these were known as 'Rehabilitated' E/1 Class tramcars. This 'rehabilitation' work continued until 1939 and the remaining unaltered E/1s were then fitted with windscreens but were not changed otherwise in appearance.

During 1933 two more accidents occurred in McLeod Road, Abbey Wood. On March 11th a down tram left the rails at Basildon Road corner and crashed into the garden of No.1 McLeod Road, while on September 22nd two trams were badly damaged in a collision and had to be run into New Cross Depot. An up No.38 tram derailed at the usual corner on

June 27th, 1935 and ran into No.77 Basildon Road.

There was a spectacular accident at Eltham on March 25th, 1934. The trolley pole of E/1 Class Tram 1103 (Service 46 for the City) became defective at Well Hall Circus and it was decided to propel it to New Cross Depot by the shortest route. Contrary to regulations it was propelled down Westhorne Avenue by another tram behind, connected by a tow cable. When the rear tram braked suddenly just before Eltham Green junction, the tow cable broke and, though No.1103's driver made frantic efforts to check its speed with the handbrake (the electric power being disconnected due to dewirement), No.1103 derailed at the trailing points, shot across the foot of Eltham Hill and overturned on the pavement by Middle Park Avenue, the roof being ripped off. Four passengers, who had wrongly been allowed to remain on the disabled car were injured, besides the conductor. (The conductor and the two drivers were fined at Greenwich Police Court for allowing passengers to remain on the faulty tram. They were asked why No.1103 had not been towed, as specified in the regulations). No.1103 was later rebuilt with a domed roof and modernised to the same pattern as Nos.982, 1260 & 1373.

An up No.66 tram and a lorry collided in Peckham Road at Camberwell Town Hall on June 13th, 1933. Other lorries ran into trams at Rushey Green, Catford (June 1st, 1934) and in New Cross Road (September 18th, 1934). A No.36 bus collided with a No.54 tram in High Street, Lewisham at night (September 3rd, 1934), while another bus and a HR/2 Class tram collided at Dulwich Library traffic lights four days later. The magnetic brakes failed on a tram approaching the 'Marquis of Granby', New Cross along Lewisham High Road causing it to crash into a stationary car standing on the track at the road junction (October 20th, 1934).

Collisions between trams occurred at New Cross Gate (December 3rd, 1934), and 'Marquis of Granby' (Autumn 1935) while two Abbey Wood trams crashed in High Street, Plumstead (September 7th 1935). At Woolwich there were collisions outside New Road Post Office (March 16th, 1936) and in Green's End (October 14th, 1936). A lorry derailed a No.72 down tram at Nightingale Place, causing it to hit an up No.46, the canopies of both cars being damaged (December 7th, 1936). A down No.72 (E/1 No.937) ran into a No.46 on the line in Grand Depot Road (October 22nd, 1937); twelve passengers, the No.72 driver and the No.46 conductor were injured, while the cars were run into Abbey Wood Depot.

Route 54 came in for its share of mishaps. Two trams collided at Grove Park terminus (January 14th, 1936) and another couple at Southover (July 22nd, 1936). The runaway tram sensation at Grove Park Station (April 21st, 1937) was re-enacted by a collision when No.977 crashed into another E/1 which finished up at the same spot overhanging the Southern Railway (November 15th, 1937). A sand drag was then installed at the terminus to prevent any further runaways. Outside the Catford Town Hall No.1282 (going towards Downham) jumped the points and crashed into No.1548 bound for Victoria (June 11th, 1937). A court case arising from this accident demonstrated the muddle-headedness of some people. About half the witnesses who had been travelling on No.1282 said that the tram had been going to Downham; the remainder said that it was going to Victoria! - And this was said on oath; the magistrate was very perplexed'.

In a disgraceful incident on Christmas Eve 1935, fighting drunks on a tram at Southend Village pushed a policeman through a lower saloon window. Christmas Eve 1936 was marred by a sad tragedy: An E/3 Class tram on Service 35 was derailed by a broken bolt in the tram rail at Malpas Road junction. Inspector W.R. Lambert of New Cross, with 32 years' service, though off-duty, was assisting to rerail the E/3 when he was pinned between the No.35 and a No.72 and fatally injured. He had driven special trams to Woolwich Arsenal during the War and had entertained at many tramwaymen's concerts. He was well-liked and many staff attended his funeral.

It must be remembered that trams are responsible for fewer accidents and are often the only vehicles operating in thick fog (as on January 1st, 1934 and October 17th, 1937), this fact being appreciated by the travelling public. Many accidents were caused between 1920 and 1940 by reckless motorists ploughing into passengers boarding and alighting from trams, so magistrates and local newspapers raised many an outcry against this dangerous driving. During the years 1930-1933 the L.C.C.T. in a 'Safety First' campaign appealed to motorists to show courtesy to tram passengers. The Metropolitan Police objection to loading islands for tram passengers did not help matters, while for many years Parliament refused to make it an offence to pass a stationary tram on the nearside at a stopping place in London, though this has always been strictly forbidden in Scottish burghs.

THE CORONATION OF H.M. KING GEORGE VI AND H.M. QUEEN ELIZABETH

Most London busmen went on strike in May 1937. The tram-men carried on, as they had inherited better conditions of service from the London County Council. On Coronation Day, May 12th, 1937, trams ran continuously from midnight; by 2.0 a.m. long queues of passengers had formed and crowded trams operated rush-hour services through the early hours of Wednesday morning.

Victoria Embankment, on the route of the Coronation Procession, was reserved for schoolchildren, so ordinary services terminated at Somerset House or County Hall. 37,000 boys and girls from London schools arrived by train, Underground, 13 steamboats and 130 special trams (which unloaded the children on the Embankment).

The trams carried coloured symbols corresponding to the sections of the processional route served by the temporary terminals, thus:-

Kingsway Subway services from North London
terminating at Aldwych : brown, blue, green.
Savoy Street via Blackfriars; Waterloo Station;
County Hall (via Elephant or Kennington): brown, green.

Victoria Station : maroon, yellow, green.

During all the festivities the trams carried the road passenger traffic, and grateful newspaper correspondents praised the goodwill and patience of tram drivers and conductors. For about three weeks, including Whitsun, tramcars were the only public service vehicles operating in London.

1937 - 1939

From September 1937 the colour of 2d. tickets was changed from purple pink to light blue and the 3d. from dark blue to light pink. Commencing September 8th, 1937 Service 66 from Forest Hill Station was diverted at Camberwell Green to Victoria Station (via Kennington & Vauxhall) instead of the Embankment, except for certain early and late journeys.

During April/May 1938 a traffic roundabout scheme was introduced at Vauxhall Cross, using the station yard and a new street - Parry Street - specially constructed. Now the trams and other traffic make a gyratory movement around Vauxhall Station (S.R.).

From 1939, instead of metal-framed windscreens, Charlton Works began fitting light timber-framed windscreens to all South London trams not already fitted. These wooden windscreens have been used ever since whenever replacements are needed.

E/3 Class Tram 170 (Service 35 for Forest Hill) was involved in a collision at St. George's Circus, Southwark, on April 27th, 1937, but damage was mainly confined to the driving platform.

Collisions between trams on the same tracks occurred at Queen's Road, Peckham (June 1st, 1938); High Street, Plumstead (October 28th, 1938) and Victoria Embankment approaching Blackfriars (November 1st, 1938). On New Year's Day 1939 E/1 Class Tram 1426 (Service 38) ran into a stationary HR/2 Class tram on Service 58 (No.128) outside St. Alphege's Church, Greenwich, 24 people being hurt. There was a collision at New Cross Gate on June 20th and a down No.40 tram ran into a stationary No.38 tram at Blackwall Lane junction, Greenwich on July 20th, 1939.

Trams ran off the line at the corner of Sunderland Road and Stanstead Road, Forest Hill (July 26th, 1938) and in McLeod Road, Abbey Wood at Cassilda Road, when the top deck of the tram was wrecked (December 2nd, 1938).

Buses collided with trams in Bromley Road, Catford at Canadian Avenue (September 18th, 1938) and at Green's End, Woolwich (November 17th, 1938). An up No.54 tram hit a No.108 bus at Lewisham Clock Tower, pushing it into a No.36 bus (July 31st, 1939). A tram was involved in a multiple collision with a heavy lorry, private car and motor van in New Cross Road near High Street, Deptford - the tram's controller was wrecked (August 26th, 1939).

A driver walking round his tram at the Lee Green changeover was struck by another tram (May 15th, 1938), while the conductor of an Abbey Wood tram was fatally injured while putting up the trolley pole at Woolwich change pit (April 21st, 1939); he was pinned by a No.40 against his own tram. A driver managed to halt his tram in Lower Road, Rotherhithe before he collapsed and died (March 4th, 1938), while a tram washer died at work in New Cross Depot (March 27th, 1939).

On the brighter side, a New Cross conductor from Downham was awarded the London Transport Meritorious Award for stopping a runaway horsedrawn dustcart passing his tram in Blackfriars Road on January 11th, 1939.

On Sunday, May 8th, 1938 the first annual parade of the No.114 (London Tramways) Division of the St. John Ambulance Brigade was held at St. Alfege's Church, Greenwich.

<u>A FRIENDLY HAUL FROM A HORSE CARMAN</u> by Driver J.T. PENNEY of New Cross.

During January 1938 we had a very cold spell with plenty of ice and snow, which was murder to trams on the conduit system if packed snow blocked the slot or salt put down by the local councils short-circuited the electric current.

One Friday afternoon I was driving on the No.68 service: Waterloo to Greenwich. This was my last run of the day and on arrival at the terminus I would be finishing my tour of duty. We had already lost about 15 minutes at Dockhead due to the current being off DEAD SHORT and we were passing through the single line at Paradise Gate, Southwark Park when the line in Jamaica Road went dead again. There we were stuck, with the live section only 50 yards ahead.

Then I noticed a pair-horse van approaching in my direction. There was a friendly feeling between tram-men and horse carmen. Noticing that his van was unloaded, I asked the driver to stop and suggested that he should back his van on to the front of my tram. He agreed and attached a rope from his back axle to the front buffer of my tram. Climbing on to the platform behind the controller, I gave the carman the go-ahead and he put his vehicle into motion, his horses pulling the tram on to the live section. We then proceeded under our own power.

I might mention that this was not an isolated event on that route and tramwaymen and horse carmen - we all helped one another.

During the War I got the crew of a Bren-gun carrier to push a tram off the 'dead' section at New Cross Gate.

FOG ! (A true tale by Mr. S.P. HARRIS)

During a real 'pea-souper' - a filthy stinking sulphurous fog which made one's eyes smart - which blotted out South London one November night in 1938, most traffic had stopped except the trams. At Camberwell depot-bound trams signed off as per their normal schedules, but around 11.30 p.m. a small group of hopefuls waited at Camberwell Green tram shelter, knowing full well that some tram would take them towards Dulwich and home, however slowly.

An HR/2 was heard approaching through the gloom. It was No.120 on Service 62 about to enter Camberwell Depot. The anxious Regulator tactfully suggested to the crew that they might like to take the huddled passengers part of the way home, say to Goose Green.

There was no argument. The points were reset, HR/2 No.120 reversed over the crossover, the grateful passengers - almost a full complement - climbed aboard and the tram vanished into the murk. All the way up Denmark Hill it picked up folk, even between stops, as it crawled along its familiar reliable steel track glinting dully in the beam of the tram's headlight.

With fog rolling past outside and windows dripping with condensation inside, No.120 nosed its way to the crest of Grove Lane, then cautiously descended steep Dog Kennel Hill into Grove Vale, East Dulwich, where the fog gathers thickest. At Goose Green the crew made no mention of reversing, but No.120 continued its steady way up Lordship Lane, passing three abandoned No.12 buses at Dulwich Library.

The fog swirled denser at Dulwich Common and an unseen Southern Railway electric train from Crystal Palace (High Level) rumbled over the bridge at Lordship Lane Station. No.120 crawled up to Horniman's Museum and down London Road to Forest Hill Station, where more abandoned buses were found littering the roadways.

Once under the railway bridge, the No.62 met a late No.35 tram taking on passengers for Brockley at Perry Vale terminus, doing yeoman service amid the wreaths of swirling fog. No.120 continued its way along Stanstead Road to Catford; the journey from Camberwell took nearly an hour, but nobody complained - the faithful tram got them home. The driver and conductor had to return No.120 to Camberwell Depot and then make their own way home afterwards, but they kept cheerful. They were proud to serve the public, even though they only received a few shillings' overtime payment.

Hardly anyone paid their fares on that tram! How could they? The tram was crammed tight with passengers and the conductor was out front most of the time, walking, armed with a torch to show the way to his motorman companion. And behind the tram followed a close formation of motor cars using the tram as a guiding star to get them home too!

Yet, in a similar fog, a motor bus on its way from Forest Hill to Dulwich was seen crawling along Crescent Wood Road in the wrong direction, a mile off its route, hopelessly lost! This is sufficient proof of the electric tramcar's superiority in thick fog.

This story of No.120 is a typical example of the L.C.C. tradition of service and loyalty to the passenger - an integral part of tramway transport.

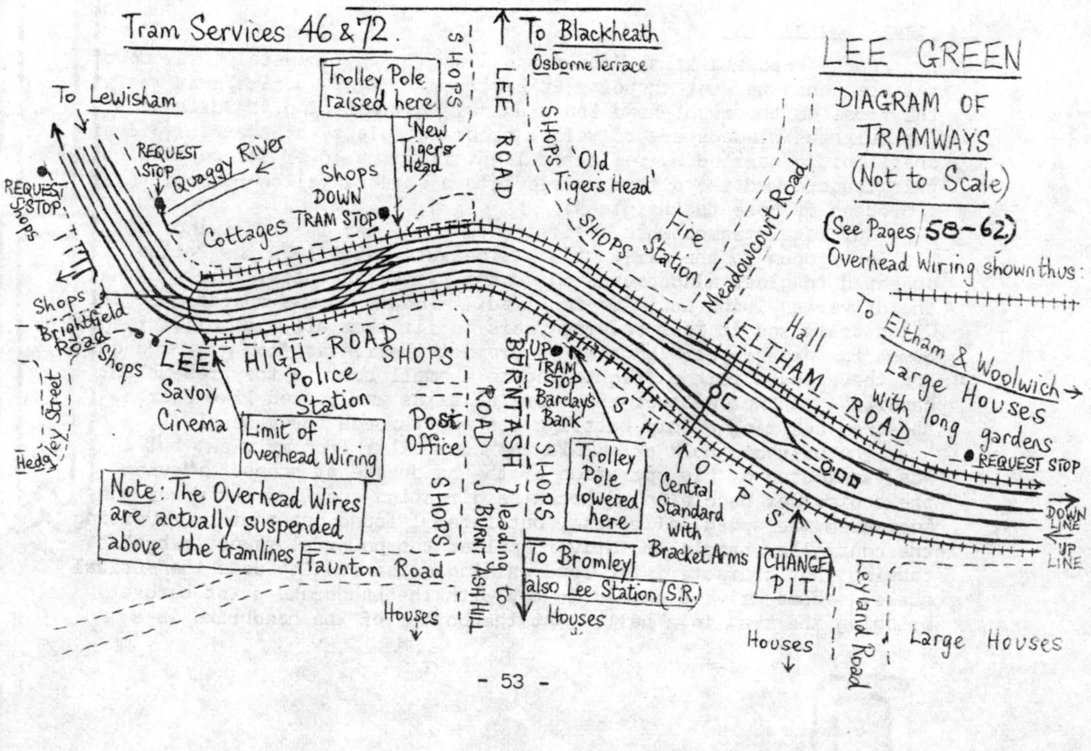

CHILDHOOD FANTASIES AND BOYHOOD REMINISCENCES

Perhaps I may be excused for these personal reminiscences, but I think that they may be of interest to the reader, particularly to boys of today. Anyone who prefers to concentrate on events and facts is welcome to pass over this section.

One of the first sounds which I heard in my life must have been that of an E/1 Class tramcar on Route 46, as I was born of Scottish stock in a nursing home situated in the High Road, Lee, just by Glenton Road crossover; that may partly account for my love of trams. Our house stands in pleasant sylvan surroundings between the Lee Green tram route and the Dartford Loop line of the Southern Railway which serves Lee Station ('for Burnt Ash'), so I have been familiar with trams and trains all my life. From my earliest days I was fascinated by trains, with Kent Coast expresses dashing by, shunting engines at Hither Green Sidings or the Loco Shed - a favourite being "the 8 o'clock Goods", usually pulled by a C Class 0-6-0 steam locomotive, waiting at the signal by our bridge every evening. I liked trams as well as trains because, after all, tramways are a kind of street railway.

Travelling by Tram

When I was small, my Mother and I sat in the downstairs saloon of the tram when we went shopping at Lewisham. My favourite seat was at the front on the right-hand longitudinal seat watching the driver. The bulkhead windows are of yellow or orange glass, so that the driver shall not be dazzled by reflected light from the lower saloon at night; this transformed the outside world into a strange yellow-hued place as I pressed my nose to the glass.

Our local trams, when I first knew them, had their driving platforms open to the air; this was because until 1930 the Police objected to glass windscreens on London trams and buses, thinking that the driver's vision would be impaired. (Route 46 was operated by E/1 Class trams and it took several years to fit them all with windscreens). Some tram drivers wore goggles to protect their eyes from grit and dust and they looked rather frightening to a small boy, as they resembled bandits! In wet weather they wore oilskins and looked like seamen, the tram becoming a ship battling its way through heavy seas!

The driver's bulk often hid the controller from my view, but I was fascinated by his operation of the handbrake at stops. Moving the controller handle in a clockwise direction supplied the power and increased the speed, of course, but later I found out that by reversing the controller handle the driver applied the powerful magnetic brakes, causing that characteristic loud whining noise running down the musical scale. Some drivers seemed to toy with the handbrake a lot before bringing the tram to a halt. At the bottom of the handbrake is a ratchet wheel which the driver secures with his foot by means of a pawl. When this is released, the brake handle spins round several times with a loud clicking noise. (Conductors also do this when the tram leaves a terminus).

Behind the driver are two pedals let into the duckboard floor: one sounding the warning gong to tell other traffic to get out of the way, the other operating the sanding gear in front of the bogie wheels. Usually the steps at the driver's end are folded up by means of a drum-shaped lever. Inside one of the dashes is painted the letter A, that at the other end being B; the word 'Interlock' used to be painted on the controller box at each end, as a reminder to drivers to interlock the controller handle in the 'off' position and remove the reversing key whenever leaving the platform for whatever purpose - an important safety measure. As a small boy this word puzzled me, as it also appeared on labels stitched on to woollen garments from Marks' and Spencer's and I couldn't see any possible connection with trams!

At points and crossings and also at feeder points there are section gaps in the live rails on the conduit system and drivers must shut off power and coast over these. They try to avoid halting on these 'dead' sections and pusher poles are kept at junctions, change pits and other strategic places so that other trams can assist stranded cars off the 'dead'. Where these poles are not available, tram crews will use the long side routeboards (unofficially) instead. Traffic policemen sometimes forget this hazard to trams on the conduit system and will halt a tram on a junction, e.g. at Lewisham Clock Tower; it is then necessary to push or tow the disabled tram on to the live section. At night, the presence of these section gaps is evident to the public as the tram's lights go out temporarily as it passes over the 'dead'. One advantage of the overhead system is that there is no interruption of current supply at junctions and section feeders. The overhead trolley wheel merely flashes as it crosses the overhead frog or insulator and the tram's lights remain on at night.

Should the driver notch up the controller too quickly on starting, thereby causing a too rapid surge of power, there is a sudden bang and a flash from the switchbox above the platform - the automatic circuit-breaker. He must then reset the switch and start off more slowly this time. Incidentally, the driver must pull this switch before he leaves the depot or the tram will not move. Nor will it move unless the driver inserts his key on to the controller and pushes it to 'forward' or 'reverse'. There is only one key for each tram which the driver carries with him when he changes ends at the terminus; that's why boys can't move the rear controller handle - it's locked. He also uses the key to operate the changeover switch on the tram platform from trolley to conduit or vice versa at change pits.

At home, I often got a row for practising my own tram-driving at the hallstand, with two old walking-sticks as handles, accompanied by sound effects! When walking along the pavement, the bonding of the paving stones represented a tram line to this small boy, when he was pretending to be a tram and not a train, as he was sometimes. Another source of annoyance to my parents were blind cords around the house tied in loops to represent trolley ropes, also strings suspended above the garden paths, tied to convenient poles and trees, which were meant to be overhead wires! Although these were high enough for me, they got the adults effectively entangled and I found it expedient to convert the garden system to an imaginary conduit line! Miniature trains were fairly easy to obtain and I have always maintained a model railway from about the age of three, but proper model trams were unobtainable in those days. However, Nanna (my Grandmother) presented me with a large tin tram, equipped with a trolley pole, which I now realise was quite a creditable copy of a Glasgow Corporation 'Coronation' tram. At her house I was also allowed to play with a fine wooden model tram, which had been made by my Grandfather, whose hobby was carpentry and cabinet-making. He once made a fine full-size rocking horse with flowing mane and tail, saddle and bridle, which still exists today. My Mother rode it as a little girl; it was passed on to me and has continued on its way round the family. Unfortunately, the wooden tram went missing, probably when Nanna was flitting (moving) to a new house.

Returning to real trams, apart from the two short longitudinal seats at each end of the lower saloon over the sandboxes, London tram seats have always been transverse on the 2-1 pattern in my lifetime (except the 2-2 transverse seats on No.1 and the 'Felthams') and all the seats have been comfortably upholstered in blue or green moquette, apart from wartime shortages. It was fun as a boy to pull over the transverse-seat backs at the terminus.

As I became older, my favourite seat became the front curved seat upstairs over the driver's head. The backing plate of the 'Venner' number stencil often carried an advertisement for All-Day Tickets or other travel facilities. (The route number on the E/1 Class is shown on a narrow black oblong metal plate with a cut-out stencil or with the white number outline picked out in perforations for the light to shine through at night). The top deck is reached by quarter-turn stairs inside a glass draught-screen at each end, closed by a door bearing the tram's number in black paint on the varnished woodwork under the glass panel. All seats in the upper saloon are upholstered in leather, though a few of the older E/1 Class trams still have slatted wooden seat backs today (1949).

To stop the tram, if the conductor is upstairs collecting fares, one has to strike the brass plunger on the bulkhead near the lower saloon door on the older E/1s, while standing on the swaying platform; this operates the driver's bell by compressed air. If the conductor is on the platform he strikes the plunger twice as the signal to proceed, but if he is upstairs he signals to the driver by blowing his whistle, usually leaning out the window to do so.

When I was nine and travelling to school at Lewisham by tram, I noticed many 'new' trams on our route. These were the 'Rehabilitated' E/1 Class, which seemed luxurious to me, with electric bell pushes and glass windscreens on the driving vestibules. Instead of stencils, the route number is shown on a roller blind in a little window above the destination indicator, both being inset. Instead of rocker panels, the sides of the tram are flush-panelled. On the open-front trams the conductor tied the trolley rope to the stair-rail when it was not in use, or looped it behind the controller when operating on the overhead section; but the 'Rehabs' had a proper cleat to which the trolley rope was attached. Later all the E/1 Class trams on our route were fitted with windscreens and cleats. I did not note individual tramcar numbers before the War, but for some reason I remember travelling on No.1377 along Lee High Road and No.1648 along Eltham Road, Lee - both 'Rehabs' on Service 46 - during Coronation Year (1937).

Even when small, I preferred trams to motor buses because they were reassuring and reliable: I expected them to keep to the lines, just like trains; buses, however, only had a steering wheel to keep them on course. The buses were bumpy and rattled along the uneven roads, which seemed to be constantly in the process of being dug up for water and gas pipes or electric cables to be altered, diverted, laid or relaid. When I was taken on the No.75 Tilling bus route to Purley or the No.136 General route to Bromley the petrol fumes and bumping often made me sick. Trams have never made me ill, nor have steam or electric trains.

(One must say in favour of the old No.75 buses before the War that they were certainly more frequent than the post-war species. Officially there is a scheduled 10-12 minute frequency, but it is common to have to wait 20-30 minutes in Burnt Ash Road for a No.75 nowadays. They are shy, elusive creatures which often travel in threes for protection and may be seen together at Blackheath Station before or after attempting the perilous crossing of the wild wastes of the 'Bleak Heath'! There is such a frequent service of sturdy trams over Shooter's Hill that they have no fear of Highwaymen!)

The Layout of Tramways

A tram journey is far more interesting than a bus ride. To me, a main road without tramlines has always seemed dull - tramlines give it character. Frequently there are crossovers and junctions; every half-mile or so there are numbered feeder boxes, sometimes quite a collection of them at important points. When a tram reaches a corner, the front appears to go straight ahead until the wheels reach the curve and then the body swings round in the new direction. Neat overhead wiring can look attractive and span wires and pull-offs at corners resemble spiders' webs.

The L.C.C. tram stop signs are very colourful: red 'Cars STOP if required'; white and blue 'All Cars STOP Here'; and brown and yellow 'L.C.C. Tramways Fare Stage: All Cars STOP Here' like the one at Lee Green. Some signs are oval with ornamental casing, others flag shaped, fixed to metal posts with fluted bases; on overhead sections the signs are mostly fixed to the overhead pole standards.

If you stand by an overhead standard, you can hear a tram approaching from quite a distance. The musical pitch changes as the trolley wheel passes the insulator on each span wire and the volume of sound increases until the tram passes your pole, then it declines gradually, span by span, till the sound dies away into the distance.

I like the independence of trams. While the other traffic takes the same path, the trams often go their own road, sometimes running between road refuges, sometimes keeping alongside traffic islands as at Lee Green and Camberwell Green, and using their own tracks on Victoria Embankment and through Kingsway Subway. When a hole is dug in the roadway, all traffic has to go round it except trams which continue straight ahead over any excavation - this feature proved invaluable in the 'Blitz'. When the warning signs 'TRACK UP' denote track repairs, red lamps and flags make the tramway look something like a railway line as tie-bars and sleepers normally hidden under the road surface are revealed to public view. The permanent way gangs with their huts, coke braziers, tar boilers and equipment create the atmosphere of a gipsy encampment. At night, free firework displays are often provided by permanent way men cleaning the conduit or welding track joints or pointwork.

<u>Lee Green Change Pit</u>

A free entertainment for boys is provided daily at Lee Green; it used to keep me enthralled for hours (when accompanied by my parents I usually had to be dragged away). This is the change pit in Eltham Road where trams change over from the overhead trolley system to conduit operation. A No.46 or No.72 tram coming from Woolwich slows or stops outside Walter Wood's the greengrocer just by Leyland Road corner. The attendant guides the plough along the conduit slot parallel to the up track, by means of a two-pronged fork, until the plough slips into the tram's carrier frame as the tram moves slowly along, the conduit slot passing meanwhile between the running rails.
The tram, still taking current from the overhead wire, then proceeds about a hundred yards to the corner of Burnt Ash Road, outside

Barclay's Bank - the Lee Green fare stage. Here the tram's changeover switch is moved from overhead to conduit operation. The conductor pulls the trolley pole off the overhead wire and if it is a tram with a single trolley boom, he runs round to the front of the tram and anchors the pole under the roof grab-hook. (This to save doing it on the return journey. Some 'lazy' conductors fix it at the back, but then they have to run round with the pole on the down journey). If the tram has two trolley booms, the conductor does not have to swing the trolley pole, unless the tram is going into New Cross Depot, when both poles have to be secured at one end, as there is limited clearance when a tram is being moved on the traverser in this depot. When the policeman on point duty at Lee Green waves the traffic on, the tram proceeds towards London on the conduit system.

Trams coming from London give a more exciting display as they get 'a good run' at the Lee Green change pit. The trolley pole is raised at the west side of Lee Road, at the traffic island opposite the Express Dairy (formerly Dennis the Butcher's). The trolley rope is pulled through the metal 'pig-tail' above the destination box and looped to the cleat on the dash, the changeover switch is thrown and the tram starts when the conductor rings the bell and the traffic policeman on point duty waves it on. The tram has to run about two hundred yards before reaching the change-pit so that the plough, following the conduit slot, shoots out of the side of the tram at speed and hits the spare ploughs in the change-pit with quite a bump!

It was not until some years later that I discovered that this scene enacted daily at the Lee change-pit is unique: until then I had imagined that this happened at all L.C.C. change-pits. Lee Green has one of the most exciting change pits owing to the velocity at which ploughs are discharged from down trams occasioned by the long distance between changeover point and change pit.

<u>Tickets</u> (For illustrations of tickets see between pages 100/101.)

Tickets were very interesting in the pre-war years as all the geographical stages were indicated; post-war tickets only show numbered stages, except for references to transfer facilities and Workman's Returns. Most boys, like myself, collected bus, tram and train tickets for their wealth of interesting information and my friends and relations helped me. My Father sometimes travelled to and from his office in Bermondsey by No.46 tram with a 6d. Return ticket to Tower Bridge Road (at other times he went by Southern Electric to London Bridge). Besides these 6d. Returns, he often brought me 2d. Cheap Midday tickets from business trips not only in South London, but also in North London and the East End (13-53-71, 43-47-49-75-83, 55-77-81).

The different colours of tickets were fascinating; bus tickets had a larger variety of coloursbecause of their higher fares, but tram tickets were more distinctive with the central white stripe and some bore coloured stripes and overprints. Tram tickets, especially returns and transfers, were longer than today and carried a wealth of information, as the 5d. and 7d. Workman's Returns and the New Cross 4d. Midday Fare still do (1949). The maximum ordinary adult fare up till June 1939 was 5d. single, 8d. return in the L.C.C. Area. One interesting event occurred in 1937 when the 2d. changed from purple pink to light blue and the 3d. from dark blue to light pink.

I understand that in the days of the horse tramway companies stage points often referred to public houses, but that the L.C.C. forbade this, except in the case of those inns that had given their names to major traffic junctions, e.g. Elephant & Castle, Angel, 'Marquis of Granby', but there were some exceptions to this rule. Thus 'Bricklayers' Arms' was shown as Tower Bridge Road on L.C.C. tram tickets, while 'The Dun Cow' in Old Kent Road became Upper Grange Road (renamed Dunton Road in L.P.T.B. days); the 'Noah's Ark' on Routes 68-70 became High Street Deptford. Similarly 'Plough', Dulwich became Dulwich Library, though 'Plough', Clapham was retained - the L.P.T.B. later renamed this stage Clapham Common Station. The 'Swan', Stockwell was allowed as an important junction (but renamed Stockwell Station by L.P.T.B.), but an exception was Stage No.9 on Routes 33-78: Dalberg Road or George Canning - perhaps this was to save space. Croydon, unlike the L.C.C., kept the names of its 'pubs' as fare stages all the way to Purley. One minor point of interest is that return tickets continued to show New Cross Station SECR until 1937 (when it became just New Cross Station), though the S.E. & C.R. became part of the Southern Railway in January 1923.

Tram routes were collected into groups for ticket purposes by the L.C.C. ticket office at Effra Road, Brixton. Each group had a code number and any alterations in the form or naming of the tickets bore a new suffix letter, e.g. successive issues of the 56-58-60-62-84 1d. ticket between 1936-1940 showed code 26L, 26M, 26N on the obverse, but 26J on the reverse of the first two and 26K on the last, as there had been less changes to the Depot Runs mentioned on the reverse side.

However, tickets of the same value would differ considerably in appearance between different groups of routes. Some 1d. to 3d. tickets showed the route numbers across the top of the ticket under the serial number but above the fare stages, e.g.

46 52 54 (Code 21D)   72 & 66EX (Code 34C)   Abbey Wood Depot Service 44 46 (Code 20F)

London Tramways Company: Horse Car No. 338 (white) at Trafalgar Road terminus, East Greenwich (1885)
(Photo: Rev. Charles Spurgeon)

New Cross Gate (c. 1906) showing D Class tramcars with open and covered tops. No. 381 (to Greenwich)
(Commercial view) *(Courtesy J.H. Price)*

Interior view of New Cross Depot (1906) showing two B Class and a D Class car.
(Photo by courtesy of the LCC)

B Class No. 131 crossing Lewisham Bridge (Loampit Vale). (July 1906).
(Photo: Perkins & Son, Lee)

C/2 No. 216 and C/1 No. 240 at Lewisham Obelisk (Loampit Vale) (February 1906).
(Photo: Perkins & Son, Lee; by courtesy of J.H. Price)

Single-decker G Class tramcar No. 589, leaving Kingsway Subway (c. 1910).
(Commercial view)

Class No. 218 in Lordship Lane at Dulwich Common (c. 1908).
(Photo: Card House)

Laying the tram tracks in the High Road, by Church Street, Lee (Winter 1906/7).
(Photo: Perkins & Son, Lee: by courtesy of Lewisham Public Libraries)

Elephant & Castle (1909) from London Road, Southwark. F Class No. 564 (to Tower Bridge); E Class No. 431 (to Waterloo Station); E Class to Streatham; D Class to Water Lane, Brixton; other E and E/1 cars.

(Commercial View)

Board of Trade Inspection of Lewisham—Lee Green tram route: April 25th, 1907. E Class No. 497 at Lee Green terminus. (Note Tilling's Blackheath—Eltham horse 'bus in background right).

(Photo: Perkins & Sons, Lee).

C Class No. 300 at Forest Hill Station terminus (London Road), (c. 1910).
(Commercial view, by courtesy of Lewisham Public Libraries)

M Class No. 1433 (to Beresford Square) on Woolwich Common (July 1910).
(Note double-trolley overhead system used until 1927)
(Photo: Perkins & Sons, Lee)

Royal procession in Walworth Road (1911). A Class No. 97 at Camberwell Gate.
(Photo by Card House)

(L to R): E/1 1098(92); M 1720 (EX); B 124(56); B104(56); C 297(60). Note traverser
(Reproduction by kind permission of the LCC)

Workmen's Cars at Rushey Green, Catford, on a misty morning in April, 1912.
(Photo by courtesy of the LCC)

Lee Green change pit (Eltham Road, Lee), (Winter 1920/1). Note double-wire overhead system (in use until 1927). E/1 Class Trams on Service 46; No. 1381 to High Street, Eltham; No. 1353 to Southwark Bridge.
(Photo: Lee Journal)

D Class No. 361 at Abbey Wood (1930)
(Photograph R. Elliott)

Lower Saloon of E/1 Class Tramcar (1929)
(Photograph by courtesy of the LCC)

M Class No. 1684 at Grove Park Terminus, Service 62 (May 1929). Note unfinished condition of roadway in Downham Way.
(Photographs by kind permission of LCC).

E/3 Class No. 1928 outside Abbey Wood Depot soon after entering service (Summer 1930).
(Photograph by kind permission of LCC)

M Class No. 1710 at Peckham Rye terminus (c. 1930) at Stuart Road.
(Photograph by courtesy of R. Elliott)

HR/2 No. 1883 at Peckham Rye terminus (c. 1933) at Stuart Road.
(Photograph by courtesy of R. Elliott)

LCC Tramways No. 1 'Bluebird' at Charlton Works (May 1932).
(Photo by courtesy of the LCC)

No. 1931, painted white, at New Cross Depot, 1931.
(Photo by courtesy of the LCC)

LCC Tramways No. 1 'Bluebird' at Charlton Works (May 1932).
(Photo by courtesy of the LCC)

ME/3 Class No. 1370 at Grove Park terminus (1933).
(Photo: R. Elliott)

HR/2 Class No. 103 at Blackwall Tunnel (c. 1933)
(Photo: R. Elliott)

Lower Saloon of HR/2 Class tram at Charlton Works.
(Photo by courtesy of the LCC)

E/1 Class No. 835, fitted with experimental bow-collector, at Grove Park terminus, Downham Way (March 1933).
(Photo by kind permission of the LCC)

E/1 Class No. 1172, fitted with experimental pantograph, at Grove Park terminus, Downham Way (March 1933).
(Photo by kind permission of the LCC)

Removing bogies from E/1 Class tramcar under overhaul:
Charlton Works
(Photo by courtesy of the LCC).

ME/3 Class No. 1444 at Charlton Works (1934)
(Photograph London Passenger Transport Board by courtesy of R. Elliott)

E/1R Class No, 1038 taking up the Plough at Lee Green change pit (Eltham Road at Leyland Road) c. 1937.
(Photo by courtesy of W.J. Wyse)

E/1R No. 1481 at Park Road Junction, Forest Hill (August 1939) (Feeder No. 727).
(Photo by courtesy of W.J. Haynes)

E/1 No. 1343 at Southend Pond, Bromley Road during the 1939-1945 War. Note protective netting against bomb blast on the windows, also whitened fender.
(Photo: W.J. Haynes)

E/1R Class No. 1763 at Grove Park terminus during wartime.
(Photo: W.J. Haynes)

E/3 Class No. 1969 at Westminster Underground Station, Victoria Embankment (Fare Stage No.3)
(Photo: K.G. Harvie)

E/1 No. 591, E/1R No. 1226, E/1 No. 1845 (34) at London Road, Elephant & Castle (Fare Stage No. 5).
(Photo: R.F. Mack)

Rebuilt Tram No. 2 in Kennington Road at Kennington Lane.

E/3 Class No. 1941 at Kennington Park junction (Feeder No. 920).
(Photo K.G. Harvie)

E/1R Class No. 978 in Camberwell New Road at Wyndham Road.
(Photo: R.J.S. Wiseman)

HR/2 No. 1880 at Camberwell Green (Feeder No. 628).

(L to R) HR/2 No. 1873, 117 and 140 at Camberwell Green (Denmark Hill).
(Fare Stage No. 7).
(Photo: W.J. Haynes)

HR/2 Class No. 120 at Denmark Hill Station (S.R.) – Champion Park. (Fare Stage No. 8)

HR/2 Class No. 1868 at foot of Dog Kennel Hill, Dulwich. Note unique four-track layout.
(Photo: J.H. Meredith)

HR/2 Class No. 1876 at Dulwich Library, Lordship Lane (Fare Stage No. 11).
(Photo: D. Scott)

HR/2 Class No. 1877, at Horniman's Museum, Forest Hill.

HR/2 Class No. 119 in Stanstead Road, Catford, at Beechfield Road.
(Photo: J.H. Meredith)

E/1 No. 1175 and E/1R No. 1088 in Old Kent Road by Leo Street. Note track repairs.
(Photo: H.B. Priestley)

E/1R Class No. 1676 and No. 1645 at New Cross Gate (Services 72 and 74). (Fare Stage No. 10).
(Photo: H.B. Priestley)

Wheel Van No. 011 in New Cross Road, outside the Depot.
(Photo: A.D. Packer)

E/1 Class No. 553, first service tram over temporary bridge, Deptford Creek: July 10th, 1949.
(Photo: J.H. Meredith)

E/1R Class No. 1422 at the 'Marquis of Granby', Lewisham Way, New Cross (Fare Stage No. 11)
(Photo: W.J. Haynes)

E/1R Class No. 1619 at Crofton Park Station (S.R.) – Brockley Road (Fare Stage No. 13)
(Photo: K.G. Harvie)

Ex-East Ham Tram 83 at Lewisham Obelisk (Fare Stage No. 13).
(Photo: W.J. Wyse)

Ex-West Ham Trams 344 and 297 in Eltham Road, Lee (Service 46).
(Photo: K.G. Harvie)

E/3 Class No. 1928 passing Lee Green change pit, Eltham Road, Lee. (Feeder No. 785).
(Photo: K.G. Harvie)

NOTE: All subsequent photographs (unless otherwise acknowledged) are by K.G. Harvie (Lee).

E/1 Class No. 1007 outside Lewisham Town Hall, Catford (Feeder Box No. 787) (Fare Stage No. 17).
(Photo: J.H. Meredith)

E/1R No. 1569 changing over from trolley to conduit at Downham Way (Bromley Road) (Feeder No. 621)
(Photo: J.H. Meredith)

E/1 No. 1629 at Valeswood Road crossover, Downham Way. (Feeder No. 622).
(Photo: J.H. Meredith)

Ex-West Ham Tram 305 at Eltham Church (Fare Stage No. 18) corner of High Street, Eltham and Well Hall Road.
(Photo: W.J. Haynes)

Ex-East Ham Tram 93 climbing Well Hall Road hill, Eltham.
(Photo: R.J.S. Wiseman)

Ex-West Ham Tram 342 in Well Hall Road at Eltham Common. Note track repairs.
(Photo: A.D. Packer)

Ex-East Ham Tram 88 at Beresford Square, Woolwich. Note Feeder Box No. 978 and telephone).
(Photo: R.J.S. Wiseman)

Some tickets had the route numbers in one corner:-	---- Others had the route numbers in a group:-		or down the middle:-			
	2-4	8-20				
	6	10	33	33	56	66
36 38 40 (Code 16K)	8-20	16-18	35	48	58	74
	2A-4A	22-24		78	60	&
	22-24	42			62	EX
12 31 (Code 5G)	CLAPHAM DEPOT	STREATHAM & THORNTON HTH			84	
	(1S)	(3G)	(Code 56C)	(37B)	(26M)	(31A)

There were two different series of tickets issued on Route 46: 44 46 series on Abbey Wood cars; 46 52 54 on New Cross cars.

Journeys by Tram

As previously mentioned, we often went shopping at Lewisham by tram. However, when aged 9-10 I travelled to school at Lewisham by tram on weekdays. The No.46s & 72s were often full during the morning rush hour, but about 8.30 a.m. every weekday a 'pirate' No.52 came up Lee High Road as far as Glenton Road crossover, showing 'LEWISHAM' on its destination blind. It reversed on the crossover and we boarded the empty tram, which now showed CITY & SOUTHWARK via Old Kent Rd and swung the seat backs over. On showing my L.P.T.B. Identity Card and offering a penny, the conductor issued me with a 1d. Scholar's Return ticket.

On my homeward journey, my ticket was available to Lee Green, but often I got off the tram at Glenton Road fare stage. As this is a request stop, I used to get up from my seat soon after the tram left 'The Rose of Lee' stop. This was necessary as I wanted to bang the bell push on the rear platform and grab the handrail before the tram reached a sharp curve in the track. The tram twists itself, then goes charging up the slight slope to the stop. Once I foolishly jumped off the tram before it stopped and landed in a heap in the road; I never tried that again!

On leaving Glenton Road stop the tram seems to hesitate, then start again - this is just the section gap in the conduit line at Feeder Box No.779 - then it roars over the crossover and goes swaying round the curve by Boone's Chapel (designed by Sir Christopher Wren in 1680). If we continue on board there is a twist in the track just after Church Street stop, then the tram gets up a fair speed after Lee Park stop before slowing down for the hump at Quaggy Bridge (built 1824), where there is a stop opposite Brightfield Road. Then the tram clangs round the curve outside the Savoy Cinema and, passing the old cottages on the left and the Police Station on the right, we clatter over the crossover and the conductor shouts "Lee Green!" and jumps off to put the trolley pole on the overhead wire.

As my brother and sister had died young, my parents quite naturally did not like me to go far by myself. So, to my regret, I was never able to explore the tramways in North and East London on an all-day ticket, for I could not expect them to ride about on trams for hours on end! To them, trams were just for travelling about; my Father had seen and travelled on horse and cable trams in the 1890s but he had no interest in them nor had the electrification of the tramways and the new L.C.C. electric tramcars stirred his imagination. My Mother's eldest brother Leslie and his cousin Douglas were fascinated by railways and made beautiful albums of steam locomotive pictures (one I still treasure), but Leslie went missing, presumed killed, in the Battle of the Somme in 1916 and Douglas fell in Flanders in 1917 - how I wish that I had known them. My Father had no real appreciation of the beauty of a S.E. & C.R. D Class 4-4-0 Locomotive in its splendour of Brunswick green, brass dome and copper chimney cap speeding through Hither Green, as I would have done. I feel that I really belong to the previous generation, as my parents married well on in life, but the year that I was born saw the highest tramway mileage in the British Isles and, sad to say, British tramways and railways have been on the decline all my life. As a boy, I had to be content with tram maps and tickets showing 'Foreign' fare stages such as Stamford Hill, Lea Bridge, Hackney Station, Victoria Park, Gardiner's Corner, West India Docks, Stratford Broadway, Wanstead Flats, Chingford Mount and Epping Forest.

However, my long-suffering parents took me over much of South East London by tram. Boarding a No.46 or 72 tram at Lee Green, we soon shed the plough and immediately plunge into the green tunnel of Eltham Road (the big old houses have long front gardens thickly studded with trees) and then at Kidbrooke Park Road we burst out into an open space, once green fields but partly covered with semi-detached houses on the right just before the 1939-1945 War; on the left playing fields and Sutcliffe Park were formed. There is an overhead feeder just before Kidbrooke Park Road and a crossover just after Sidcup Road junction.

There is another crossover at Eltham Green. The new Route 72 commenced operation when I was nearly five and avoids the centre of Eltham by the Westhorne Avenue cut-off, a new wide road built through a council housing scheme. The continuation of this road through Horn Park to Burnt Ash Hill, Lee (unfortunately destroying a local beauty spot - the picturesque farm and duckpond were surrounded by orchards) was opened about 1938 as a dual carriageway, but the planned tramway extension to Grove Park Station was never laid. At Middle Park Avenue and Rochester Way roundabouts were made and the trams have to proceed slowly round the perimeter; occasionally the automatic points do not function and the driver has to change them with his point-iron.

If we are on a No.46, our tram climbs Eltham Hill, passing the Swimming Baths on the left and the Gaumont Cinema on the right, then makes a double bend round the churchyard, with St. John's Church on its knoll above, and turns left into Well Hall Road. Here Service 44 used to terminate at the facing crossover just by the passenger shelter, but since May 1948 it has been extended down Eltham Hill to Eltham Green crossover and now only an occasional tram reverses at Eltham Church.

At Eltham we can visit Prince John's Palace, full of historical interest, or run down Well Hall Road hill and under the railway bridge at the Station to the newly-opened Pleasaunce at Well Hall, with the old Tudor Barn, moat, beautiful rose gardens and scenic rock gardens and goldfish pools. This was once the home of Margaret Roper, daughter of Sir Thomas More, and her husband William Roper. The Tudor Barn today houses an art gallery and a tearoom (very welcome!) On the way to Woolwich were a number of wartime shacks, still inhabited, on the southern slopes of Shooter's Hill, but about 1937 they were replaced by a northward extension of Woolwich Borough Council's Page Estate (commenced 1920) which embraces Westhorne Avenue. On the right of the tram route lie Eltham Common, Jack Wood and Castlewood, which we like to visit sometimes; there is a tearoom in Severndroog Castle.

From the crossover at Shooter's Hill Road there are no buildings on the left side of the tram for a mile - just the wide expanse of Woolwich Common. On the right is the Royal Military Academy, standing in its spacious grounds, then we pass the Prince Imperial Monument (commemorating the French Emperor Napoleon III's son killed in the Zulu War of 1879). There are several terraces of Regency houses on the right to Nightingale Place, one being the birthplace of General Charles Gordon (1833-1885) of China and Khartoum fame.

Entering the one-way section and passing the Garrison Church (later bombed in the 1939-1945 War) on the right and the Royal Artillery Barracks, we descend a steep hill into Woolwich (up trams climb gradually up New Road on the other side of the church). Scarcely have the tracks met at Anglesea Road crossover when they part again and make a loop round Green's End and through the Market in Beresford Square crowded by stalls and shoppers on either side, turning again into New Road for the return journey to London. There are several connections with the Abbey Wood route, including an interlaced curve, used mostly for depot journeys.

Twice we crossed Woolwich Free Ferry in my Uncle's motor-car on our way to visit a distant relative at Westcliff on Sea. On these occasions we saw open-balcony East Ham trams on Route 73 to Wanstead Park. The trams at Southend on Sea were bogie cars something like London's in appearance, though on a narrower gauge (3ft. 6ins.) and all on the overhead system. My Uncle had an argument with a tram driver when the car strayed on to the tramlines on Southend Esplanade, which were semi-reserved like those on Victoria Embankment. I shall never forget the sight of the curious tram passengers gazing down at us in the car - for once my position was reversed; normally I was in the habit of looking down on motor cars from my seat in a tram! No wonder that many motorists dislike trams, which give them an inferiority complex: trams are so solid and powerful towering above them. On one occasion when we went there by train, I managed a tram-ride from Westcliff to Southend and return, but when we went by car I just couldn't get my parents to take me on the Southend trams.

To return to the London trams, sometimes we continued our journey from Lee Green and went on from Woolwich to Bostall Woods. The route through Plumstead is interesting because of several single-track sections (though most of them were eliminated in the 1914-1919 War). In places the double track can be operated as a single line by means of facing crossovers when other vehicles obstruct the tracks in these narrow streets. At Wickham Lane junction, just beyond St. Nicholas's Church, the trams to Dartford used to branch right, but since 1936 this route and the route to Erith have been operated by trolleybuses.

The school had a half-holiday on Empire Day: May 24th, 1937, so I persuaded Mum to take me to Abbey Wood by tram; previously I had never been beyond Bostall Hill. We were fortunate to get a No.46 tram running right through from Lee Green to Abbey Wood. Here we saw the Depot, which houses many of our local trams, besides enjoying the beauty of the nearby woods. On our return journey, however, we had to change trams at Beresford Square, Woolwich.

On trips to Bromley by No.136 (later No.94) bus, we glimpsed the Grove Park tram terminus in Downham Way, but we did not often use the No.54 & 74 trams before the War, as they do not run near our home. Sometimes, however, we would take a tram from Lewisham or Catford along Bromley Road to Peter Pan's Pool at Southend Village (Routes 52,54,74).

During the school holidays we often went up to London by tram using the 2d. Cheap Midday Fare (1d. for me). We could go all the way to the Embankment by No.72 tram up Loampit Hill, past three junctions and a fascinating glimpse of the depot at New Cross, then through Peckham and Camberwell, round Kennington Park and over Westminster Bridge, passing Big Ben and Boadicea. Occasionally we met strange single-deck trams scuttling about like large beetles - these were the permanent way works cars. For some obscure reason, which I don't now remember, I attributed sinister motives to these works cars during my earlier years, probably because they were 'different' from the other trams - this was certainly a calumny that they did not deserve, being very useful members of the tramway fleet.

Sometimes we changed at New Cross Gate or Camberwell Green to a No.35 tram which went up Walworth Road and negotiated the busy junctions at the Elephant & Castle, in those days surrounded by large shops, like Isaac Walton's and Tarn & Company, not the wilderness of bomb-scarred ruins it now is. Tram drivers have to be skilful at junctions not to get stuck on the 'dead' (the gap in the conductor rail), especially if a traffic policeman suddenly holds up his hand.

The trams on Route 35 are more modern than our E/1s: they are quieter and run with a more mellow D-d-d-D sound. They have large illuminated boxes of white pearl glass over which a big route number stencil is fitted. They run through the mysterious Kingsway Subway to Bloomsbury (where the Milbro model railway shop stands in Southampton Row). In pre-war days they disappeared along Theobalds Road into the then unknown world (to me) of North London. I was always impressed with the courtesy and interest shown by Mills Bros. staff. At the Model Railway Exhibition at the Central Hall, Westminster in April 1939. I was shown one of their Southern Railway wooden corridor coaches with real glass windows and told that the price was 35/6 each. I was determined to have the authentic model and it took me half my pocket money (6d. a week) for seven months and my birthday money to reach this tremendous sum. When we went to the Milbro shop at the end of July, the gentleman told me that the correct price was 36/6. "Oh!" I said with disappointment, your representative at the Model Railway Exhibition said that the price was 35/6." "Well, sir," the gentleman replied," if he told you that, you may have it for 35/6" and so I did. I have never forgotten that pleasant episode when this gentleman honoured the word of a 12-year-old boy. Perhaps he was a Scout too.

Sometimes, on our way home from Bloomsbury, we enjoyed the exhilarating plunge down the ramp in Kingsway into the inky blackness below before shooting up into Holborn Tram Station. On other occasions we would descend the steps to the tram stations at Holborn and Aldwych, listen for the approaching thunder and watch the moving lights grow larger, till with a roar a No.31, 33 or 35 reveals its splendour in the lighted station. What fun to use the driver's platform (and stairs) for boarding and alighting at the central platform - What a pity they never built the intended Strand station! How thrilling to watch the tunnel walls zoom by, especially in the winding single-line tunnels under Aldwych where the tram seems almost to brush the walls! The signal lights make it seem like an underground railway. Then the speck of daylight suddenly appears straight ahead and rapidly grows larger - a framed picture of the River Thames, with tugs and barges proceeding upstream and downstream across which the Embankment trams pass to and fro.

While Waterloo Bridge was being rebuilt, a new entrance was made to Kingsway Subway about 1938 and the trams entered and left the tunnel under a maze of steelwork and scaffolding until the stonework was completed. When I first knew the Subway, 'Tubby' the tramwayman used to stand in the middle of the Embankment, wave a red flag to stop other traffic and blow his whistle to tell the trams to cross the roadway to and from the tunnel. Later, the present traffic lights were installed.

Occasionally we went to the City by No.46 tram or to Victoria by a No.54, but most of our pre-war trips to London crossed Westminster Bridge. I was especially intrigued by the No.14s for Wandsworth and the No.26s for Kew Bridge, as I never got the chance to ride on them to those faraway places! On Victoria Embankment a continual procession of E/1s, E/3s, HR/2s and 'Felthams' invite the public to visit every part of South London, and you can get really close to the trams as they glide safely beside the pavement under the riverside trees. As a boy I was never afraid of trams or trains because I trusted them to keep to their rails. I have been fortunate in that I have never seen a tramway or railway accident in my life, but I have always been wary of motor vehicles with their huge unprotected wheels.

Besides our local trams, my favourite route was, and still is, 'via Dulwich'. I have to thank my Grandmother - 'Nanna' - for introducing me to the HR/2 Class trams when she took us to Dulwich Park. These modern trams make a very musical sound (due to their helical gears) as they glide smoothly up and down the steep hills or hum along the more level stretches. When I was very young, I preferred the No.62s 'with arms' to the No.58s, which had 'no arms'. It must have seemed to me that the 101-159 series, which were equipped for conduit working only, had something vital missing as they had no trolley poles - until the War Nos.101-135 at Camberwell Depot were usually kept on Service 58, perhaps because No.62 had worked on the overhead section to Grove Park at one time (and there may have been thoughts of doing so again). Nos.136-159 operated from Holloway Depot on Routes 11 (Highgate Hill) and 35 until 1940. Once, after visiting Gamages' we saw an older tram 'without arms' on Route 3 at Holborn terminus in Gray's Inn Road, opposite the Tudor buildings of Staple Inn - it must have been an E Class tramcar.

Watching the driver on an HR/2 via Dulwich is even more interesting than on an E/1 or E/3 on other routes. At Horniman's Museum and at the top of Dog Kennel Hill, also at Goodrich Road, Dulwich, on the descending journey, he winds round the curved wheel of the slipper brake set at right angles to the handbrake handle; this works the special track brakes for these steep hills. The interior of the HR/2 Class tram is light and attractive, with blue moquette seating in the lower saloon and cheerful red leather seats upstairs (brown leather covers were used during the War).

If I was lucky I could get a trip from Lee to London via Dulwich or vice versa, but usually the HR/2s took us to Dulwich or Greenwich. Sometimes we went to Horniman's Museum at Forest Hill, one special attraction being the German clock from the Black Forest, on which moving figures representing Our Lord and the Twelve Apostles appear every afternoon at four o'clock; then Jesus and eleven Apostles go in through one door, while Judas Iscariot turns his back on Christ and goes off through another door. On several occasions we went to Peckham Rye Park (change to No.56 or 84 at Goose Green, but I have never seen a goose there!), but usually we got off the tram at Dulwich Library in Lordship Lane and walked down Eynella Road to Dulwich Park.

This was my favourite local outing and I still enjoy it today: No.62 tram to Dulwich Library, visit Dulwich Park with a row on the lake, then tea at the Park refreshment room or the baker's shop in Dulwich Village. The beautiful wooded scenery around Dulwich has always appealed to me and there are picturesque old cottages and gracious old houses and mansions, besides historic buildings like those of Dulwich College and the Picture Gallery, though unfortunately some were damaged or destroyed during the war by enemy action. Apart from that, even in Dulwich Park one can hear the musical sound of the HR/2s in Lordship Lane, anticipating the pleasure of the tram journey home.

Special attractions of the No.58/62 tram route between Catford and Camberwell are the railway stations at Catford Bridge, Catford, Forest Hill, Lordship Lane, East Dulwich and Denmark Hill (with the chance of seeing a passing train); triangular tramway junctions at St. Laurence's Church, Catford, Brockley Rise/Cranston Road and Goose Green; the No.35/66 terminus at Forest Hill Station; the unique four-track layout on Dog Kennel Hill; the many leafy roads; the numerous curves (especially those in Sunderland Road and Devonshire Road, Forest Hill) and the frequent changes of gradient requiring many different techniques of tram driving.

In the tearoom at Dulwich Park there used to hang on the wall a London County Council Tramways map which must have been issued some year between 1927 and 1930. This fascinated me, as it showed Services 76, 78, 80 terminating at West Norwood, whereas my tram maps at home showed Nos. 33, 48, 78. On my first visit to Brockwell Park one Bank Holiday, I was surprised to find the trams at Herne Hill operating on the overhead system, even the No.33s which I had previously met on the Embankment and in Kingsway Subway. I was also reminded of the Embankment by the way that the trams run by the kerbside outside Brockwell Park railings. An original L.C.C. overhead standard with elaborate scrollwork stands in the middle of the road at Herne Hill junction.

A visit to Greenwich Park and Greenwich Pier, usually approached by No.75 bus, often meant a return trip on an HR/2 tram between Greenwich and Lewisham, then an E/1 tram to Lee.

This section of the No.58/62 tram route consists of several stretches of single track with passing loops in South Street and Lewisham Road; in London Street, Greenwich there is a stretch of single track with double conduit - a centre hatch makes it possible to push a plough across from one conduit to another should a tram have to be reversed here. The No.68/70 route was explored as far as Deptford Creek Bridge and I had seen No.68s around the Elephant and No.70s down below London Bridge Station, but I did not travel on 'the slow road' via Rotherhithe until my teens.

(Note to Second Edition: E/1 Class Tram 599 'starred' in the 1951 film 'Pool of London', several quite lengthy shots in Tooley Street being taken, also interior views of the tram. There was also a brief glimpse of Camberwell Green with HR/2s).

In Greenwich Park there is the Royal Observatory and the 'meridian line', besides flower gardens, a deer enclosure, large open spaces for games, a boating lake and a tearoom. It is bordered by several 18th Century houses in Chesterfield Walk, including the Ranger's House; on the east side is 'Vanbrugh Castle'. There were naval relics (including Admiral Lord Nelson's uniform worn at the Battle of Trafalgar in 1805 still stained with his blood) and models of sea battles in the Painted Hall of the Royal Naval College, which were on show to the public. About 1937 they were moved across Romney Road to the Queen's House and placed in the National Maritime Museum, which was opened there by H.M. King George VI.

Once we went through Blackwall Tunnel on a No.108 bus and I had my only glimpse of trams operating on Routes 65 & 67 at Poplar. We came home on a HR/2 to Lewisham Obelisk, where we changed to a Lee tram.

When I was nearly eleven, I became a boarder at Caterham School in Surrey, partly for health reasons, so for the next seven years I was only at home at weekends and during the school holidays. During the 1939-1945 War I did not realise that All-Day facilities had been withdrawn, as wartime was not a suitable time for joy-riding on trams in London all day long, especially during the flying-bomb and rocket raids. When we had several days' holiday in May 1945 to celebrate VE Day (Victory in Europe), I decided to buy a 1/- All-Day ticket on the trams. Imagine my disappointment when the woman conductor, after consulting the elderly driver, informed me that 1/- All-Day tickets had been withdrawn during the War! Still, tram travel has remained cheaper for longer mileages than journeys by motor-bus or trolleybus in London, so we are fortunate in that respect.

STREET LIGHTING ON TRAMWAY ROUTES

In many parts of South London the South Metropolitan Gas Company suspended gas lamps on span wires over the conduit tramway tracks. The lamps were wound to the pavement for maintenance by turning a crank lever. Around Kennington and in S.W. London, however, they suspended their lamps from bracket arms on standards at the side of the road. In the Borough of Woolwich, however, electric lamps were fixed to the tramway overhead standards or slung on span wires across the road above the overhead tram wires, as in Eltham Road, and are still in use.

About 1937 the Lewisham Borough Council installed elegant square electric lanterns on columns at alternate sides of the roads in London Road and Stanstead Road, around Forest Hill Station and in Brockley Rise and Stondon Park as far as the borough boundary in Brockley Road, also down Loampit Hill and Vale and along Lewisham High Street. Just before the 1939-1945 War similar columns but with semi-circular lanterns were erected up Downham Way between Bromley Road corner and Grove Park Station. At the time of the Coronation in 1937 flags, garlands and coloured bunting were hung from lighting standards at Lewisham, Lee Green, Catford, Downham (Bromley Road) and Forest Hill Station. Only recently (1949),have electric light standards of a utilitarian design replaced gas lighting in Lee High Road, Rushey Green, Catford Road and Bromley Road. All these lanterns give a blue mercury-vapour glow.

Just before the War, Camberwell Borough Council installed electric lighting standards (of the same design as those used by the L.B.C. in Downham Way) on tramway routes and other main roads. This design was also used in Norwood Road between Herne Hill and West Norwood in the Borough of Lambeth, though the rest of the borough has been lit by gas until very recently - utility electric standards are now being installed in Kennington Road. Deptford prefers concrete columns for electric lighting, but the Boroughs of Greenwich and Southwark retain gas lighting for main roads, also Bermondsey, except in Southwark between Elephant & Castle and St. George's Church, also in Newington Butts, Walworth Road, New Kent Road, Great Dover Street, where elegant electric lanterns are used. Finally, the elaborate standards on Victoria Embankment, bearing the coats-of-arms of the Cities of London and Westminster, which support electric lights on span wires, are worthy of note.

The various types of lighting standards are an essential part of the South London tramway scene; hence this digression from real tramway matters.

THE 1939 - 1945 WAR

On the night of August 11th, 1939 a blackout test was held in the London area. Trams were praised as having the safest blackout measures; 'the trams' hooded lights were very successful.'

The evacuation of London schoolchildren began on Friday, September 1st, 1939 - the date of the German invasion of Poland - and was almost complete by the time that Great Britain declared war on Nazi Germany on Sunday, September 3rd. 533 London trams helped to convey the children to railway stations, where they boarded trains for the country. In a further evacuation of children and mothers in June 1940 (after Dunkirk) 54 trams were used.

When the blackout was imposed at the outbreak of war, tram headlights were masked and the fenders painted white. Schedules had to be lengthened to cope with lower speeds during blackout hours; the reduced lighting made the task of drivers and conductors very difficult. Women conductors were employed again from October 1940. Fortunately, the trams were able to maintain good services during daylight hours (apart from air raids), as they were free from fuel restrictions.

As the side route number stencils under the stairs could not be seen in the blackout, these were moved to a new position at the bottom right corner of the lower saloon window nearest to each driving platform. They remain in this position today (1949) (when the crews remember to carry them), as the original platform signal lights (disused during the war) were damaged or removed from the trams. For this reason also, blackout masks are still retained on the trams today as these are now the sole means of displaying a rear red light at night. (Compare pre-War and post-War views of London trams).

During Autumn 1939 motor-bus services were reduced, owing to petrol rationing; the public were exhorted to 'use the trams instead.' London Transport published advertisements in local newspapers giving alternative tramway services. During successive years of the War, as the provision of fuel oil became more difficult, quite a number of bus services were withdrawn where they paralleled tramway routes.

Tram track maintenance had to be carried out in daylight owing to the blackout; work at junctions had to be confined to weekends, when traffic was lighter and single-line working could be instituted. Later during the War some night work was allowed, using screened equipment, except during air raid warnings. From time to time, replacement of special work (points and crossings) was temporarily delayed by a shortage of manganese steel supplies.

In spite of the national emergency, London Transport persisted in completing their trolleybus programme in North and East London till only the Kingsway Subway routes (Nos.31, 33,35) remained. The last 'conversion' was carried out at the weekend after the Dunkirk Evacuation was completed in June 1940 - not a very patriotic move. (During the 'Blitz' many lengths of trolleybus wiring along conduit tramways in East London were blown down by bombing. Engineers wired up a half-mile diversion in the Commercial Road and erected 43 overhead standards. One wonders if the trams might not have done better in East London had they been allowed to continue operating there - they certainly proved more versatile in South London during the Blitz than most folk expected. In the Summer of 1943, miles of tramlines capable of use were lying disused in the roadways of East Ham and West Ham). Fortunately, however, many trams from West Ham and Poplar Depots were stored at Hampstead Depot in case of emergency, quite a number being used to replace blitz casualties.

The fare increases of June 11th, 1939, anticipating the War, raised the 8d. Return to 9d. and the 2d. Cheap Midday Fare to 3d., while the 5d. and 6d. Returns were withdrawn. From July 1940 the penny fare single was raised to $1\frac{1}{2}$d. and the 2d. Workman Return became $2\frac{1}{2}$d. Other results were the raising of the 5d. maximum in the L.C.C.

Area south of Bloomsbury to 6d. single, another stage being added, and the disappearance of the 1/- through fare on Service 35; knowing passengers purchased a 1/- All Day ticket now. (The 9d. Return was still available on Service 35 for a 6d. journey, e.g. Forest Hill Station - Bloomsbury; Camberwell Green - Nag's Head, Holloway; Elephant & Castle - Highgate (Archway Tavern).

From May 1940 certain rush-hour journeys on Service 46 were extended from Woolwich to Wickham Lane, Plumstead. From January 24th the rush-hour service on Route 46 had been augmented to give a 3-minute service (instead of a 4-minute service as previously), while a 4-minute service operated during 'normal' hours, making 15-20 trams an hour. This was to cater for workers' traffic to and from Woolwich Arsenal and other local factories.

The tramway staff had received training in air raid precautions. Over a thousand tram drivers had been trained to drive motor buses to maintain emergency diversion services if tram routes were cut. A special device was made available to the L.C.C. Fire Brigade and Auxiliary Fire Service so that they could cut off the overhead electric current in the neighbourhood of any fire. The Tramway Control telephone exchange was transferred from Camberwell to the Oval Tube Station, Kennington.

When air raids first began, tram crews stopped their cars and took shelter with their passengers, but soon they were only taking cover when things got 'too hot'. Conductors were issued with lists of public shelters on their routes for the benefit of passengers. Sleeping accommodation was provided for staff on early turns or any bombed-out or unable to get home.

Though Nazi air raids on London commenced in August 1940, tram services were not affected until September. Some tram drivers risked passing delayed action bombs and many crews had a special bell code whether to 'stop' or 'step on it' when bombs were falling. When baskets of incendiary bombs burst over trams, the crews used poles to knock them off the roof.

Continuous air raids occurred from September 1940 until the end of the year and then fairly frequently during the first four months of 1941 (the last major raid being on the night of May 10th/11th). Incidents disrupting tram tracks during that period were as follows:-

<u>1940:</u>

<u>Thursday, September 5th</u> : A high-explosive bomb falling at the corner of Westhorne Avenue and Briset Road, Eltham brought down the overhead wires on Route 72. The Overhead Gang worked through the night so that full services were operating next morning.

Friday, September 6th : Store collapsed across Borough High Street - trams diverted via Southwark Bridge Road. Route reopened on September 15th.

Saturday, September 7th : UXB by points at Lewisham Obelisk about 6.0 p.m. - exploded about 11.30 p.m. - track damaged. (Restored within a week). High Street, Lewisham blocked near Albion Road - debris soon cleared off tramlines and services restored. High explosive and incendiary bombs on Camberwell Depot destroyed 20 trams and damaged others.

Sunday, September 8th : Unexploded bomb at New Cross Gate Station. Trams from London reverse at New Cross Gate; trams from suburban termini reverse at 'Marquis of Granby'. Trams stored at Hampstead Depot sent to S.E. London to maintain services. More H.E.s and incendiaries on Camberwell Depot.

Monday, September 9th : Camberwell New Road blocked; trams diverted via Walworth Road & Elephant (Nos. 54, 58, 66 continuing to Victoria via Lambeth Road & Vauxhall). Southwark Bridge closed; trams diverted to Hop Exchange (reopened during evening). Daylight hit on St. Thomas's Hospital - Westminster Bridge closed (reopened 6.0 p.m.). An unexploded bomb at Well Hall Circus cut Routes 44, 46, 72 for three days until it was removed; meantime trams reversed at a safe distance on each side.

Tuesday, September 10th : E/1R Class Tram 1385 (Service 40) blown off down line in Kennington Road at 'The Horns'. Harleyford Road blocked: Nos. 54, 58, 66 via Elephant as yesterday. No.46 from 'Marquis' reversing at Lee Green. H.E. on Victoria Embankment at Charing Cross Station during night, blocking road. Another crater on the Embankment at the Temple blocked tram track until 18th September.

Thursday, September 12th : All tram services suspended - probable hit on main feeder cable outside Greenwich Power Station, but No.70s from Tooley Street restored during evening. Damage to main cable from Greenwich Power Station later confirmed. New Cross sub-station working again nine hours later.

Friday, September 13th : River service between Westminster and Woolwich began, using 15 river steamers and tugs. 36-38-40 tram tickets issued by tram conductors on board. (River service continued until November 2nd, 1940 except when adversely affected by tides, fogs and mines in the Thames). Tram track on east side of Peckham Rye damaged: Nos.56 & 84 reverse at Nunhead Lane (line reopened by end of month). Victoria - Kennington and Camberwell - New Cross Gate tram services restored. H.E. in Lower Road, Rotherhithe cut Routes 68 & 70 until early January 1941. Romney Road and Trafalgar Road, Greenwich blocked (until December 14th), also Bromley Road, Catford (until October 4th).

Saturday, September 14th : All services restored, except on the Embankment, Camberwell New Road, New Cross Gate - 'Marquis'; Greenwich - Charlton. No.66 working Vauxhall - Stockwell - Brixton - Coldharbour Lane - Camberwell - Peckham - New Cross Gate.

Sunday, September 15th : H.Es fell at Shooter's Hill Road and Well Hall Road (Eltham Common), destroying tracks and overhead wires. Nos. 46 & 72 terminated at the Odeon, Well Hall Circus and a single-line shuttle service worked from there to Eltham Common (Arsenal Road). Inadequate emergency 'bus service (every 20 minutes during rush hours) from Woolwich to Eltham. (185 German aircraft shot down today).

At this time, the roads between Lewisham and Greenwich and between Lewisham and Catford were also blocked. No.54 diverted via Brockley to Catford (terminus). Nos. 58 & 62 terminated at Catford. Bromley Road closed; several trams destroyed by fire at Bellingham Road when H.E. hit a gas main. Emergency 'bus services from Catford to Blackwall Tunnel and to Grove Park using diversion routes. The Lewisham - Catford section was soon reopened. Unexploded bombs were causing breaks in tram services.

Monday, September 16th : High tension cable damaged: five sub-stations out of action.

Tuesday, September 17th : Vauxhall Bridge Road blocked: Nos. 54,58, 66, terminate at Vauxhall. (Temporary bridge being constructed on Victoria Embankment by Charing Cross Station).

Wednesday, September 18th : Through running resumed on Embankment using temporary bridge over crater (for trams only). Camberwell New Road reopened. Unexploded bomb on Denmark Hill - no trams between Camberwell Green and Champion Park. Nos. 36, 38, 40 from 'Marquis' terminating at Greenwich - craters in Trafalgar Road and Woolwich Road, etc. Trams working between Woolwich Ferry and Abbey Wood. No.74 working from 'Marquis' to Brockley Cross only.

Thursday, September 19th : New Cross Gate - 'Marquis' reopened. Up line in Kennington Road reopened, but trams return via Elephant and Kennington Park Road.

Friday, September 20th : Nos. 68 & 70 still working from London to Rotherhithe only. H.E. at Well Hall Circus, Eltham brought down overhead wiring, which was soon replaced. Unexploded bomb on Eltham Hill further afected No.46: bomb exploded some days later, making crater in tram track.

Monday, September 23rd : No.74 extended from Brockley to Catford.

Thursday, September 26th : Two H.Es at Kennington Gate. Nos.40,54,58, 66,72 diverted via Walworth Road to Embankment. Nos.46 & 72 extended from Lee to Eltham.

Saturday, September 28th : Open-fronted trams (ex-Poplar Depot, stored at Hampstead) working Service 35 between Bloomsbury and Highgate, also No.33 between Bloomsbury and Balls Pond Road. These services were operated whenever E/3s from South London could not reach North London and also to augment trolleybus services affected by 'incidents'. Among the E/1 Class noted on these duties were Nos.1000, 1005, 1049, 1050, 1073, 1107, 1124, 1166, 1217, 1252, 1259, 1262, 1302 & 1304.

Tuesday, October 1st : Trams to Vauxhall again, continuing over the bridge to Grosvenor Road, thence emergency 'buses to Victoria.

Wednesday, October 2nd : Tramlines damaged in High Road, Lee (by Glenton Road) - soon reopened.

Thursday, October 3rd : Adhesive window netting to prevent flying glass first fitted to trams, though 'buses had it a fortnight before.

Friday, October 4th : H.Es in Woolwich Road and at New Cross Gate (east side of triangle). Old Kent Road tram services run into Queen's Road, reverse on crossover there and use western spur. Bromley Road, Catford reopened to trams.

Monday, October 7th : Shardeloes Road, Brockley blocked: No.35 worked via Lewisham and Catford to Forest Hill; No.66 via same route to Brockley Cross: No.74 working Brockley - Catford only. By October 12th, No.35s were using Malpas Road en route for Forest Hill, but returning to London via Catford & Lewisham.

Tuesday, October 8th : Two trams damaged near Elephant by low-level daylight raid during morning. (Two 'buses wrecked, but road soon reopened).

Wednesday, October 9th : Through services via Denmark Hill resumed on Dulwich routes.

Thursday, October 10th : H.E. in Bromley Road, near Southend Village (line reopened by October 22nd).

Monday, October 14th : Through services restored to Victoria terminus.

Early in October a high-explosive bomb fell outside the Odeon Cinema, Well Hall Circus, Eltham. This caused a reduced No.72 service and No.46 terminated at Eltham Church. In mid-October, Eltham Hill was blocked. Bus route 21 was strengthened to replace Tram 46, and No.72 was augmented between Lewisham and Middle Park Avenue. By this time, No.44 had been restored between Woolwich and Eltham Church.

For weeks no trams had operated beyond St. Laurence's Church, Catford, except for a few days after October 4th, owing to damage in Bromley Road, or between Lewisham and Greenwich, three craters blocking the road at Lewisham Road, South Street and Romney Road. Emergency 'Buses worked on diversion routes to Grove Park and Blackwall Tunnel.

Nos. 58 & 62 worked to Catford and Lewisham only, 52, 54, 74 to Catford only. Several damaged trams were parked outside St. Laurence's Church on the south and east sides of the triangle and in Bromley Road.

Tuesday, October 15th : H.E. had caused damage to the roof of New Cross Depot and several trams standing below.

Thursday, October 17th : H.E. scored direct hit on New Cross Gate Station railway bridge about 7.30 p.m., severing S.E. London tram routes. 'Buses were diverted via Pepys Road and Brockley Cross. Trams from London reversed at New Cross Gate; trams from suburban termini reversed at the 'Marquis'. E/1 No.1499 was abandoned on the up line about twenty yards east of the station with all its windows broken and debris on the front platform - it had been moved there from Lewisham High Road, where it had been disabled. (The bridge was not fully rebuilt until three months had elapsed). Next day the following services were operating from the 'Marquis':- to Greenwich Church; to Lee & Westhorne Avenue; and a circular service 'Marquis' - Lewisham - Catford - Stanstead Road - Brockley - 'Marquis' and vice versa. Trams often carried no route numbers or else incorrect ones. An emergency 'bus service operated Greenwich - Charlton. Trams were also working from Church Lane, Charlton to Abbey Wood. A high explosive bomb blocked Old Kent Road at Dunton Road; the line reopened on October 22nd. Holloway Depot had been hit and some trams damaged.

Monday, October 21st : Blackfriars Road blocked (soon reopened); also Southwark Bridge Road (reopened November 15th), Vauxhall Cross (restored by October 26th) and Old Kent Road (soon reopened). Route 46 was working in three sections: Southwark Bridge - Dunton Road; shuttle service down Old Kent Road to New Cross Gate; 'Marquis of Granby' - Eltham. HR/2 on shuttle service: Vauxhall Bridge - Victoria.

Friday, October 25th : H.E. scored direct hit on centre of five southbound trams waiting for the traffic lights at Blackfriars Road railway bridge during morning rush hour. (Two E/1s from Clapham Depot were practically destroyed; HR/2 Class Tram 1863 (Service 56) lost its windows). Services were restored by the evening. Trams were unable to proceed beyond Brockley at this time.

Saturday, October 26th : Walworth Road up line blocked: trams diverted via Vauxhall or Kennington & Elephant. Services to Victoria terminus were restored. Camberwell Depot under repair.

Tuesday, October 29th : Huge crater in Lordship Lane, outside St. Peter's Church at Dulwich Common. Nos. 58 & 62 from London to Dulwich Library only. The down line was reopened on November 7th on the edge of a vertical drop. Single-line working on the railway staff system was instituted between Horniman's Museum and Grove Hotel. As this section was half a mile and curved, a stationary tram was parked on the up line near Sydenham Hill to remind drivers to reverse on to the down line when proceeding towards London. Drivers carried a baton between the pointsmen at each end of the single line. Service 58 was now restored through to Greenwich.

Friday, November 8th : Walworth Road blocked: trams diverted via Vauxhall (up) and Elephant & Kennington (down). Only the southbound curve at Kennington Park junction on Routes 40 & 72 had been relaid owing to the difficulty in obtaining special manganese castings for the up line. The up curve was relaid on November 25th. Abbey Wood Depot had been hit the previous night (7th) and eight trams damaged. H.Es in High Street, Lewisham (through services restored by December 14th) and Church Street, Woolwich (through services restored by January 11th, 1941).

Friday, November 15th : Waterloo Road blocked: No.68 reverses in Blackfriars Road at Stamford Street siding. (line soon reopened).

Monday, November 18th : Unexploded bomb in Queen's Road, Peckham. Trams from London terminated at Harder's Road, just beyond Rye Lane. Road between Lewisham and Catford blocked: trams worked shuttle service from 'Marquis' to crater. No.54 diverted via Brockley.

Wednesday, November 20th : Kingsway Subway closed - H.E. at south end. Hole through tunnel; water and gas mains burst. Up line reopened next day (single-line working).

Saturday, November 23rd : Up line over New Cross Gate railway bridge restored for trams on depot workings and workmen's specials only. During the weekend, Abbey Wood Depot was hit, several trams being destroyed.

Sunday, December 8th : Kennington Gate hit again: Nos. 40 & 72 diverted via Vauxhall.

Friday, December 13th : Temporary crossovers laid at the 'Horns', Kennington (in use on Christmas Eve).

Tuesday, December 17th : H.E. at corner of Walworth Road and New Kent Road. Camberwell trams used Short Street (Elephant) in both directions. Normal service at Elephant on December 19th.

Wednesday, December 18th : Normal double-track working through Kingsway Subway.

Friday, December 27th : Several trams were destroyed when a land mine fell on New Cross Depot. The front was demolished and the entrance blocked by thirty tons of debris. Fortunately about 150 trams from the depot were out on the road at the time. Trams were able to enter and leave the depot by December 30th, after a magnificent clearance and repair job by the gangs.

Monday, December 30th : After the great fire raid on the City: Blackfriars Bridge and Victoria Embankment closed as far as Somerset House because of firemen's hoses - reopened by evening. Destroyed tram on the Embankment near Westminster. Theobalds Road blocked (until January 5th). Great Dover Street blocked: shuttle service City - Elephant (Nos. 46 & 52 normal on January 15th).

Wednesday, January 1st, 1941 : Nos. 40 & 72 diverted from Kennington Road to Blackfriars (via Lambeth Road curve) owing to damage between there and Westminster (normal next day).

Saturday, January 4th : Nos. 58 & 62 to Blackwall Lane (Woolwich Road) only.

Sunday, January 5th : Theobalds Road reopened to trams: No.35 restored at noon.

Monday, January 13th : Large crater in St. George's Road: Nos.35, 56, 62 via London Road, Southwark.

Tuesday, January 14th : Blackfriars Bridge closed (reopened next day)

Wednesday, January 15th : Great Dover Street reopened: Nos. 46 & 52 now normal.

Thursday, January 16th : Walworth trams again diverted via Kennington. Unexploded bomb - exploded later - in Old Kent Road at Dunton Road but tramlines laid across crater and tram services restored.

Monday, January 20th : New Cross Gate railway bridge reopened for trams (but paving of down line still incomplete on March 15th). Routes 46 & 72 working normally once more. New Kent Road blocked: Nos.36, 38, 40 work to Blackwall Lane via Walworth Road or Kennington (later some trams returning from Blackfriars via Borough Road and High Street, thence Great Dover Street). During much of January Old Kent Road was closed to motor traffic - only trams allowed. Blackwall Lane, Greenwich - Church Lane, Charlton section reopened on January 27th.

Tuesday, January 28th : H.E. on down single track at Grand Depot Road, Woolwich Barracks. Single-line working (44,46,72) via New Road, using signalling system. Down line reopened by February 4th.

At this time, Holloway Depot was cut off by an unexploded bomb in Holloway Road. Two trams provided a shuttle service between Highgate and Holloway. Trams from South London (via Kingsway Subway) had to reverse at Highbury Station and, owing to some E/3 Class trams being marooned in Holloway Depot, a number of E/1 Class trams (including No. 1623) worked through the Subway daily until Holloway Road was cleared, despite the official regulation. St. George's Road, Southwark was reopened to trams on February 14th.

During March the following open-fronted E/1 Class Trams were noted operating rush-hour services from New Cross Depot (service numbers in brackets):- Nos.1049 (40), 1163 (66), 1217 (66), 1252 (72), 1259 (40), 1277 (66), 1288 (40 & 72), 1302 (66), 1304 (66), 1312 (68), 1588 (72), 1754 (36, 40 & 72). No.1288 later became a staff car at Charlton Works.

After the Wednesday night raid of April 16th, Nos. 54,58,66 had to turn back at Kennington. Nos.52,54,74 terminated at Catford - emergency 'buses to Grove Park.

A land mine on Hungerford Bridge (affecting Charing Cross Station).

was removed by 11.0 a.m. on April 17th, but a crater blocked Victoria Embankment outside Somerset House (trams restored on April 23rd). Nos. 36 & 84 reversed at Blackfriars; 38,40,56,62,72 at Savoy Street. London Road (Southwark) was closed on account of firemen's hoses - reopened on Thursday evening. Walworth Road closed; 56,60,62 via Kennington. Newington Causeway blocked by debris near the railway bridge: 60 diverted via Southwark Bridge Road. Nos. 46 & 52 worked to Southwark Bridge or the Hop Exchange via New Kent Road and St. George's Circus. Two trams were marooned at St. George's Church, Borough. H.E. in Rosebery Avenue, Clerkenwell: single-line working 6.0 p.m.

After the Saturday night raid of April 19th, the Goose Green - Peckham Rye branch (56 & 84) was closed (reopened by April 29th). Catford was still the southern terminus of Routes 52,54,74. The tram shelter at St. Laurence's Church had been damaged by blast. Nos. 36 & 38 terminated at St. Nicholas's Church, Plumstead because of craters at Basildon Road and Wickham Lane. Blackwall Lane was blocked and a temporary 'bus service worked between Blackwall Tunnel and Woolwich Road. Trams 58 & 62 reversed in Trafalgar Road.

Peckham High Street was blocked; next day, single-line working was resumed between Rye Lane and Harder's Road. By April 25th both tram tracks were in use, spanning the crater by means of a temporary bridge. Craters between Kennington and Vauxhall and Westminster caused Nos. 54 & 58 to be diverted to Savoy Street via Kennington Park Road & Elephant, No.66 to Blackfriars via Walworth Road and No.72 worked to Savoy Street via Old Kent Road & Elephant. Service 35 terminated at Holborn Tram Station in Kingsway Subway, owing to dangerous ruins in Theobalds Road, Bloomsbury and a power failure north of Bloomsbury; No.35 was normal by April 24th. By April 23rd Kennington - Victoria was reopened and Nos. 40 & 72 worked via Vauxhall. They were restored to Kennington Road soon after.

Track was being laid across the crater at the 'Horns', Kennington on Friday, April 25th.

Monday, April 28th : No.46 working from City to Lee Green only; (restored to Woolwich next day).

Friday, May 2nd : Unexploded bomb found in Eltham Road, alongside Sutcliffe Park. Nos.46 & 72 terminated at Sidcup Road; No.44 at Middle Park Avenue. Emergency 'buses operated between Eltham Church and Sidcup Road corner via Middle Park Estate.

Sunday, May 4th : Double-line working at the 'Horns', Kennington again.

The last major air-raid of the 1940/1941 Blitz occurred on the night of May 10th/11th (Saturday/Sunday), when the Luftwaffe tried to burn London to the ground, but fortunately were thwarted in their efforts by the firemen, civil defence workers, night-fighter pilots and the A.A. gunners - the R.A.F. and A.A. guns shooting down 33 German aircraft. The raid badly affected transport communications.

Crater on Victoria curve at Vauxhall roundabout and unexploded bomb in Parry Street: shuttle service to Victoria terminus.

Southwark Bridge closed: trams terminated on south side of bridge.

Unexploded bombs in London Road, Southwark and Old Kent Road. The Elephant & Castle district had been brightly illuminated by hundreds of coloured flares and heavy loads of incendiaries and H.Es were dropped. All water supplies were hit and the firemen had to lay miles of hoses, often only to have them rendered useless by sparks and falling debris. The fire at the Elephant grew into a huge conflagration, finally controlled by relaying water from the River Thames and Surrey Canal the next day.

Dangerous buildings blocked Blackfriars Road. Victoria Embankment closed to all traffic.

Tram tracks damaged in Westminster Bridge Road, Waterloo Road, Walworth Road, Camberwell Road (down line), Peckham Rye, Peckham Road, New Kent Road, Great Dover Street, Greenwich Road, and Trafalgar Road, also in Tooley Street, Tower Bridge Road and Creek Road, Deptford. Emergency 'bus service between Greenwich Church and London Bridge.

Direct hit on southern entrance of Kingsway Subway. Dangerous ruins in Theobalds Road, Bloomsbury. Trams from Highgate to Holborn Hall only.

The overhead wires in High Street, Plumstead at Lakedale Road were damaged, but these were quickly repaired.

The tramways in the central area were badly affected by this raid, as no trams could approach the Central London termini. However, by Monday, May 12th the situation had improved somewhat, as unexploded bombs were removed and dangerous ruins made safe.

The situation on May 15th was as follows:-
Westminster Bridge Road blocked (reopened on the 16th): Services 40, 56 & 62 worked either to County Hall via Vauxhall, or to Christ Church via Walworth Road, returning via Kennington Park Road (owing to damaged down line in Walworth Road). Nos. 36 & 84 ran to Westminster via Blackfriars. Service 35 operated in two parts: Forest Hill - Blackfriars via Walworth Road, returning via Kennington Park Road (jointly with No.74) and Highgate - Aldwych Station. On May 18th Kingsway Subway was reopened throughout (with a hole in the roof). Victoria services were divided at Vauxhall, but through tickets were issued. No.60 terminated on the south side of Southwark Bridge, but there were no 46s & 52s to Town.

Routes 36 & 38 worked in several sections: Embankment - Old Kent Road via Borough Road and High Street (owing to a crater in New Kent Road); from the south side of a crater near Canal Bridge (Old Kent

Road) to King William Street, Greenwich (crater in Trafalgar Road); from Blackwall Lane to Abbey Wood. Relief 'buses worked from Greenwich Church to Blackwall Tunnel.

Route 68 worked from Greenwich Church to Bricklayers' Arms only, No.46 from Woolwich (via Eltham) to Canal Bridge only. The Old Kent Road line was reopened on May 20th and Walworth Road down line on May 22nd. No.54 was working from County Hall via Vauxhall to Catford (emergency 'bus service to Grove Park for some days).

Single-line working was resumed on the down line in Trafalgar Road, Greenwich on May 27th, but the road was still closed to all traffic other than trams. During June 1941 all tram services were restored to normal, but the tram terminus at the City end of Southwark Bridge had to be cut back about a hundred yards and has remained there ever since. This was caused by a huge crater in Queen Street, which had to be traversed by the girder bridge which remains to this day.

It will be seen that the tramways fared better in the 'Blitz' than might have been expected. Damaged tracks were speedily repaired and trams crossed craters on temporary bridges, while engineers repaired electric cables and gas and water mains below. Debris could soon be cleared off tramlines, but other traffic had to meander round diversion routes - the sign "Diversion -- Trams Only" became very familiar. If the track was blocked or torn up you travelled with a through ticket up to the brink of the crater, walked round it and got on another tram the other side. The only thing that really interfered with tram services was the delayed — action or unexploded bomb, but not usually for long!

Among the trams transferred from store to assist South London services were bogie cars built for West Ham Corporation Tramways (Nos. 295-312) and East Ham Corporation Tramways (Nos.81-100) between 1925 and 1931. These trams were based on the L.C.C. E/1 design. Another batch of West Ham trams (Nos. 326, 327, 330-344) entered regular service again at the end of the War, to make good wartime losses. Nos. 326, 327 & 330 are used as staff cars. All the other trams are normally housed at Abbey Wood Depot, but occasionally assist New Cross services also.

The War was taken as an excuse to abolish the 1/- All Day Ticket, 6d. Child's Day Ticket, and 6d. Evening Tourist Ticket after October 9th, 1942, while from October 12th the availability of the 9d. Return fare was reduced. In order to save paper, the numbered geographical stages on single tickets (except references to transfer facilities) were replaced by plain stage numbers from about October 1940, e.g. on Route 46 the stages: 13 Clock Tower, Lewisham; 14 Glenton Road; 15 Lee Road; 16 Courtlands Avenue; 17 Middle Park Avenue; 18 Eltham High Street; were henceforth shown only as 13, 14, 15, 16, 17, 18.

Tickets were further shortened in length about 1942.

Service 62 was curtailed to operate from Savoy Street via Dulwich to Forest Hill (Park Road) only from Autumn 1941 - an erroneous decision, as two services are needed between Forest Hill and Greenwich (via Catford & Lewisham). It was soon found that Services 58 & 38X were unable to cope with the Greenwich traffic at rush hours and, following local complaints and a question asked in Parliament in February 1943, Service 62 was restored to Blackwall Tunnel at rush hours only, though still terminating at Forest Hill during slack hours.

From June 1941 until May 1944, though there were occasional air raids on the London area, the tramways seem to have escaped serious damage. On July 27th, 1941 H.E. bombs in Blackwall Lane, East Greenwich curtailed Nos. 58 & 62 for several days, but the services were soon restored. An air raid on Sunday night, January 17th, 1943 badly affected tram services in the Southwark Bridge and Surrey Docks areas; things were normal again by February 1943. A H.E. bomb at Vauxhall roundabout (South Lambeth Road junction) on Tuesday/Wednesday night, March 21st/22nd, 1944 caused single-line working on Services 54, 58, 66 under Kennington Lane railway bridge for some days.

Flying bombs and rockets during 1944/1945 did not cause damage to the tramways to the extent of the 1940/1941 'Blitz'. Roads were blocked by fallen debris, but in most cases this was speedily cleared and the tracks reopened to trams. By this time during the War, owing to reduced maintenance, some older trams had inevitably become rather noisy and many passengers preferred to travel by tram as the nöise of the motors drowned the ghastly sound of flying bombs rattling overhead.

In the Summer of 1944, during the Nazi flying-bomb (V1) offensive, 363 trams carried evacuee children and mothers from all parts of South London to the railway stations, where they boarded trains to the Midlands, North, West Country and Wales.

Incidents caused by V1 flying bombs which affected S.E. London tramways were as follows:-

On the night of Thursday/Friday, June 15th/16th, 1944, a flying bomb which fell on the railway embankment near Camberwell New Road caused superficial damage to the west side of Camberwell Depot including the temporary roof. 64 trams were slightly damaged, mainly glass being blown out of the windows. After any glass splinters had been removed from the interiors, several trams went into service in this state, as it was fortunately a fine warm day.

Ex-Walthamstow Tram 2044, on loan from Streatham, was operating on Service 66 that day. A curious passenger asked the conductor why there were no windows in the tram and received this witty reply: "We're operating a skeleton service, so this is a skeleton car!" Owing to a temporary shortage of E/3s, No.2056 operated on Service 35 for a few days - this is the only municipal wooden car known to have worked through Kingsway Subway on regular service. Also at this time, Jamaica Road, Bermondsey was blocked for a day or so.

After Bexley Heath trolleybus depot was badly damaged by a flying bomb on the early morning of June 29th, 1944 and all the trolleybuses unusable, Driver 'Bert' Summers and all his mates who could drive trams were taken by coach to New Cross Depot. On arrival, he and Driver 'Dolly' Grey encountered 'Scarface', the Superintendent, who sent the Bexley crews up to the Canteen and later told them off in pairs (driver and conductor) to take trams to Abbey Wood.

When it came to Driver Summers's turn, he told the Superintendent that he was unable to do that as he had never driven a tram over the conduit system in his life and was not licensed to do so. So he and his conductress had a return trip to Abbey Wood on a mate's tram and then spent the rest of his duty in the Canteen at New Cross Depot while most of the other Bexley men were running to and from Woolwich! (They should have sent him to Abbey Wood Depot instead: at least he could have worked the No.44s between Woolwich and Eltham on the overhead system!)

New Cross Depot suffered next, on Wednesday, August 2nd, 1944, when the roof at the rear of the depot was damaged and 112 trams slightly damaged. Two hours later, 141 trams were operating from the depot. Owing to damage in Newington Causeway during August, No.60 was diverted via Southwark Bridge Road.

On Saturday, August 5th, 1944 an HR/2 on the No.58/62 route was travelling south along Lordship Lane, East Dulwich, when the driver noticed a flying bomb approaching. Ignoring the stop at North Cross Road, he notched up to full power and drove his tram at maximum speed. As he reached the hill leading to Dulwich Library the flying bomb fell on the 'Co-op' shop at North Cross Road corner.

On Thursday, August 24th three Streatham trams were destroyed at Kennington Gate and the tracks blocked for some time.

Nazi V2 rockets were responsible for three incidents affecting tramways in S.E. London. The up line in Shardeloes Road, Brockley was damaged on Wednesday, November 1st. The track was repaired and Services 35, 66, 74 were normal again by November 11th. 'Woolworths' at New Cross Road received a direct hit at noon on Saturday, November 25th, when there was a heavy death toll, but debris was soon cleared from the tramlines.

On Friday, March 2nd, 1945 a V2 rocket damaged both tracks in Parker's Row, Bermondsey, making a crater in the down line. Normal services were resumed on Routes 68 & 70 on May 14th, using a temporary pair of points and single-line working past the site. This was the last war damage caused to S.E. London tramways.

During the last year of the War an arrangement was made that Southern Railway workmen's tickets between Woolwich and Deptford and intermediate stations were available for return by train or by L.P.T.B. tram services 36, 38, 40. Also to help workmen, a connecting curve and junctions were put into use from Green's End into Beresford Street, Woolwich on August 27th, 1944 for early morning trams between Eltham and Greenwich; 5d. & 6½d. Workmen's Return tickets were specially introduced for this journey, with the peculiarity of being transfers in one direction only.

The tramway staff's devotion to duty during the War deserves the highest praise. Drivers, conductors, conductresses, inspectors, controllers and depot staff stuck to their posts during the heaviest of air raids. 'Spotters' risked their lives to warn crews of imminent danger. Permanent way staff and overhead linesmen worked wonders relaying track and supply cables and re-erecting overhead equipment to restore tram services. Casualties among tram and trolleybus staff <u>on duty</u> were 48 killed and 803 injured.

Among those who received awards for gallantry were Driver Alfred E. Sharman O.B.E. of Camberwell Depot for several brave deeds, including helping to save 'buses from burning at Camberwell Garage on the night of November 1st, 1940, and Mr. E. Fox, Labourer, awarded the special London Transport certificate for bravery - he extinguished incendiary bombs and resultant fires at a tram depot, thus saving the building, tramcars and valuable stores. 68 London trams were destroyed by enemy action during the War: 36 E/1 Class cars, 16 HR/2 cars, both HR/1 cars and eight E/3 cars, also two 'Felthams', two Walthamstow trams, Croydon car No.396 and West Ham car No.303, while damaged trams were stored at Purley Depot awaiting repair. It was stated that every tramcar in the operating fleet of about 1000 vehicles was damaged on at least one occasion. 33 special trams were used to carry returning evacuees during June/July 1945, after War in Europe ended. (V.E. Day was May 8th).

<u>BLITZ STORIES by Inspector J.T. PENNEY of Downham</u>

During the big Nazi air attack on London on the afternoon of Saturday, September 7th, 1940 I was on duty at Lewisham when a load of bombs was dropped into the Quaggy River opposite the Obelisk, throwing a lot of debris over the tram track. A gas pipe running up the wall of a shop at the corner of the High Street and Rennell Street was fractured setting the gas alight.

I also noticed a hole in the road about two feet from the nearside up tramline. After notifying the authorities concerned, I set about clearing the tram track; luckily there was not a great weight of material to shift.

I had just finished this job when a No.72 tram came out of Lee High Road into the High Street, proceeding towards New Cross. I stopped the driver and cautioned him to go slow over the Obelisk junction, due to the possibility of obstruction in the slot rail; however, this tram got through all right and so did several others.

When the Fire Brigade arrived to deal with the flaming gas, I was standing by the hole to warn the drivers of the fire engines and was quickly told to 'get the hell out of it!' - I had been standing over a delayed-action bomb!

The fire was damped down and the fire engines went away. A message had told me of another delayed action bomb at New Cross Gate Station, so I knew not to expect any more trams coming in the down direction, but I went back to the Clock Tower in case there were more trams coming my way which must be stopped and warned of these incidents.

About 11.30 p.m., during the long night raid when everything was lit up by the vast Dockland fires, that bomb went off, blowing the roadway and tram track sky high - and to think of those trams being driven safely over it some hours before!

One Sunday night I was on duty at the Elephant and a raid was in progress at the time. Several bombs were dropped at Bricklayers' Arms and my section inspector and myself made our way towards the scene of the incident.

On arriving there we found utter chaos: a Green Line coach and other motor vehicles had been blown on to the pavement. There was a broken water main flooding the road, shutting off the electric current. About five trams were standing on the down track with various amounts of damage, mainly broken windows. On the rear one, however, a piece of bomb casing had gone clean through the rear bay of the upper deck, striking the back seat and killing a male passenger outright.

While I contacted the Breakdown Gang, my colleague rang up the A.R.P. from the police 'phone box' in Great Dover Street. The Gang soon arrived and towed the trams on to the live section of track in Old Kent Road, the crews taking their cars back to New Cross Depot with the crew of the rear car as passengers. The rear car was left behind for the A.R.P. to remove the body.

Well, things began to 'warm up' and we were anxious to get away from that neighbourhood, which was none too healthy, but we couldn't leave our former passenger behind unattended. As there was no sign of an ambulance, we went back to the 'phone box and were told that an ambulance was on the way. One did pass us as we were walking back to the tram. For some unknown reason I went upstairs and found to my surprise that the body had been removed.

We took the tram back to the depot, showering broken glass all over Old Kent Road en route. We managed to pick up a soldier and a railwayman on the way. Suddenly, the soldier shouted that there was a hole in the road! Immediately I slammed on the magnets and the tram nearly stood on its head! All the remaining glass from the windows crashed into the road. He then explained that he was referring to an incident at New Cross which we already knew about and which would not prevent us reaching the depot. My record down Old Kent Road stands at three minutes flat from Bricklayers' Arms to New Cross Gate returning to the depot one night, but naturally I took it a bit easier on this particular Sunday, especially after this shock, and we reached the depot safely. I think that this was one of my most hectic nights and I was glad to get home.

One moonlight night I was again on duty at the Elephant when I was instructed to go to Tower Bridge as it was feared that one of our inspectors had been hurt. After collecting my section inspector we both walked the length of New Kent Road and most of Tower Bridge Road before we found the trouble - a bomb had dropped near the 'Dundee Arms'. The road was covered with debris.

We went to Tower Bridge Police Station where we were informed that our colleague had died and his body had been taken to the mortuary. The next thing was to inform Tram Control by 'phone from the section box in Tower Bridge Road; we had some difficulty in getting through.

Jerry was dropping everything including the kitchen sink and, to make matters worse, although it was a bright moonlight night a S.R. steam locomotive was standing on the railway bridge blowing off steam to its heart's content. If Jerry couldn't see that he must've been blind!

Well, things got too hot, so we decided to take shelter in the basement of the police station, which I believe was being used as a canteen. Then Jerry dropped a beauty right behind the building, which blew the doors open. What struck me as funny was that one man of pre-Great War vintage had just picked up his pint from the counter and got it halfway to his mouth when the bomb dropped and his arm stopped poised in mid-air. Then, realising that he was still alive, he carried on drinking - not even Jerry could upset him!

WARTIME ACCIDENTS (OTHER THAN AIR RAID INCIDENTS)

Quite a number of accidents involving tramcars during the War were caused by blackout and 'Blitz' conditions or by bad track, maintenance arrears and brake failures due to wartime shortages of staff and materials.

HR/2 Class Tram 1903 (Service 56) was involved in a collision on Victoria Embankment at Westminster on April 20th, 1940, the driving platform being damaged.

Collisions between trams on the same track occurred in New Kent Road (three trams: September 22nd, 1939, blackout); outside Lewisham Hospital (July 28th, 1940) three staff and 25 passengers were injured when lights were extinguished because of an air raid warning. Other collisions between pairs of trams were at: Nightingale Place, Woolwich Common (October 18th, 1941); Bromley Road, Catford (June 12th, 1943); Well Hall Road up track, Eltham (July 6th, 1943) and Greenwich Road (May 13th, 1944).

There were two crashes at Downham change pit during the War. On February 5th, 1940 an up No.54 tram ran down Downham Way from Glenbow Road and hit a stationary tram at the changeover point; 17 passengers and a tramwayman were injured and the line was blocked for three hours (this was during the exceptional bitter Winter of early 1940, when the country was covered with snow for weeks). On July 6th, 1944 another up No.54 tram ran away, failed to stop at the change pit and overturned at Bromley Road corner (this was E/1 Class No.1605); the driver and 13 passengers were hurt.

A tram was derailed outside St. Alphege's Church, Greenwich (December 18th, 1941), and a woman on the pavement was killed when an up No.66 tram overturned at Brockley Lane railway bridge due to snow, ice and grit in the rails, the driver and seven passengers being injured (January 22nd, 1942).

A No.94 'bus skidded into an oncoming tram outside Forest Hill Station (November 23rd, 1939). During the blackout a 'bus hit a tram travelling in the opposite direction head-on in Woolwich Road, East Greenwich; 18 were hurt (December 17th, 1943). Other collisions between 'bus and tram occurred at St. Laurence's Church, Catford (November 4th, 1944, blackout) and in New Cross Road at Tanner's Hill, when a No.53A 'bus hit a No.40 tram (December 22nd, 1944).

A motor car collided with a tram at the Clock Tower, Lewisham on Christmas Eve 1939; the tram caught fire and the private car was burnt out. An army lorry crashed into two trams in Stanstead Road, Forest Hill (November 29th, 1941), while another hit a tram at Academy Road, Woolwich Common (December 29th, 1941).

A tram went on fire in Church Street, Woolwich at Warspite Road stop (October 11th, 1944), while another tram caught fire in New Cross Depot (January 15th, 1945).

On January 15th, 1944, in thick fog, a tramwayman from Forest Hill stopping bolting horses in Greenwich Road. A conductress reversing the trolley pole at Wickham Lane, Plumstead was struck by a motor cycle (January 25th, 1945).

FOREMAN JOE AND THE No.84 TRAM - another true tale by S.P. HARRIS

One sunny Friday evening on Peckham Rye during the Summer of 1946 a crowd of building workers boarded an HR/2 Class tram on Service 84 at Stuart Road terminus, after a day's work erecting 'pre-fabs'. The tram starts and is soon speeding alongside Peckham Rye Common, fresh air streaming through the open bulkhead door.

Suddenly, with a loud hooting and a terrific rattle, Joe, the building foreman, in a pre-war Ford 8, overtakes the No.84. Amid the jeers and catcalls of the home-going crowd, he pulls ahead, doing about 50 m.p.h., and disappears in a cloud of blue smoke round the corner of Nunhead Lane. A few years previously Joe had chased Rommel's retreating Afrika Korps in his tank across the Libyan Desert.

The tram rounds the curve and runs up to the stop by the ruined 'King's Arms'. The traffic lights show red; right in front of the No.84 sits Joe in his Ford 8 on the tram track. The signal lights change through amber to green, but Joe's car doesn't move. He fiddles with the controls in vain - it won't start. The workers on the tram shout sarcastic banter and the air is full of Cockney wit. The lights change back to red. Cars and buses pile up behind, honking impatiently as the lights change back to green. In vain Joe appeals to his mates to come and give him a shove; they stay fast on the tram.

Joe's eyes almost pop out of his head as he sees the huge red bulk of the tram slowly bearing down on his little motor car, but the motorman leans out and shouts something to him. Joe jumps back into his Ford with alacrity and releases the handbrake. The tram driver inches his controller handle gently forward and the great red leviathan softly pushes the Ford across the road junction like a gentle elephant helping a cheeky monkey. The car engine catches, the Ford springs to life once more and careers up East Dulwich Road towards Goose Green, closely pursued by the No.84 tram, with cheers from the building workers and laughter all round!

1945-1949 : PUBLIC AND STAFF COMPLAIN OF NEGLECT TO TRAMS

The trams and tramwaymen and women contributed much towards Victory by keeping South London on the move during the War. Bombing and shortage of supplies caused deterioration of vehicles and tracks, but when materials became available trams and tracks were neglected, as were the tram-men and women (who came out on strike over this in May 1945). Noisy motors, rattling windows, leaky roofs, dropped rail joints and sunken paving were still in evidence during 1949, four years after the Victory). (Birmingham, Sheffield and Glasgow's tramways also suffered from bombing and a lack of materials, but they were in good shape again by 1949). However, things have improved in London since 1947.

During 1946 waterproof shelters were provided for tramway pointsmen in exposed places. From June 26th, 1946 All-Night Services were numbered (using spare stencils from Hampstead Depot):-

No.5 Downham (Bromley Road) - Savoy Street via Old Kent Road & Blackfriars;

7 New Cross Gate - Savoy Street via Walworth Road & Blackfriars.

By 1947, though 'buses had been getting priority of new material, London Transport had to take notice of public complaints about the bad state of tram tracks and tramcars, especially as questions were asked in Parliament. A programme of thorough overhauls on tramcars was instituted at Charlton Works in the Summer of 1947; in some cases repair work was done at running depots and certain electrical firms overhauled electric motors on contract work. London Transport announced "The Board's policy will be to maintain all trams at the highest standards of safety".

BAD WEATHER

During the severe Winter of January-March 1947 trams were delayed by frozen points (e.g. at Forest Hill Station: January 28th) and frozen slush and ice in the conduits; on overhead sections trams were hardly affected and operated almost normally. A L.T.E. official stated on the B.B.C. Light Programme on December 5th, 1948 - a day of dense fog - "In the morning no trolleybus could leave the depot. It was the same all over North London. Things were much better in South London. We still have the trams there!" (It should be mentioned that the London Passenger Transport Board became the London Transport Executive on January 1st, 1948, when the Railways were nationalised by the Labour Government).

1947-1949 : SOME IMPROVEMENTS, BUT HIGHER FARES!

On August 13th, 1947 New Cross Depot staff arranged a coach outing to Brighton for bombed-out and orphan children. Similar treats and parties have been given by this and other depots since the War.

During 1948 new indicator blinds were fitted to trams (there had been complaints about the use of old illegible ones since 1946). Following a dispute, staircase mirrors were fitted on trams from New Cross Depot so that conductors when upstairs could see when to give the driver the signal to proceed.

In July 1948 London Transport told the tramwaymen that they were making "a valuable contribution to the travelling facilities of London and towards National recovery."

Automatic signals were installed on the single-track sections in High Street, Plumstead in June 1948 and in August illuminated signs with the wording "TRAMWAY CROSSING" in white lettering on a black ground were fixed at the Embankment entrance of Kingsway Subway.

An intensive programme of track repairs was also started in 1947, much work being done on Routes 36, 38, 40 between Greenwich and Woolwich. On May 12th a permanent way gang replaced a broken rail in four minutes; there was only a slight delay to the trams. There was an unusual occurrence on February 4th, 1948 when a section of the conductor T-rail in the conduit of the up track on Old Kent Road dropped out of position so that the ploughs of the trams could not pick up current. This happened when passengers were on their way to work in the morning and up trams on Services 36, 38, 46, 52, 74 had to be diverted via Peckham & Walworth Road until the fault was rectified.

Since January 1948 track repairs have been carried out at many places, including Victoria Embankment, Westminster Bridge Road, Victoria terminus, Vauxhall Cross, Kennington Road, 'Horns' Kennington, Camberwell New Road, Walworth Road, between Camberwell Green and Peckham Rye, Lewisham Way, Brockley Road, Stondon Park, Brockley Rise, Downham Way, New Kent Road, Old Kent Road and Basildon Road (Plumstead). New tracks have been laid in Eltham Road, Lee on concrete foundations covered with tar macadam up to rail level, giving an excellent road surface, comparable with Sheffield Corporation Tramways. About 800 men are now employed throughout London on this important job of bringing tram tracks up to standard.

In 1946, at a public enquiry, London Transport asked for a 2d. minimum fare, but this was not sanctioned. (The L.C.C. representative suggested a return to the penny fare). However, a new fare increase came into operation on February 9th, 1947; the minimum fare remained at 1½d. but the 2d. fare was raised to 2½d. and is now available for only two stages instead of three stages as previously. 3d., 4d., 5d. and 6d. fares were increased by a penny; the 9d. Return became 11d. Return and the 3d. Cheap Midday Fare rose to 4d. after four stages, though the 3d. Cheap Midday Fare is still available for shorter journeys. The maximum tram fare between London and suburban termini in the County of London is now 7d. single, 11d. Return - still quite cheap. (Ordinary return fares on motor-buses and trolleybuses disappeared during the War).

During the last two years several slight extensions have been made to four local services. From January 3rd, 1948 Service 74 was extended from Downham to Grove Park from 9.0 a.m. on Saturdays instead of 12 noon. More Saturday morning trams for shoppers have been provided since January 31st, 1948: seven more on Nos. 36 & 38; five more on No.46; and three more on No.54.

On May 5th, 1948 Service 44's terminus was extended from Eltham Church to Eltham Green (Middle Park Avenue); during June 1948 the suburban terminus of Service 40 was extended from Parry Street a quarter of a mile eastwards along Plumstead Road to Perrott Street, Woolwich. (At rush hours No.40 still continues to Wickham Lane, Plumstead). From November 13th, 1948 Service 62 was altered to run from Elephant & Castle to Lewisham Hill via Dulwich on Saturday afternoons and evenings only.

By May 1949 Service 74 was extended to Grove Park terminus as a regular daily service. At Deptford Creek a new bridge is being built and a temporary bridge carrying tram tracks for Routes 68 & 70 came into use in July 1949. Since August a second loading island has been provided at Victoria terminus for Services 54, 58, 66, the original island being used by S.W. London services.

POST-WAR ACCIDENTS 1945-1949

An up No.52 tram ran into the back of a stationary No.54 in heavy rain at Headcorn Road stop, Downham Way; both crews and twelve passengers were injured (October 23rd, 1945). Similar accidents happened at Downham change pit (up track) when two staff and 13 passengers were hurt (February 25th, 1946); and at Grove Park terminus involving E/1 Class Trams 557 (Service 54) & 1404 (April 12th, 1947). An up No.74 failed to stop at Downham change pit and twelve were hurt (January 6th, 1946), while an up No.52 (No.1593) ran into a stationary No.74 (No.1009) at Glenbow Road stop, Downham Way during heavy rain, nine being hurt (November 5th, 1949). Theseaccidents resulted from brake failures and possibly careless driving. The cars involved belonged to the older E/1 Class type which had borne the brunt of two world wars - the newer E/3s and HR/2s were more reliable - but one wonders if these accidents might have been avoided if the E/1s had been fitted with slipper brakes. In the early days of the L.C.C.T. C Class and M Class cars, both fitted with slipper brakes, were used on Loampit hill and New Road hill, Woolwich respectively, yet these were replaced with E/1 Class cars using only magnetic and hand brakes, when these routes were extended.

Collisions between trams on the same track occurred at Deptford Broadway - down No.38 hit No.36 (December 18th, 1947); Old Kent Road at East Street - No.46 & No.52 collided (March 3rd, 1948); Lewisham Way at Malpas Road junction (June 12th, 1948); St. Alphege's Hospital, Woolwich Road, East Greenwich (June 1948); on Bromley Road, Catford during fog (December 1st, 1948); and at Well Hall Road, Eltham - E/1 Class Tram 565 (Service 46) and another up tram collided (January 7th, 1949).

At Brockley Rise junction, Forest Hill, the driver of an up No.74 tram (E/1R No.827) was at fault when he hit a down No.58 (HR/2 No.1862) which was crossing the points (January 8thm 1947). A pointsman's error caused a down No.36 tram to collide with an up No.33 at County Hall junction (June 17th, 1947).

E/1 Class Tram 576 (Service 72) ran down Grand Depot Road hill, Woolwich, derailed at Anglesea Road and crashed into the Co-op shop (April 18th, 1946). As the top deck was embedded in the masonry of the shop-front, it had to be cut off to release the tramcar. No.576 remains presently as a single-decker in New Cross Depot and is used to train new drivers.

During this period there were three derailments in New Cross Road: A No.38 tram (September 27th, 1947); a No.36 by a broken rail (April 5th, 1948); and an empty tram on July 26th, 1949. An E/1 Class tram on Service 40 derailed at Woolwich change pit (December 11th, 1947); a similar mishap befell a No.38X tram bound for Woolwich at Ladywell Road, Lewisham (March 14th, 1949).

There was a peculiar derailment of a down No.58 outside Whitbread's Bottling Yard in Lewisham Road, caused by broken glass in the groove of the tram rails (March 21st, 1947). An up tram left the rails in Shardeloes Road, Brockley, careered forty yards along the pavement and hit a wall (February 7th, 1948); this accident was caused by faulty track, the rail having previously been damaged. The driver of this tram, an E/3 from Holloway Depot on Service 35, was very upset, as he had a clean driving record, but it was proved that he was NOT to blame. He had applied the magnetic brakes fully, which failed to act on the damaged track.

A down No.38 tram jumped the points outside St. Alphege's Church, Greenwich and killed an invalid in a wheelchair on the pavement (March 24th, 1948). An all-night tram ran off the line in Lewisham Way outside the Welsh Presbyterian Church due to a bolt lying in the tram rail (February 4th, 1949).

Thirteen people were hurt when a 'bus and tram collided in Bromley Road, Catford (September 13th, 1947). A motor car was sandwiched between a No.72 and another tram at New Cross Gate Station (September 12th, 1947), while another car was squashed between a No.47 'bus and E/1R Class Tram 1216 (Service 54) outside the Plaza Cinema, Catford (January 21st, 1949). A motor car collided with E/1R Class Tram 1608 (Service 40) at the 'Horns', Kennington (April 10th, 1949).

A grocer's van charged across Stondon Park, Forest Hill from Honor Oak Park right into the path of a No.74 tram and came off the loser (December 10th, 1947). An army lorry collided with E/1R Class Tram 1310 in Bromley Road, near Southend Lane (March 9th, 1948). During thick fog on November 30th/December 1st, 1948 there were two pile-ups; Grand Depot Road, Woolwich (two lorries, two trams and a pedal cyclist) and at Tunnel Avenue, East Greenwich (tram, motor-cycle and sidecar, motor van and motor coach).

I hope that the tram-men will pardon me for saying that among some of the newly-demobilised tram drivers there was an air of recklessness during the years 1945-1948. This could also be seen among ex-servicemen recruited as tram drivers. Many of them had driven military motor vehicles at high speeds during the War and were inclined to be impatient of the L.P.T.B. tramway speed restrictions and compulsory stops, which cover ten pages and six pages respectively in the Rule Book. In fairness, one may say that their comrades who took to driving motorbuses and civil motor vehicles on the road during these years were a far worse menace. Nor did these younger tram drivers share the tradition of the L.C.C. Tramways as the older men did. Furthermore, the attitude of 55, Broadway towards trams did not encourage them to take a pride in their work. An example of this reckless spirit is typified by a tram driver known to a friend of mine who allowed him to drive the tram along Bromley Road on quiet evenings at the age of fifteen on several occasions. This driver would leave the controls, go upstairs to look for a discarded newspaper or to shut the door while the tram cruised gaily along - but, of course, only when the road seemed clear. The great advantage of a tram to its driver over every other vehicle, apart from a railway locomotive, is that one can drink tea and eat sandwiches, a pie or cake while the tram is in motion in absolute safety. One is glad to say that the L.C.C.T. tradition dies hard and most of the younger men have acquired this noble tradition of good service from their older comrades by now.

It has to be said that tramcars from New Cross Depot seem to have been involved in many of the accidents recorded. However, this depot is rather a 'Cinderella' for several reasons, mainly its size and also the average age of its rolling stock. Holloway only operates a small number of trams,all modern; Camberwell operates mostly modern trams (E/3s and HR/2s); Abbey Wood Depot operates mostly ex-East Ham and West Ham trams with modernised equipments; also it only houses 86 cars (compared with New Cross's 326) so that the staff know the individual trams better and a driver may have the same car day after day. Abbey Wood is confined to the Woolwich routes and has only two routes to London, both via Old Kent Road - in a way it is more like a small-town system working through to a nearby city. At New Cross every tram is a common-user and though drivers usually have a regular 'road', they may be called to work any one of eleven routes with E/1 and E/1R Class cars. These remarks are not intended to belittle the work and faithful service of men at any depot, but to explain the particular problems at different depots.

Recital of these accidents may seem depressing, but in the interest of history they should be recorded. It should be noted that considering the frequency of tramway services and the large number of passengers conveyed safely each day, tramcars have been responsible for fewer accidents than any other type of road vehicle. Speaking more particularly about pedestrians, the Lewisham Coroner said at a fatal inquiry: "In regard to the number of miles run, singularly few accidents have been caused by trams. The electric tram's record from a safety point-of-view.... has been very good."

If I may be permitted a personal word, as a regular traveller by tram during the 22 years of my life, I have never seen a tram accident (1949). (Sixteen years later, I can say that the only tram incident in my life so far occurred in 1959 when Glasgow Corporation Tramcar No.812 (Service 25 from Rouken Glen to Bishopbriggs), on which I was travelling, was derailed by a bolt in the tramline at Renfield Street/ Sauchiehall Street junction. Even then, the driver brought the tram safely to rest against the kerb and no damage was done - 1965 note to Fourth Edition).

Turning to natural occurrences, lightning struck a No.46 tram at Well Hall railway bridge, Eltham on June 14th, 1948. Fire broke out and the fire brigade was called; the tram had to be taken out of service. The driver and three passengers were injured by this freak bolt from the sky. During the first week of July 1948 trams were delayed by floodwater in the High Road, Lee, when a water main burst; other traffic was diverted for ten days or so.

A thrilling episode occurred in April 1946 when a woman and two men robbed passengers and assaulted the conductress on an up No.54 tram between the Prince of Wales Cinema, Lewisham and the 'Marquis of Granby', New Cross. After a chase they were caught by the Police and were duly sentenced at Greenwich Magistrates' Court. In May 1948 a man was arrested for persistently begging on tramcars in High Street, Lewisham.

TRIALS AND TRIBULATIONS ON THE 54s by Conductor H. ELLIS of New Cross Depot.

When I entered service at New Cross Depot in January 1946 as a conductor on Route 54, my motorman was a character nicknamed 'Country Bill', who despite thirty years as a London tram driver still spoke with a Gloucester accent you could cut with a knife! His performance was hardly suited to the No.54, one of the fastest tram routes in London, and as he never could get that controller handle past the 'series' notches the net result was frequent 'turns' (short-workings) by the Regulators. However, when due to run into the depot about 11.0 p.m. and he thought he could get a ride home to Brockley on a No. 66 or 74, I swear that he could find an extra four 'parallel' notches on that controller and nobody could push a tram along faster!

On one occasion when we were working the first run to Victoria, leaving the depot about 4.30 a.m., the car allocated was down at the New Cross Road end of the 'runway'. Obviously it must have been of the last to enter the depot the previous night, for before we had even reached Camberwell Green we had not one but two 'hot boxes'. By the time we were at Kennington they were well alight and drew frequent shouts from passers-by: "Oi, mate! Yer on fire!" However, we made Victoria and changed cars on our return to New Cross Gate.

The standard of maintenance at New Cross Depot just after the War left much to be desired, probably due to the large numbers of cars there, and all too often the last ones in at night were the first out the next morning. The most common causes of running in, out of service, were 'hot boxes', 'tight blocks' or 'twisted magnets'. If it was a minor defect like a broken driving mirror we did not run the car in for that, as the Regulators at New Cross Gate kept a large stock of mirrors in their box, plus a spanner. So we used to repair to the lay-by at Harder's Road, Peckham and indulge in a spot of 'do-it-yourself'!

Another unusual reason for running a defective car into the depot - and this one really caused a sensation - was a broken reversing key! The key was on an English Electric controller and we had just switched from trolley to conduit at Downham change pit and my mate (a spare man) was replacing the key into the keyway when one of the prongs just fell off! - all this before he could put the key into the forward position. The only tram at hand was a Westinghouse car and its key was too open to operate on an English Electric controller.

Then I hit upon the idea of opening the tool box and using the adjustable spanner to do the trick. It worked and eventually we got the car into the depot. When I reported the car as 'run-in' at the Traffic Office and told them the reason, nobody could believe their ears and even Mr. Dunn, the Divisional Superintendent, had to go up into the depot to see for himself!

During the great 1947 'freeze-up' there was one duty that we worked which left the depot about 6.15 a.m., turned at Camberwell Green and was the last 'Workman' car from Grove Park. Our progress was very slow to Downham change pit, where we were met by the Section Inspector who informed us that after 'shooting the plough' we were to reverse over the adjacent crossover and proceed to Grove Park terminus via the up track, as the points at Grove Park were frozen up. Frequently we lost the'juice', as many stretches of the trolley wire were covered with ice.

We reached Grove Park about 8.0 a.m. - the first car through for over an hour. When I asked the Inspector what I should do about Workman tickets, he replied: "If they ask for one, give them one!" It transpired that on this up journey I was to issue Workman, Ordinary and even Cheap Midday fares!

At Lewisham Clock Tower we were informed that there was a tram with a broken plough carrier on Loampit Hill, so we would have to go via South Street to Greenwich, reverse there and come via Greenwich Road to the 'Marquis' to regain our line of route. This we did, making a slow but uneventful journey as far as Hill Street, Peckham, where once again it was "Halt! 'broken carrier' just beyond Rye Lane!"

This time fortunately we had stopped outside the 'Dining Rooms', so I quickly went and bought a jug of tea and some sandwiches. My mate and I did full justice to these, as it was long past our meal relief time.

Eventually we arrived at Victoria just before midday and by the time we had returned to the 'Gate' for our relief the Regulator told us to pay in and go home. This was one of the blackest days for 'broken carriers', for 96 trams ended up in New Cross Depot with this trouble. Also one could see many strangers around New Cross Gate: No.16s, 18s, 34s and 48s all trying to get on their own roads by long diversions.

Another adventurous run of a different nature happened one afternoon when we took a No.52 out of the depot. Now it was the practice of Regulators to take two of these cars to run off route, one via Brockley as a No.74, the other to run as a 36/38 'Circle'; we were asked to do the latter.

Everything went well from New Cross to the Embankment and down to Woolwich Ferry, then the fun started! My mate, who had not worked that road for over twenty years, found that many stops had been moved and was unaware that trams and trolleybuses shared the overhead as far as Bostall Hill. Frequently I had to play the National Anthem on the bell to prevent him trying to overtake trolleybuses. After completing a round journey and running into the depot, my mate said: "Blow that! I'm not going down there anymore!"

SOME AMUSING ANECDOTES

On October 3rd, 1946 trams were held up on Blackfriars Bridge by a swan alighting on the track. It followed the conduit towards Victoria Embankment and, resisting all efforts at removal, the swan rounded the corner and continued as far as John Carpenter Street between the tramlines before taking off and flying back to the Thames.

Passengers on a Brockley tram during Easter Week 1948 were much amused when a little girl of seven, who had hauled a huge dog up the stairs to the upper saloon, on sitting down asked the conductor for "a dog and a half, please."

Mr. W. Johnston, a New Cross conductor, recalls that one morning his driver unwittingly drove the tram out of the depot without him and he had to chase his tram along New Cross Road, waving his rack of tickets and clasping his ticket box under his other arm.

Two similar incidents involved conductresses from New Cross Depot. One left her money satchel at home during the dinner-break and had to race upstairs while the tram waited at the corner of her road till she returned, red-faced and exhausted. The other left her tickets at the depot, and, as her driver could not hold up the following trams in New Cross Road, he drove the tram to the crossover in Queen's Road, where he reversed and shuttled backwards and forwards over the crossover to let other trams pass, much to the amazement of passengers and passers-by, till his conductress arrived on another tram.

This is perhaps the place to mention a source of contention, namely delays to traffic caused by trams waiting to enter New Cross Depot. Most folk are unaware that this is not the fault of the tramways, who have to make the best of an awkward situation. The L.C.C. planned two entrances to this huge depot, but residents in nearby roads objected successfully to a line entering the depot by 'a back door' and subsequent efforts of the L.C.C. were also resisted and doomed to failure. In comparison, it may be noted that Holloway, Clapham, Streatham and Camberwell Depots all have two entrances, which expedite the entry and exit of trams considerably.

FAITHFUL SERVICE

A praiseworthy record is held by Messrs. A. Beningfield, W. Bolton, W. Cody, W. Lawrence and A. Pedley of New Cross Depot who hold awards for over 20 years' safe-driving. Tribute should be paid to Motormen T.W. Cooling and George Cunningham who have driven trams from New Cross Depot since 1906; Mr. Tom Lazell of Greenwich, traverser driver and shunter at New Cross since 1906; and Mr. Frank Smith of Honor Oak Park, traverser driver and shunter at Camberwell Depot since 1908. They are representative of the L.C.C. tramwaymen who have given a lifetime of loyal service to the travelling public of London and, whether named here or not, they all deserve our gratitude.

When a well-liked tramwayman retires, it is usually the custom to send him home on a decorated special tram, often festooned with paper garlands and balloons and sometimes flags.

LOCAL SERVICES, 1949

The following tram services are now operating in South-East London (1949):-

Route No.			Journey Time
H/L	35	Forest Hill Station -- Highgate(Archway Tavern) via Walworth Road & Kingsway Subway.(Daily Service)	(86 mins)
A/X	36 & 38	Abbey Wood -- Victoria Embankment via Greenwich & Old Kent Road(Daily Services): (36 up via Blackfriars, down via Westminster; 38 up via Westminster, down via Blackfriars). (also extra rush-hour service - usually No.38X: Plumstead & Woolwich - Catford via Lewisham Road, some trams working through to the Downham Estate).	(75 mins)
X	40	Woolwich (Perrott Street) -- Savoy Street,Strand via Greenwich, Kennington & Westminster(Daily Service) (extended to Wickham Lane, Plumstead at rush hours(73 mins)	(65 mins)

A	44	Eltham Green(Middle Park Avenue)--Beresford Square,Woolwich (Weekdays only)	(21 mins)
A/X	46	Beresford Square,Woolwich -- City & Southwark via Eltham & Old Kent Road (Daily Service)	(65 mins)
X	52	Grove Park Station -- City & Southwark via Lewisham & Old Kent Road (Rush hours only).	(54 mins)
X	54	Grove Park Station -- Victoria Station via Lewisham & Peckham (Daily Service)	(62 mins)
L	56 & 84	Peckham Rye -- Victoria Embankment via Walworth Road (Weekdays) (56 up via Westminster, down via Blackfriars; 84 up via Blackfriars, down via Westminster).	(39 mins)
	56	Peckham Rye -- Savoy Street, Strand via Walworth Road & Westminster (Sundays)	
L	58	Blackwall Tunnel -- Victoria Station via Catford & Dulwich (Daily Service)	(73 mins)
L	60	Dulwich Library -- City & Southwark via Walworth Road (Rush hours only)	(34 mins)
L	62	Forest Hill(Park Road) -- Savoy Street, Strand via Dulwich & Westminster (Weekdays only)	(45 mins)
		(extended to Blackwall Tunnel at rush hours	(79 mins)
		(works Lewisham Hill -- Elephant & Castle via Dulwich on Saturdays after 3.0 p.m.	(52 mins)
L/X	66	Forest Hill Station -- Victoria Station via Brockley & Peckham (Weekdays only). (Certain workings to Blackfriars at rush hours)	(48 mins)
X	68	Greenwich Church -- Waterloo Station via Rotherhithe & Tower Bridge Road (Daily Service)	(36 mins)
X	70	Greenwich Church -- London Bridge Station (Daily Service) (works to Bermondsey Street only at certain hours)	(25 mins)
X	72	Beresford Square,Woolwich -- Savoy Street,Strand via Westhorne Avenue & Kennington (Weekdays)	(73 mins)
		Beresford Square,Woolwich -- New Cross Gate via Westhorne Avenue. (Sundays)	(39 mins)
X	74	Grove Park Station -- Blackfriars(John Carpenter Street) via Brockley & Old Kent Road(Daily Service)	(65 mins)

All-Night Services 5 and 7 operate as in 1946, when they were numbered.

The code letters shown above refer to the tram depots which operate these services, thus:-

A - Abbey Wood; H - Holloway; L - Camberwell; X - New Cross Depot

(These code letters are my own reference and are not carried on the trams, which show a duty number plate only).

Destination blinds used on trams in South East London (1949):-

CAMBERWELL DEPOT (1) (continued)

S P E C I A L

ST GEORGES CH

ELEPHANT & CASTLE

GROSVENOR RD

CLAPHAM JUNC

PLOUGH CLAPHAM

CAMBERWELL GRN

via New Cross
CAMBERWELL GRN
via Dulwich

DULWICH LIBRARY

B R I X T O N R D
via Camberwell
CITY & SOUTHWARK
Brixton & Camberwell
KINGS RD CHELSEA
via Clapham
CAMBERWELL GRN

V I C T O R I A
via Kennington & New X
F O R E S T H I L L

NEW CROSS GATE

W O R K M A N

B L A C K F R I A R S
via Camberwell

V I C T O R I A
via Dulwich
F O R E S T H I L L
via Catford
BLACKWALL TNL
via Dulwich
C A T F O R D

via Dulwich & Westr
SAVOY ST STRAND
Walworth Rd & Westr
E M B A N K M E N T
Walworth Rd & Blackfrs

PECKHAM RYE
via Walworth Rd

GOOSE GREEN

C A T F O R D

LEWISHAM Clock Tr
via Dulwich

GREENWICH CH

BLACKWALL LANE
(Woolwich Rd)

(continued above -top right)

LEWISHAM Clock Tower
via Dulwich
C A T F O R D

via Dulwich & Westr
SAVOY ST STRAND
Walworth Rd & Westr
EMBANKMENT
Walworth Rd & Blackfrs

PECKHAM RYE
via Walworth Rd

GOOSE GREEN

GREENWICH CH

BLACKWALL LANE
(Woolwich Rd)

CAMBERWELL DEPOT (2)

S P E C I A L

ST GEORGES CH

ELEPHANT & CASTLE

VAUXHALL STN

CAMBERWELL GRN

via New Cross
CAMBERWELL GRN
via Dulwich

DULWICH LIBRARY

CITY & SOUTHWARK
via Camberwell
B L A C K F R I A R S

W O R K M A N

FOREST HILL
via Brockley & New X
V I C T O R I A
via Dulwich
FOREST HILL
via Catford
BLACKWALL TNL
via Dulwich

N A G S H E A D

Angel
ISLINGTON
Green

BLOOMSBURY

WESTMINSTER

H I G H G A T E
Walworth Rd & Westr
NEW X & FOREST HILL
Westr & Walworth Rd
NEW CROSS GATE

ELEPHANT & CASTLE
via Westminster
H I G H B U R Y

NEW CROSS GATE

NEW CROSS & ABBEY WOOD DEPOTS (1)

S P E C I A L

P L U M S T E A D

BERESFORD SQ

WOOLWICH FERRY

BLACKWALL LANE
(Woolwich Rd)

GREENWICH CH

KENNINGTON

WESTMINSTER

GROSVENOR RD

CAMBERWELL GRN
via Walworth Rd
NEW CROSS GATE
via Old Kent Rd
CAMBL TOWN HALL
via Kennington
HARDERS RD PECKM

BLACKWALL TNL

BERESFORD SQ
via Kennington

via Old Kent Rd & Blackfrs
E M B A N K M E N T
via Old Kent Rd & Westr

via Old Kent Rd
A B B E Y W O O D
via Kennington & Westr
SAVOY ST STRAND
via Walworth Rd & Westr
E M B A N K M E N T
via Walworth Rd & Blackfrs

W O R K M A N

(Continued)

NEW CROSS GATE

via Kenn & Westhorne Ave
BERESFORD SQ
via Lewisham & Eltham
CITY & SOUTHWARK
via Old Kent Rd

V I C T O R I A
via Lewisham
G R O V E P A R K
Old Kent Rd & Brockley
SOUTHEND VGE

B L A C K F R I A R S
via Brockley Old Kent Rd
SAVOY ST STRAND

D O W N H A M
(Bromley Rd)

B R O C K L E Y

ST GEORGES CH

ELEPHANT & CASTLE

TOWER BRIDGE RD

L E W I S H A M

C A T F O R D

L E E G R E E N

ELTHAM CHURCH

WESTHORNE AVE

WATERLOO STN

NEW CROSS & ABBEY WOOD DEPOTS (2) (Continued)

S P E C I A L

Wickham Lane
PLUMSTEAD

BERESFORD SQ

FREE FERRY
via Woolwich Rd
BLACKWALL LANE

GREENWICH CH

KENNINGTON
WESTMINSTER

VAUXHALL STN

BLACKWALL TNL

WOOLWICH PERROTT ST
via Kennington

via Old Kent Rd & Blckfrs
EMBANKMENT
via Old Kent Rd & Westr

via Old Kent Rd
A B B E Y W O O D
via Kennington & Westr
SAVOY ST STRAND
via Brockley Old Kent Rd
B L A C K F R I A R S

W O R K M A N

NEW CROSS GATE

via Kenn & Westhorne Ave
BERESFORD SQ
via Lewisham & Eltham
CITY & SOUTHWARK
via Old Kent Rd
NEW CROSS GATE

V I C T O R I A
via Lewisham
G R O V E P A R K
Old Kent Rd & Brockley
DOWNHAM Bromley Rd

ST GEORGES CH

ELEPHANT & CASTLE

BRICKLAYERS ARMS

LEWISHAM Clock Tower

C A T F O R D

L E E G R E E N

ELTHAM CHURCH

MIDDLE PARK AVE

WATERLOO STN

R E D L I O N
Rotherhithe
T U N N E L

H I G H S T
Deptford

LONDON BGE
Tooley St
BERMONDSEY ST

WATERLOO STN
via Tower Bridge Rd
G R E E N W I C H

TOWER BRIDGE

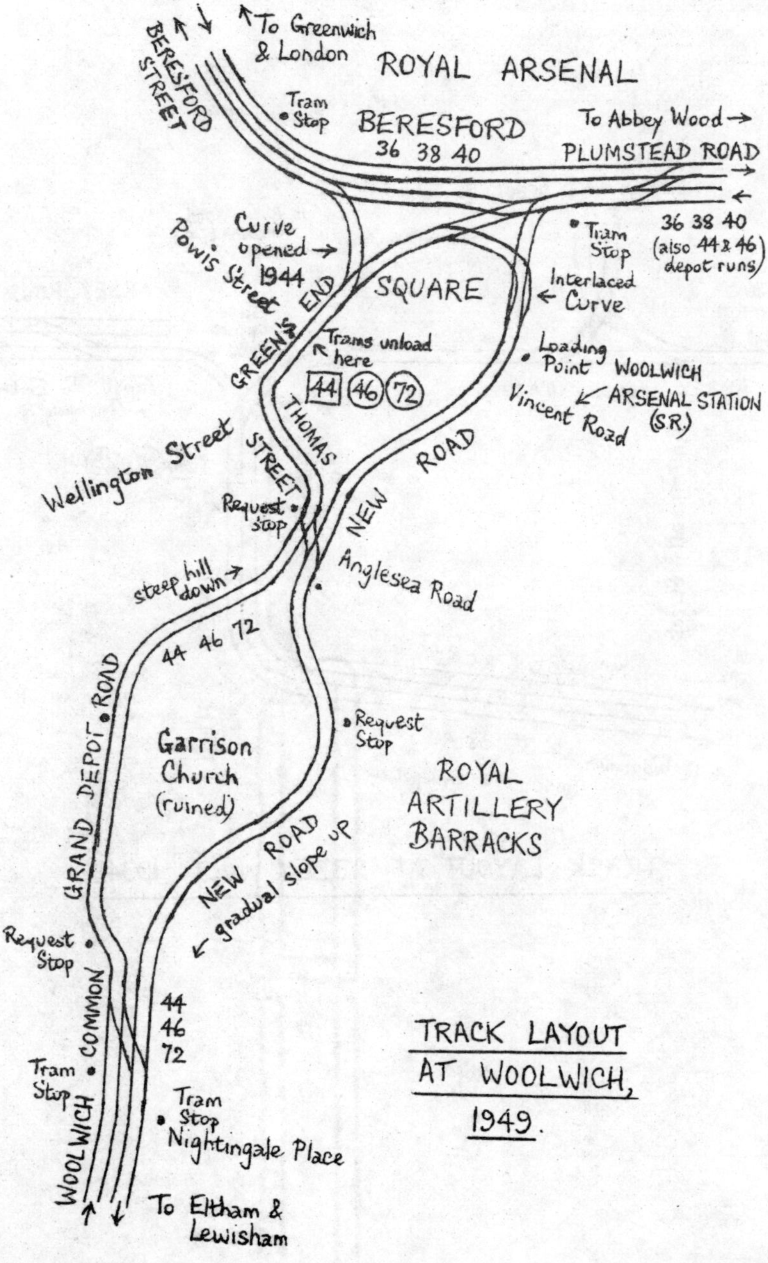

TRACK LAYOUT AT WOOLWICH, 1949.

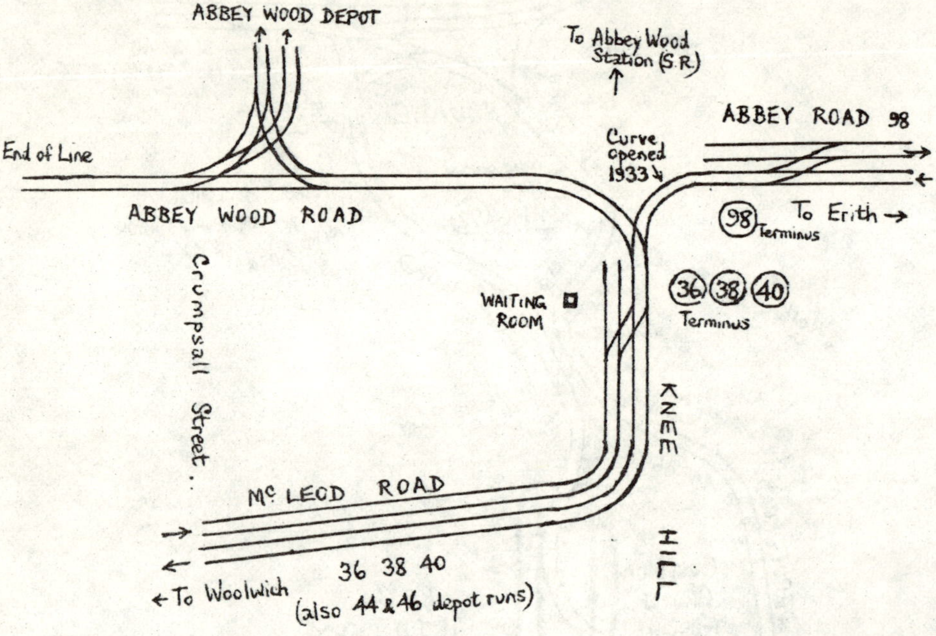

TRACK LAYOUT AT ABBEY WOOD, 1934.

L.C.C. TRAMWAY TICKETS ALSO CROYDON (Bx 6629) AND LONDON, CAMBERWELL & DULWICH TRYS COY (CB 3698)

(1d) Tickets with Diamonds ◆ are Cheap Fare; (1d) MJ 3907 1d Child's Ticket; ST 1888 ½d Child's Ticket.

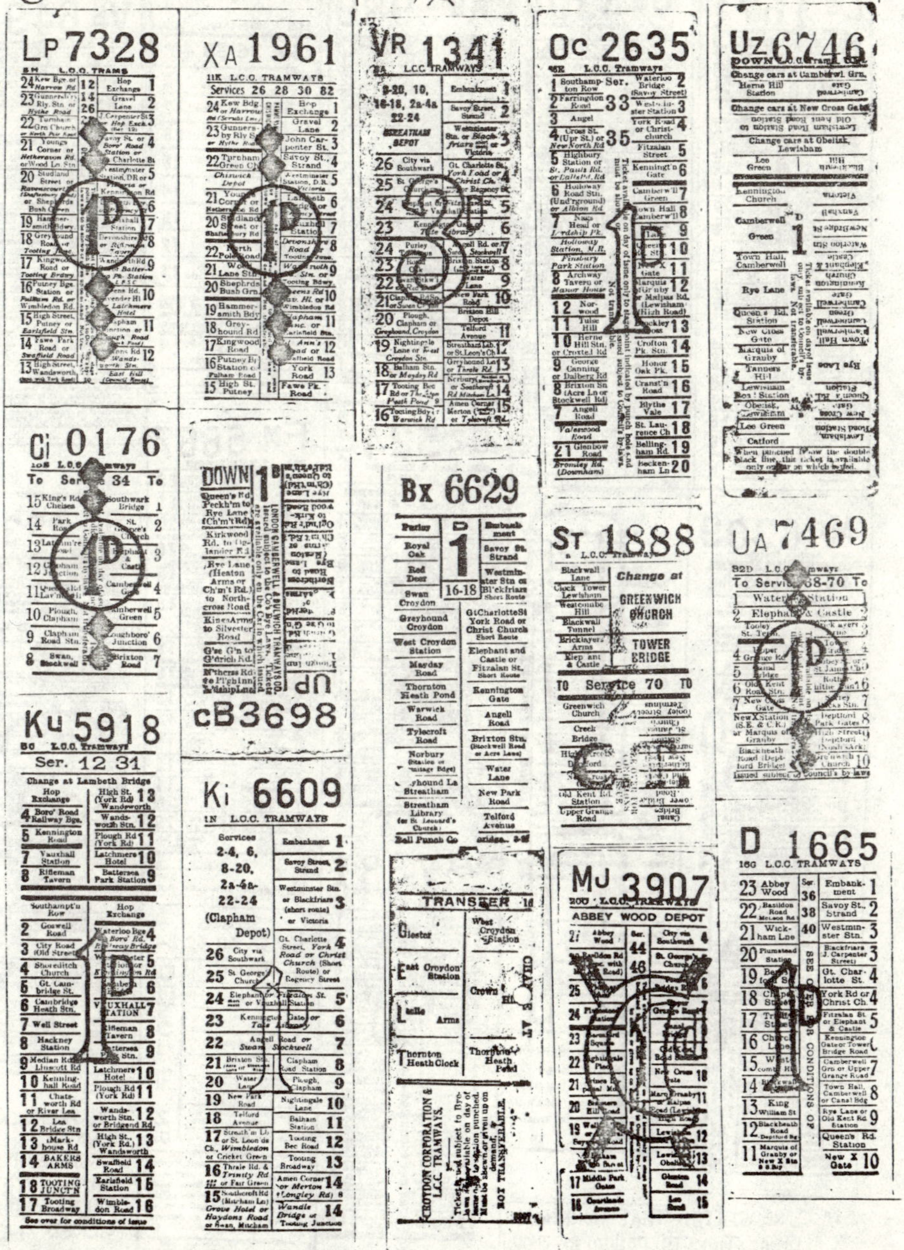

LONDON TRANSPORT TRAMWAY TICKETS 1934-1938 (SELECTION)

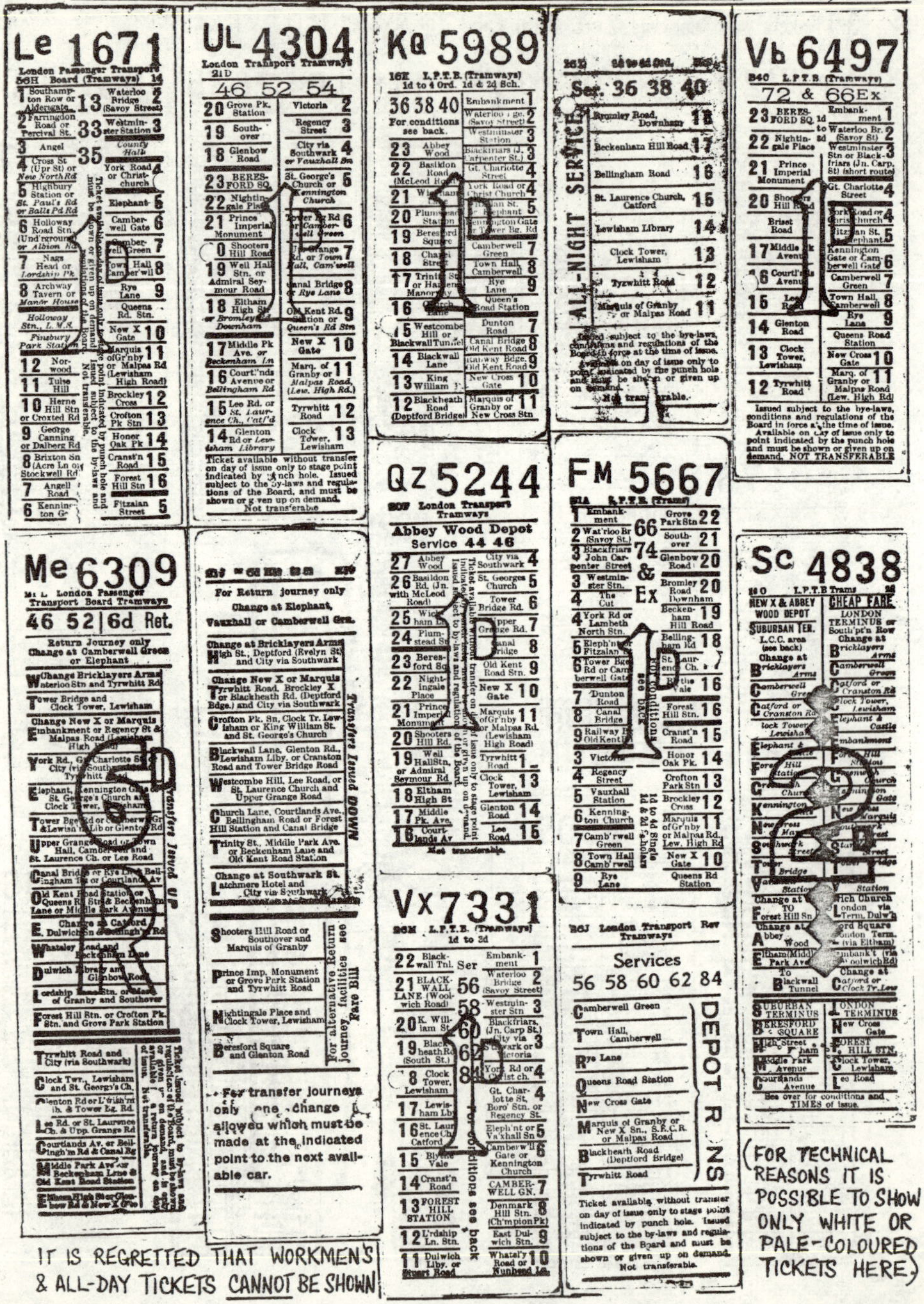

IT IS REGRETTED THAT WORKMEN'S & ALL-DAY TICKETS CANNOT BE SHOWN

(FOR TECHNICAL REASONS IT IS POSSIBLE TO SHOW ONLY WHITE OR PALE-COLOURED TICKETS HERE.)

THE TRAMWAYS OF SOUTH LONDON AND CROYDON 1899-1949

by K. G. HARVIE

PART TWO: THE WANDSWORTH, TOOTING, STREATHAM AND NORWOOD ROUTES OF THE L.C.C. TRAMWAYS AND THE TRAMWAYS OF CROYDON 1899-1949

HORSE AND CABLE TRAMWAYS

The London Tramways Company operated double-track routes from London to Tooting and Streatham. The first section of horse tramway was opened between the 'Horns', Kennington and Brixton Station (L.C. & D.R.) on May 2nd, 1870, later extended southwards to Water Lane, Brixton Hill on August 21st, 1871. Northwards the line was extended to Christ Church, Lambeth on October 5th, 1870 (the scene of G.F. Train's Kennington Road tramway of 1861/1862, which had been compulsorily closed by order of the Sheriff of Surrey after ten months, due mainly to the use of the 'step' rail obstructing horse-drawn carriages and carts, though the trams were popular with local passengers as fares were cheaper than on the omnibuses. The adoption of the grooved rail by the tramways of 1870 removed this objection to lines in the roadway).

Further sections of horse tramway were opened as follows:-
Kennington Gate - 'Swan', Stockwell via Clapham Road(December 7th, 1870);
Christ Church, Lambeth - Westminster Bridge Road at Belvedere Road (December 23rd, 1870);
'Swan', Stockwell - 'Plough', Clapham Common (May 1st, 1871);
'Horns', Kennington - Elephant & Castle (routes to Blackfriars and the Borough (December 28th, 1874).

The Clapham route was later extended to Nightingale Lane on July 28th, 1889 and then via Balham to Totterdown, at the north end of High Street, Tooting on December 16th, 1889. Horse tramway depots were situated in Kennington Road (by Upper Kennington Lane); at the 'Plough', Clapham; and at Marius Road, Balham. The London County Council took over all these tramways from January 1st, 1899.

On December 19th, 1892 cable traction replaced horse traction between Kennington Church and Water Lane, Brixton and the cable tramway was extended up Brixton Hill to Telford Avenue, Streatham Hill. A depot was provided in Brixton Road (near Kennington Church) and another depot was erected at Telford Avenue, where the engine winding house was situated. From Kennington the tramcars were hauled by horses to termini at Westminster Bridge Road (red cars), Blackfriars Road (blue cars), and Old Kent Road - via St. George's Church, Borough (yellow cars). The cars were hauled by tractor 'dummies' fitted with gripper mechanism on the cable section south of Kennington.

In December 1895 the cable route was extended to Streatham Library. The passenger cars were fitted with gripper mechanism in 1898 and the use of tractors was discontinued. A change pit was installed at the north end of Brixton Road, Kennington, where the gripper apparatus could be inserted or removed from the cars. The cable system seems to have worked quite well both in company days and during the first four years of L.C.C. operation from 1899.

The South London Tramways Company, which opened its first section of route on January 1st, 1881, operated the following tram services regularly with horse traction:-

East Hill, Wandsworth - Hop Exchange, Borough (brown cars),
East Hill, Wandsworth - Westminster Bridge Road (yellow cars),
(both services via Wandsworth Road);
North Street, Wandsworth - Hop Exchange, Borough (green cars),
North Street, Wandsworth - Westminster Bridge Road (blue cars),
(both services via Battersea Park Road);
Queen's Road, Lavender Hill - Chelsea Bridge (red cars);
Clapham Junction - Chelsea Bridge via Falcon Lane (chocolate cars).

There were other odd branches and spurs which did not carry regular services.

This company owned depots in Borough Road, Southwark; Queen's Road, Battersea; Jew's Row, Wandsworth; and at Clapham Junction, with additional stables in Gonsalva Road, South Lambeth. The routes were mainly single track with passing loops, except for double line along Albert Embankment and in Battersea Park Road. 'Chain horses' ('Cock horses') assisted trams on Lavender Hill and St. John's Hill. The L.C.C. acquired the routes and depots from November 22nd, 1902.

Another company - the London Southern Tramways - also operated horse trams in the Brixton district. The original two services from Camberwell Green via Coldharbour Lane to the 'Swan', Stockwell, opened on December 20th, 1883 (green cars) and to Tulse Hill, opened on July 10th, 1884 (blue cars) were joined by a third: Tulse Hill to Stockwell (red cars). They were extended to St. Luke's Church, West Norwood on June 4th, 1885 and Vauxhall Station on August 21st, 1887. Horse trams also operated occasionally from Camberwell to Brixton Town Hall (brown cars). These open-top trams had a tilted board placed at the top of the stairs to prevent passengers hitting their heads on a low railway bridge at Loughborough Junction.

Depots were provided at Stockwell Green and Lansdowne Hill, West Norwood, while sick horses were cared for at stables in Eastlake Road, Camberwell. All the routes were single track with passing loops except for some double track between the "Swan', Stockwell and Vauxhall Station. The L.C.C. took these routes over on October 2nd, 1906.

THE INAUGURATION OF ELECTRIC TRACTION

The L.C.C. had erected a housing estate at Totterdown Fields in the 1890s; this may be one reason why the L.C.C. electrified the Tooting tramway first, another being the extension of the City & South London Underground Railway from Stockwell to Clapham Common in 1900. Reconstruction of the tramway began in 1902 and took a year, owing to the diversion of sewers and the massive conduit construction work entailed. Meanwhile the horse car services used temporary tracks (see also notes in S.E. London section on this interim period).

The new electric tramway to Tooting was ceremonially opened on May 15th, 1903 when H.R.H. The Prince of Wales (later King George V) drove a decorated white tramcar from Westminster Bridge Road part of the way to Tooting. Princess May (later Queen Mary) and two of their sons, Prince Edward and Prince Albert (later King George Vl) were among the distinguished passengers. Special tickets were issued, one of which is preserved at County Hall; the Royal party paid with specially-minted coins. It is said that the young princes were reprimanded by their father for playing with the destination blind at the front of the car! (In 1924 Prince Albert himself drove Glasgow Corporation Tramcar No.38 at Parkhead). The Royal party visited the Totterdown Fields Estate and also alighted at Marius Road Depot, Balham, during their return journey to London in the 'White Car'.

Some of the new A Class tramcars (Nos. 1-100) operated first from the depot at Marius Road, Balham until the new Clapham Depot was ready to house all the electric cars. A small boy went to the stables by the 'Plough' Inn and offered ninepence from his moneybox to buy one of the tram horses made redundant by the new electric tramcars!

A temporary power station at Loughborough Junction supplied electric current until Greenwich Power Station was opened in 1906. The new electric services operated to Westminster Bridge Road (Belvedere Road), Waterloo Station and Blackfriars Road (Stamford Street.) The chief offices of the L.C.C. Tramways were at 62, Finsbury Pavement E.C., but moved to 23, Belvedere Road, S.E.1. about 1914.

The L.C.C. experienced many teething troubles on this its first electric tramway route, mainly due to conduit operation. The conduit slot was found to be too narrow and a wider slot had to be substituted; certain weaknesses in the original conduit-construction were also remedied. Other road users (mainly horse-drawn traffic) frequently obstructed the tramway track, which was the only part of the roadway adequately paved in those days: a number of prosecutions followed. There were speed restrictions varying between 4 m.p.h. and 12 m.p.h. on this route at first, and policemen with stop watches lurked on Clapham Common to trap 'speeding' drivers!

THE EXPANSION OF ELECTRIC TRACTION

After the electrification of the Tooting route, Streatham residents were eager for electric trams. The L.C.C.T., wishing to remove horse trams from Kennington Road and Kennington Park Road as soon as possible (as the slower horse trams delayed the speedier electric trams) decided to equip several tramcars of the B Class (Nos.102-201) with cable grippers to operate on the route to Streatham Library. Up till this time the cable cars had worked quite a reliable service, but the heavier electric trams now used imposed too great a strain on the cable and, after several breakdowns, a runaway tram on Brixton Hill compelled the L.C.C. to abandon these experiments. Meanwhile, the cable cars maintained the Streatham service.

Electrification of the Streatham route was immediately decided and the line was closed for reconstruction on April 15th, 1904. So rapidly was this work done that electric trams began to operate on the conduit system between London termini and Brixton Station on May 25th, 1904 and the complete route to Streatham Library was opened to electric trams on June 18th/19th, 1904.

On August 1st, 1904 the lines between the Elephant & Castle and Southwark Bridge via Southwark Bridge Road and also via Borough High Street to St. George's Church were reopened for electric traction. Through services were inaugurated between Southwark Bridge terminus and the termini at both Tooting and Streatham, also from St. George's Church, Borough to Streatham Library.

The Tooting route was extended from Totterdown Street to Tooting Broadway and round the corner into Defoe Road on August 8th, 1905. A cash office was opened at No.8 Defoe Road (now part of Garratt Lane), which subsequently became a private house.

The following year a continuation of this line along Garratt Lane, through Earlsfield and Wandsworth, via York Road to Plough Road, Battersea was opened on August 5th, 1906. A further extension was opened to Battersea Park Station (L.B. & S.C.R.) on October 13th, and through services from Tooting via Wandsworth & Vauxhall to St. Thomas's Hospital, Lambeth and Hop Exchange, Borough operated from December 22nd, 1906. Electric services commenced on the Falcon Road route from the 'Prince's Head', Battersea to Clapham Junction on October 13th, 1906.

The route between Tooting and Wandsworth had never been served by horse tramcars, but between Wandsworth and London the former horse routes of the South London Tramways Company (acquired by the L.C.C. on November 22nd, 1902) were reconstructed for electric conduit traction. Jew's Row Depot at Wandsworth was enlarged to house the electric trams. The Clapham/Tooting and Streatham services were extended over Westminster Bridge and along Victoria Embankment to John Carpenter Street on December 15th, 1906, but the connecting curve and junction at Stangate, Lambeth for the Wandsworth service was not opened until February 4th, 1907.

Only open-top A Class cars could be used on the direct Tooting route for several years owing to the low railway bridges at Clapham and Balham Stations. The roadway was then lowered under both bridges so that the E Class cars, which were built with top covers, could operate on Clapham Road through to Tooting. (The roadway was further lowered in 1921/1922 to permit the passage of tramcars fitted with trolley poles). Afterwards, top covers were fitted to A Class cars.

Two conduit extensions were opened from Tooting Broadway on October 13th, 1907: along the High Street to the west end of Longley Road, where it met the London United Tramways overhead electric route from Kingston on Thames; and via Amen Corner to Tooting Junction Station (L.B. & S.C.R.), where the L.C.C. trams met the South Metropolitan trams on the overhead system from West Croydon Station.

At this time there was no through running between the L.C.C.T. and both the L.U.T. and S.M.E.T. owing to the different systems of electric traction, so passengers had to change tramcars at both boundaries. The L.U.T. had been operating to Longley Road since June 27th, 1907; they called the boundary terminus 'Tooting' while the L.C.C. referred to it as 'Merton'. The S.M.E.T. cars had been running to Tooting Junction since May 28th, 1906 (see Croydon section).

Electrification now came to the routes of the former London Southern Tramways. On April 4th, 1908 the Vauxhall - Stockwell - Brixton route was reopened for electric conduit operation, and on November 21st the Brixton - Camberwell route for electric overhead trolley operation. Change pits were provided at Gresham Road(Brixton Road corner) and Coldharbour Lane (Denmark Hill corner). The spur line from East Brixton Station to Brixton Town Hall was never electrified.

The branch from Loughborough Junction (S.E. & C.R.) along Milkwood Road was also equipped for electric overhead trolley operation. Electric trams began running to Herne Hill Station (S.E. & C.R.) on May 28th, 1909 and to St. Luke's Church, West Norwood on May 30th, 1909. The horse tram depots were closed and the electric trams used Camberwell Depot and a new depot erected by the L.C.C.T. in Norwood Road, just south of Tulse Hill Station (L.B. & S.C.R.). A trolley reverser was provided at the original terminus at West Norwood, outside the 'Thurlow Arms', until the 1920s, when the line was extended several hundred yards to a stub terminus in the High Street, by the church gate.

The L.C.C. was able to use the more efficient overhead system on these routes as municipal opposition to overhead wires had now declined, and also the trams traversed quiet roads. The horse trams had run along Hinton Road, but the electric trams were routed via Herne Hill Road and Wanless Road to avoid a low railway bridge. The L.C.C. devised an ingenious one-way system using Poplar Walk Road and Lowden

Road for the down line while the up line continues along Milkwood Road. Opposite Herne Hill Station the up line runs alongside the western pavement and it also 'hugs' the kerb by Brockwell Park. By these means double track is provided all the way to West Norwood except for two short single-track sections at Hinton Road and Trinity Rise. The original tramway junction at Loughborough faced towards Brixton, but after 1912 only occasional workings used it. The awkward corner by the railway bridge necessitated the single-line junction in the Camberwell direction and Norwood-bound trams have to cross on to the wrong (up) line in Coldharbour Lane, branch off on to the up line in Herne Hill Road, then cross over on to the correct (down) track.

The Streatham route was extended along the High Road past the Common to Hermitage Bridge, Norbury on July 31st, 1909. A change pit was installed just north of Streatham Station (L.B. & S.C.R.) - at Gleneagle Road, whence trams used the overhead trolley system to Norbury terminus, where there was one of the few trolley reversers on the L.C.C.T. system, situated at the boundary of the County of London with the Borough of Croydon.

Only a few yards separated the L.C.C. trams from the Croydon trams (the gap between the tracks being only six inches), but, although both were standard gauge, there was no through running for over sixteen years - a sad mistake from which the motor-bus companies profited. Through tram tickets were issued, however, between the L.C.C. Tramways and Croydon Corporation Tramways from 1909.

CROYDON

Horse trams commenced to run in Croydon in 1879. Twenty years later, the following routes were operating:-

Thornton Heath - Thornton Heath Pond - North End (green cars);
South Norwood - Selhurst - North End (white and blue cars);
Addiscombe - George Street, Croydon (red single-deck cars);
'Red Deer', South Croydon - 'Green Dragon', South End, Croydon (double-deck cars).

A short length of line connecting North End and South End had been opened in 1897 after the High Street had been widened. Horse tram depots were at Thornton Heath Pond and 'Swan and Sugar Loaf', South Croydon.

The Corporation acquired the system in 1900 and leased it to the British Electric Traction Company from January 1st. The main line was relaid for electric traction and extended at each end to Norbury and Purley respectively, horse trams working over the new tracks from May 2nd, 1901. The new electric tramway service was ceremonially opened by the Mayor and Corporation on Thursday, September 26th, 1901, leading a procession of twenty new tramcars. The full service of electric trams began to operate between Norbury and Purley in the evening and vast

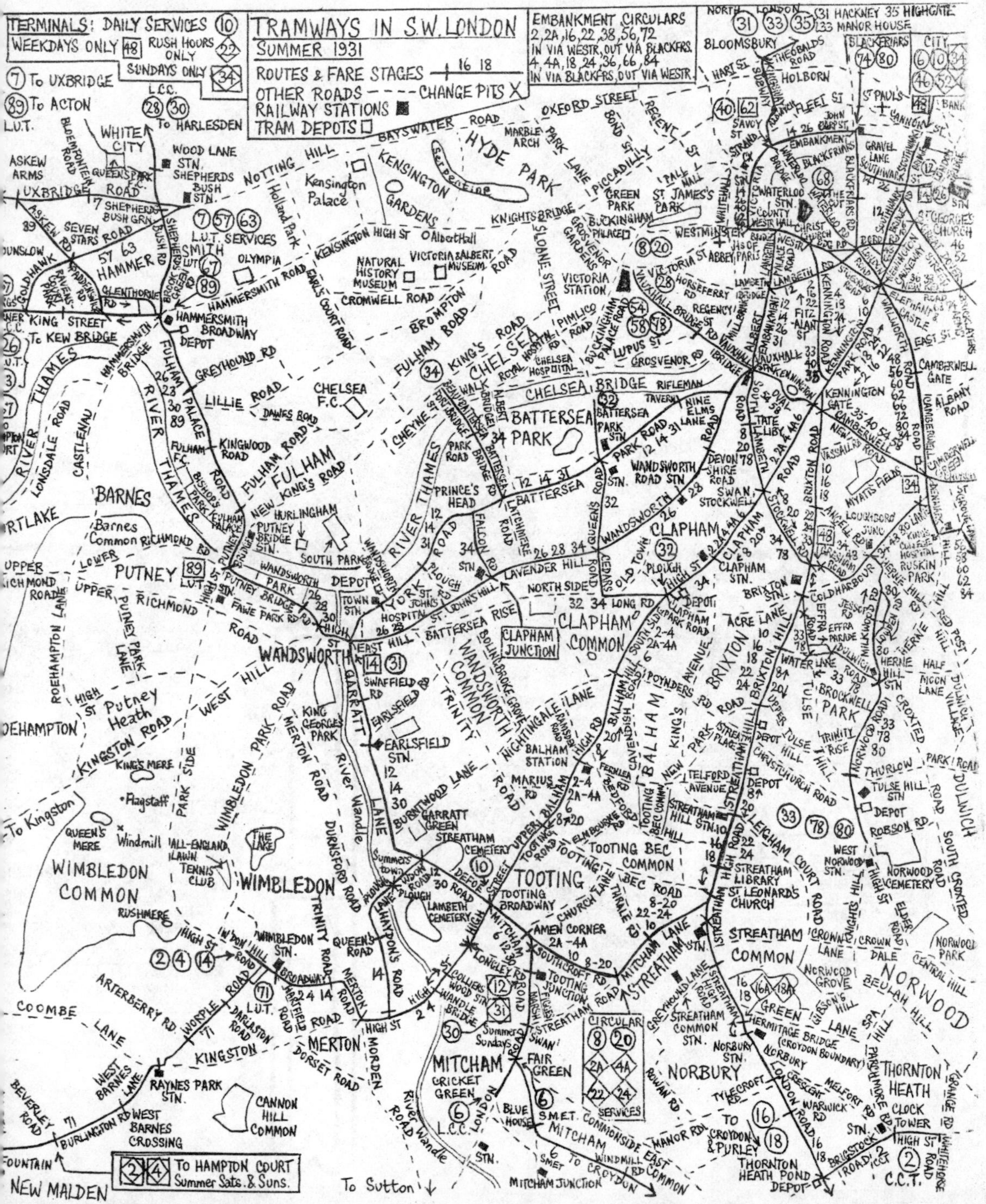
TERMINALS: DAILY SERVICES 10
WEEKDAYS ONLY 48
RUSH HOURS ONLY 22
SUNDAYS ONLY 34
TRAMWAYS IN S.W. LONDON
SUMMER 1931
ROUTES & FARE STAGES 16 18
OTHER ROADS
CHANGE PITS X
RAILWAY STATIONS
TRAM DEPOTS
EMBANKMENT CIRCULARS
2, 2A, 16, 22, 38, 56, 72
IN VIA WESTR, OUT VIA BLACKFRS.
4, 4A, 18, 24, 36, 66, 84
IN VIA BLACKFRS, OUT VIA WESTR.
NORTH LONDON
31 HACKNEY 35 HIGHGATE
33 MANOR HOUSE
7 To UXBRIDGE
89 To ACTON
L.U.T.
L.C.C.
28 30 To HARLESDEN
BLOOMSBURY
THEOBALDS ROAD
HOLBORN
HART ST
FLEET ST
ST PAUL'S
CANNON ST
BANK
BLACKFRIARS
CITY
OXFORD STREET
BAYSWATER ROAD
MARBLE ARCH
PARK LANE
BOND ST
REGENT ST
HYDE PARK
KENSINGTON GARDENS
Kensington Palace
Serpentine
PICCADILLY
GREEN PARK
ST JAMES'S PARK
BUCKINGHAM PALACE
WESTMINSTER
WHITEHALL
STRAND
SAVOY ST
EMBANKMENT
WATERLOO STN.
COUNTY HALL
BLACKFRIARS RD
ST GEORGE'S CHURCH
WHITE CITY
WOOD LANE STN.
SHEPHERDS BUSH STN.
NOTTING HILL
ASKEW ARMS
UXBRIDGE ROAD
SHEPHERDS BUSH GRN
SEVEN STARS ROAD
L.U.T. SERVICES
HAMMERSMITH
OLYMPIA
KENSINGTON HIGH ST
Albert Hall
KNIGHTSBRIDGE
NATURAL HISTORY MUSEUM
VICTORIA & ALBERT MUSEUM
CROMWELL ROAD
SLOANE STREET
GROSVENOR GARDENS
VICTORIA STATION
VICTORIA ST
ABBEY
HORSEFERRY RD
REGENCY ST
LAMBETH BRIDGE
VAUXHALL BRIDGE RD
HAMMERSMITH ROAD
KING STREET
To KEW BRIDGE
HAMMERSMITH BROADWAY
DEPOT
HAMMERSMITH BRIDGE
EARLS COURT ROAD
BROMPTON ROAD
FULHAM ROAD
KING'S ROAD
CHELSEA
PIMLICO ROAD
BUCKINGHAM PALACE ROAD
LUPUS ST
GROSVENOR RD
CHELSEA HOSPITAL
CHELSEA BRIDGE
RIFLEMAN
NINE ELMS LANE
VAUXHALL
KENNINGTON
KENNINGTON ROAD
ELEPHANT & CASTLE
EAST ST
CAMBERWELL GATE
ALBANY ROAD
KENNINGTON GATE
CAMBERWELL NEW RD
OVAL
TATE LIBY
GREYHOUND RD
LILLIE ROAD
DAWES ROAD
CHELSEA F.C.
CHEYNE WALK
ALBERT BRIDGE
BATTERSEA BRIDGE
BATTERSEA PARK
BATTERSEA PARK STN
PARK ROAD
WANDSWORTH ROAD STN
DEVONSHIRE ROAD
SWAN, STOCKWELL
RIVER THAMES
CASTELNAU
LONSDALE ROAD
FULHAM PALACE ROAD
KINGWOOD ROAD
FULHAM F.C.
FULHAM
NEW KING'S ROAD
BISHOPS PARK
BARNES
Barnes Common
RICHMOND RD
HURLINGHAM
PUTNEY BRIDGE STN.
SOUTH PARK
PRINCE'S HEAD
BATTERSEA
FALCON RD
LATCHMERE ROAD
QUEENS ROAD
WANDSWORTH
CLAPHAM
CLAPHAM STN.
BRIXTON ROAD
STOCKWELL RD
LOUGHBORO JUNC
MYATTS FIELDS
COLDHARBOUR LANE
RUSKIN PARK
PUTNEY
UPPER RICHMOND ROAD
WANDSWORTH PARK
DEPOT
TOWN STN
YORK ROAD
PLOUGH
LAVENDER HILL
NORTH SIDE
OLD TOWN
CEDARS ROAD
LONG RD
HIGH ST
DEPOT
CLAPHAM PARK ROAD
BRIXTON STN
EFFRA ROAD
ACRE LANE
HERNE HILL
RED POST HILL
FAWE PARK RD
EAST HILL
HOSPITAL
ST JOHN'S HILL
BATTERSEA RISE
CLAPHAM JUNCTION
CLAPHAM COMMON
SOUTH SIDE
BRIXTON HILL
WATER LANE
HERNE HILL STN
HALF MOON LANE
DULWICH VILLAGE
ROEHAMPTON LANE
WEST HILL
WANDSWORTH COMMON
BOLINGBROKE GROVE
TRINITY ROAD
SWAFFIELD RD
EARLSFIELD RD
GARRATT LANE
KING GEORGE'S PARK
EARLSFIELD STN.
NIGHTINGALE LANE
BALHAM HIGH RD
POYNDERS RD
KING'S AVENUE
NEW PARK ROAD
TULSE HILL
BROCKWELL PARK
CROXTED ROAD
Putney Heath
KINGSTON ROAD
ROEHAMPTON
PARK SIDE
WIMBLEDON PARK ROAD
MERTON ROAD
King's Mere
Flagstaff
BALHAM STATION
BALHAM
TELFORD AVENUE
DEPOT
CHRISTCHURCH ROAD
NORWOOD ROAD
THURLOW PARK ROAD
DULWICH
TULSE HILL STN
BURNTWOOD LANE
MARIUS RD
UPPER TOOTING ROAD
STREATHAM HILL STN.
TOOTING BEC COMMON
To Kingston
Queen's Mere
Windmill
ALL-ENGLAND LAWN TENNIS CLUB
THE LAKE
DURNSFORD ROAD
River Wandle
GARRATT GREEN
STREATHAM CEMETERY
ROBSON RD
WEST NORWOOD STN.
NORWOOD CEMETERY
SOUTH CROXTED ROAD
WIMBLEDON COMMON
WIMBLEDON
Summerstown
PLOUGH
LAMBETH CEMETERY
TOOTING
TOOTING BROADWAY
CHURCH LANE
THRALE RD
STREATHAM LIBRARY
ST LEONARD'S CHURCH
LEIGHAM COURT ROAD
KNIGHTS HILL
CROWN LANE
CROWN DALE
NORWOOD PARK
RUSHMERE
HIGH ST
WIMBLEDON STN.
QUEENS ROAD
HAYDON'S ROAD
AMEN CORNER
MITCHAM LANE
STREATHAM STN.
STREATHAM COMMON
NORWOOD GROVE
CENTRAL HILL
NORWOOD
BEULAH HILL
ARTERBERRY RD.
WORPLE ROAD
BROADWAY
MERTON ROAD
COLLIERS WOOD STN
LONGLEY ROAD
TOOTING JUNCTION
SOUTHCROFT RD
STREATHAM ROAD
GREYHOUND LANE
GREEN LANE
SPA HILL
COOMBE LANE
DARLASTON ROAD
KINGSTON ROAD
MERTON
MORDEN ROAD
HIGH ST
WANDLE BRIDGE
Summer Sundays
SWAN
CIRCULAR
SERVICES
STREATHAM COMMON STN.
NORBURY STN.
HERMITAGE BRIDGE (CROYDON BOUNDARY)
PARCHMORE RD
THORNTON HEATH
WEST BARNES LANE
RAYNES PARK STN.
CANNON HILL COMMON
DORSET ROAD
MITCHAM
CRICKET GREEN
FAIR GREEN
NORBURY
ROWAN RD
TYLECROFT RD
WARWICK RD
MELFORT RD
CLOCK TOWER
BEVERLEY ROAD
BURLINGTON RD
WEST BARNES CROSSING
L.C.C.
LONDON ROAD
BLUE HOUSE
S.M.E.T.
COMMONSIDE EAST
MANOR RD
To CROYDON & PURLEY
THORNTON HEATH POND
DEPOT
BRIGSTOCK ROAD
WHITEHORSE ROAD
C.C.T.
FOUNTAIN
NEW MALDEN
To HAMPTON COURT Summer Sats. & Suns.
To Sutton
MITCHAM JUNCTION
To CROYDON
WINDMILL RD
COMMON

TRAMWAYS IN THE CROYDON AREA
1927 – 1934
ROUTES & FARE STAGES thus: 16 18
OTHER ROADS
L.C.C.T. CHANGE PITS
TERMINAL POINTS
TRAM DEPOTS
RAILWAY STATIONS (SOUTHERN RAILWAY)
C.C.T. Service 2 renumbered No 42
S.M.E.T. Service 6 renumbered No 30
by L.P.T.B. in October 1934
To Wandsworth
To Clapham & London
To London
ST. LEONARD'S CHURCH
To Dulwich
To Forest Hill
To Catford
TOOTING
TOOTING BROADWAY
TOOTING BEC RD
AMEN CORNER
TOOTING JUNC.
STREATHAM
STREATHAM COMMON
NORBURY
NORBURY STATION
CIRCULAR ROUTES
NORWOOD
THORNTON HEATH
CLOCK TOWER
CRYSTAL PALACE
HIGH LEVEL STN
SYDENHAM
PENGE
PAWLEYNE ARMS
BECKENHAM
BECKENHAM JUNCTION
BECKENHAM ROAD
ELMER'S END
MITCHAM
FAIR GREEN
MITCHAM COMMON
MITCHAM JUNCTION STN
MERTON
MORDEN
ST HELIER
Rosehill Park
HACKBRIDGE
BEDDINGTON PARK
BEDDINGTON
WADDON
Waddon Marsh
ADDISCOMBE
ADDISCOMBE ROAD
SHIRLEY
SHIRLEY PARK
WICKHAM ROAD
To West Wickham
ADDINGTON HILLS
COOMBE LANE
GRAVEL HILL
SUTTON
CARSHALTON
WALLINGTON
CROYDON AIRPORT
PURLEY WAY
SELSDON
SELSDON ROAD
FARLEIGH ROAD
SANDERSTEAD
SANDERSTEAD ROAD
SOUTH CROYDON STN.
CROHAM HURST
DAVIS THEATRE
L.P.T.B.
RED DEER
PURLEY OAKS STN.
BRIGHTON ROAD
DEPOT
FOUNTAIN
PURLEY STN.
PURLEY
RUSSELL HILL
FOXLEY LANE
WOODCOTE GREEN
COULSDON
OLD COULSDON
RIDDLESDOWN
MITCHLEY AVENUE
GODSTONE ROAD
To Caterham Valley
To Caterham on the Hill
To Redhill & Brighton
Farthing Downs
HAMSEY GREEN
To Warlingham
To Banstead & Reigate
To Woodmansterne
To Cheam
Carshalton Beeches

crowds sampled the service during the first week.

Most of the route through the centre of Croydon was single track and passing loops on account of the narrow North End, High Street and South End. Between Thornton Heath Pond and Norbury terminus each overhead wire was supported by its own standards with short bracket arms on each side of the road. At Norbury Station (L.B. & S.C.R.) the roadway had to be lowered under the railway bridge for the trams. Between South Croydon and Purley the overhead wires were supported by bracket arms on the west side of Brighton Road, the standards being in the Borough of Croydon. (The east side was in the area of the Coulsdon and Purley Urban District Council). The tram track was paved with wood blocks covered with tar, instead of the usual granite setts employed by most councils at this time.

The offices and main depot, accommodating 43 tramcars, were erected at Thornton Heath Pond, while another depot was built at Purley, at the corner of Purley Downs Road; this was extended in 1907 to hold 36 tramcars. The Purley tram terminus at Godstone Road corner, by the Fountain, was a quiet place until the shops on the west side were built; in those days, the long gardens of big houses occupied the site. In November 1902 a scissors crossover was installed at Purley terminus, enabling two cars to load at a time, and about 1906 another scissors crossover was laid at Norbury terminus. Electric power was supplied by the Generating Station at Pitlake to both the Croydon Corporation Tramways and the South Metropolitan Tramways.

Single-track branches, with passing loops and bracket-arm overhead, were reopened for electric traction from High Street (Crown Hill) to Bingham Road, Addiscombe on January 4th, 1902; from Thornton Heath Pond to Thornton Heath Station (L.B. & S.C.R.) via Brigstock Road on January 10th, 1902, extended along the High Street to Whitehorse Road (after the bridge over the railway had been rebuilt) on June 13th, 1903; and from West Croydon Station (L.B. & S.C.R.) to Selhurst Station on January 24th, 1902. The Selhurst route was extended to Norwood Junction on March 14th, 1902 and to Selby Road (Borough Boundary) on December 14th, 1905. A former horse route along Whitehorse Road north of the 'Gloster' was electrified in 1906, opening on November 9th, but did not prove a success and was closed on July 5th, 1908; reopened on July 28th, 1911, it was finally closed on March 8th, 1913.

At West Croydon, from 1902 until 1925, cars on the Selhurst route worked in a loop via Oakfield Road, London Road and back via Station Road. A separate overhead wire was used along London Road and a pointsman was stationed on West Croydon Station railway bridge to work the points for the Selhurst line.

Coloured lights were carried on the tramcars at night to indicate the different services, thus:-

Norbury - red	South Norwood - green
Thornton Heath - green	
'Red Deer' - red	Addiscombe - red
Purley - green	Crown Hill - green

Croydon Corporation now decided to operate their tramways themselves from June 1st, 1906 and terminated their lease with the B.E.T. The Tramways Manager, Thomas Boyce Goodyer Esq., continued in the Corporation's service until his retirement in June 1928.

From June 1st, 1906 the B.E.T. concentrated on developing the South Metropolitan Electric Tramways instead. The "South Met" had running powers from West Croydon Station to Selby Road over the Croydon Corporation system and opened its own route to the 'Pawleyne Arms', Penge on February 10th, 1906. This line was extended along High Street, Penge to Thicket Road (entrance to Crystal Palace Park) on April 11th, a branch from the 'Robin Hood', Anerley to Crystal Palace (Low Level) Station (L.B. & S.C.R.) being opened the same day. After certain modifications to the tramcars imposed by the Board of Trade had been made, the route was extended up steep Anerley Hill to the Crystal Palace itself, passing by the South Tower, on May 28th, 1906. The depot for these routes was in Oakgrove Road, Anerley, a turning just beyond the 'Robin Hood', and still stands today.

The original service run was alternate cars from the Crystal Palace to Penge and Selby Road, with through tickets to West Croydon, until June 24th, 1907, when by agreement Croydon cars began to operate the Penge - Croydon service, while S.M.E.T. cars worked the Crystal Palace - Croydon service.

Other S.M.E.T. routes were opened from West Croydon (Canterbury Road) across Mitcham Common to Tooting Junction on May 28th, 1906 (with a depot at Aurelia Road), extended at the Croydon end to Church Street on June 2nd and West Croydon Station on October 9th; and from West Croydon to Carshalton on November 10th, extended to High Street, Sutton on December 21st, 1906 (with a depot at Westmead Road, Sutton). Ruskin Road and Beynon Road, Carshalton, together with three adjacent roads, were specially constructed with the new tramway, and Ringstead Road and Westmead Road widened.

Most of the S.M.E.T. system was double track (though the Selby Road - West Croydon section used by the S.M.E.T. was mainly single track and passing loops with one-way working at West Croydon), but an awkward junction at Pitlake made automatic signals necessary. This junction consisted of double track on the Sutton route, but a single line from Mitcham joined the wrong line in Tamworth Road and cars regained the correct track by a crossover. A single line also connected the Mitcham and Sutton routes in the reverse direction originally, but this curve was removed by 1920.

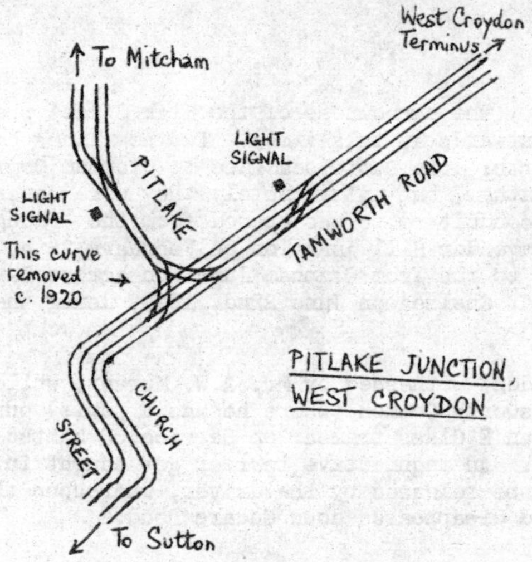

The Croydon Corporation tramcar livery was brown and white. On July 22nd, 1908 Thornton Heath Depot provided a decorated and illuminated car for Croydon's Lifeboat Day. The S.M.E.T. cars were originally painted green and white, later red and ivory from 1921. Both systems operated open-top tramcars, both bogie cars and single-truck cars (four-wheelers). The S.M.E.T. cars on the Crystal Palace route were fitted with special track brakes for Anerley Hill. Among the S.M.E.T. bogie cars were four originally built for Gravesend, which were kept mostly on the Mitcham route, though it seems that on Saturdays in the 1920s they also operated extras between West Croydon Station and Woodcote Road, Wallington.

On Easter Monday: April 1st, 1907 S.M.E.T. Car No.19 ran away on Wallington railway bridge and overturned at Park Lane corner; two people were killed and 30 injured. A fitter, who did not know the route, had been driving the car, due to heavy holiday traffic.

At one period the S.M.E.T. operated an internal baggage service by passenger tramcar with offices at Sutton Depot and Church Road, Waddon, but this ceased at the end of 1911. The Company's main offices were in Lower Church Street, Croydon until June 1913, when the S.M.E.T. was transferred to the Underground Railways Group.

BATTERSEA ELECTRIFICATION COMPLETED (L.C.C.T.)

The horse tram route along Queen's Road, Battersea was reopened for electric traction with single-deck cars from Chelsea Bridge to Lavender Hill on January 25th, 1909, while the Wandsworth Road horse line was reconstructed the same year. The Wandsworth Road route was reopened for electric double-deck cars from Nine Elms to Queen's Road on September 23rd, down Lavender Hill to Clapham Junction on October 9th and to East Hill terminus, Wandsworth, at Alma Road on

December 16th, 1909. (The narrowness of the High Street prevented further extension westwards at this time). Two new lines had been planned from Wandsworth: via Battersea Rise to Clapham Common and via Trinity Road to Streatham, but unfortunately they were never constructed.

However, a new conduit route was opened from the 'Plough', Clapham via Cedars Road to Lavender Hill junction on February 26th, 1910 and electric trams began to run from Clapham Junction across Battersea Bridge to King's Road, Chelsea on June 22nd, 1911, using the conduit system.

An amusing incident witnessed by Mr. A.W. Morant, while walking to Emanuel School, Wandsworth Common (where he was a pupil) one day about 1913, occurred when an E Class tramcar on Service 30 halted on North Side, Clapham Common. An inquisitive terrier got caught in the lifeguard and had to be released by the driver, whereupon the dog shot off like an arrow and disappeared down Cedars Road.

Another E Class car climbing Cedars Road hill had a circuit breaker 'blow' and ran back downhill. Fortunately no traffic was passing as it shot across Lavender Hill junction and hit a single-deck car waiting at Queen's Road terminus, nobody being injured.

L.C.C. TRAMWAY SERVICES IN 1909

The following tramway services were operated by the L.C.C. in S.W. London and the Herne Hill district during the Summer of 1909. The services were grouped into routes for administrative purposes, but no route numbers were carried on the tramcars, though the services were denoted by a three-colour light code shown above the destination boxes at night.

Route 15 :		St. Paul's Road, Canonbury - Lavender Hill, via Kingsway Subway & Queen's Road.
24 :	(-R-)	Norbury - John Carpenter Street via Westminster;
	(RRR)	Streatham Library - Blackfriars Road;
	(WWW)	Streatham Library - Southwark Bridge (rush hours only);
	(R-R)	Streatham Library - St. George's Church, Borough;
		Water Lane, Brixton - Blackfriars Road (all-night service).
25 :	(GGR)	Norbury - Victoria Station via Brixton.
26 :	(-G-)	Merton - John Carpenter Street via Westminster;
	(GGG)	Merton - Blackfriars Road;
	(G-G)	Tooting Broadway - Waterloo Station;
	(RWG)	Tooting Broadway - Southwark Bridge;
		Tooting Broadway - Savoy Street, Strand (all-night service).
27 :	(W-G)	Merton - Victoria Station via Clapham.

Route 28 : (-GG) Tooting Junction - Hop Exchange, Borough
via Wandsworth & Lambeth Road.
29 : (WGG) Clapham Junction - John Carpenter St. via Battersea;
(WWR) Lavender Hill - Chelsea Bridge;
(-RR) East Hill, Wandsworth - Savoy Street, Strand,
(horse and electric traction - under reconstruction).
30 : (WGW) Victoria Station - St. George's Church, Borough,
via Brixton & Camberwell;
West Norwood - Savoy Street, Strand,
via Camberwell & Westminster.

(Colour-code reference:- B - blue; G - green; R - red: W - white;
Blank or Black shown thus -, e.g. (---).

The white code sometimes appeared as yellow and the blue code as purple, depending upon the state of the electric light bulbs and the glass shades used in the destination boxes.

The L.C.C.T. services from Merton and Norbury previously terminating in Blackfriars Road at Stamford Street were extended over Blackfriars Bridge on September 14th, 1909, while the Battersea and Wandsworth Road services previously terminating on the Embankment were extended over the bridge and along Southwark Street to the Hop Exchange.

About 1910, a new service was started between West Norwood and Victoria Station via Loughborough Junction (colour code: green, red, green), so the service from St. George's Church was curtailed at Brixton Road (Gresham Road) instead of working through to Victoria. The Norwood - Victoria service was diverted via the new Effra Road route in 1912.

At the same time (1910), a rush-hour service was started between East Hill, Wandsworth and Victoria Station,(colour-code: red, green, red); later this became a daily service.

Driver Green of Wandsworth Depot had been one of the crew of H.M.S. Discovery and had sailed with Captain Robert Scott on his voyages of Antarctic exploration.

CONNECTIONS AT TOOTING AND BRIXTON

A conduit branch was opened on November 5th, 1910 from St. Leonard's Church, Streatham down Mitcham Lane to Amen Corner, Tooting, where it joined the Tooting Junction route. In its early days Southcroft Road was only a rough track alongside the tramlines and the tramwaymen nicknamed this section "the prairie".

On the same day a conduit spur was opened from Garratt Lane, Tooting along Wimbledon Road to Summerstown, where it met the L.U.T. Haydon's Road branch (overhead system), which had been opened on June 27th, 1907; there was no through running at this time.

The L.C.C. opened a new overhead trolley route from Brixton Town Hall to Herne Hill Station on April 5th, 1912, to shorten the distance between West Norwood and Victoria. A one-way system was used on part of this route also, the down line using Morval Road, the up line Water Lane. A change pit was installed in Effra Road outside St. Matthew's Church.

The L.C.C. Tramways established their Ticket Printing Works in Effra Road, Brixton. At first, rolls of different-coloured card were used for varying fare values and types of ticket, but during the Great War it became impossible to obtain coloured card. Instead, white card had to be used and the borders of the tickets were tinted with different colours to represent various fare values and special types of ticket, except the penny white. This proved so acceptable that the practice has continued ever since and this is the origin of the conspicuous L.C.C. (and L.P.T.B.) tram ticket bearing coloured borders and a white stripe down the middle.

TRAILER CARS

During the Summer of 1913 trailer cars began operating on the Victoria Embankment circular routes to Merton and Norbury. The trailers (Nos. T1-T8) were converted horse cars, but in the next two years 150 new trailers were built (Nos. T9-T158). Trailers for the Merton route were kept at Marius Road Depot, Balham and at Clapham Depot. At Balham a proper shunting system was operated by petrol-electric tractors, but at other depots service cars had to shunt the trailers on and off; this sometimes led to delays.

A turning circle was provided on Clapham Common, near Nightingale Lane, round the triangle at the end of the Avenue. Permission was granted in 1914 to use trailers on Routes 14 & 26, but none were ever used on these services.

About 1913, with the incursion of women into business life, the L.C.C.T. experimented with tramcars reserved for Ladies only, some operating on the Tooting - Embankment circular route.

L.C.C.T. ROUTE NUMBERING

From September 1912 the L.C.C. numbered its tramway services. The route numbers were first shown on metal plates hung from the canopies of the trams, but these were soon replaced by oblong stencils of the 'Venner' type inside the front and rear end upper-saloon windows of the tramcars. Narrow route boards were carried outside the lower-saloon windows, in addition to the roller blinds fitted in the end destination boxes.

After the introduction of route numbers, the following services were operating in this area during the Summer of 1914:-

Route 2 : Merton (Longley Road)- Victoria Embankment via Westminster;
4 : Merton - Embankment via Elephant & Blackfriars;
6 : Tooting Broadway - Southwark Bridge (rush hours only);
8 : Merton - Victoria Station via Clapham;
10 : Merton & Tooting - Southwark Bridge via Streatham & Brixton;
12 : Tooting Junction - Hop Exchange, Borough via Battersea;
14 : Tooting Junction - John Carpenter Street via Battersea;
16 : Norbury (Hermitage Bridge)- Embankment via Westminster;
18 : Norbury-Embankment via Elephant & Blackfriars;
20 : Norbury - Victoria Station via Brixton;
X 22 : Southcroft Road - Embankment via Streatham & Westminster;
X 24 : Southcroft Road - Embankment via Streatham & Blackfriars.

(Note: X - Routes 22 & 24 operated during rush hours only).

Route 26 : East Hill, Wandsworth - Hop Exchange via Lavender Hill & Embankment;
28 : East Hill - Victoria Station;
30 : East Hill - Waterloo Station via Cedars Road & Clapham Road;
32 : Lavender Hill - Chelsea Bridge via Queen's Road;
34 : Clapham Junction - King's Road, Chelsea;
74 : Brixton Road - Southwark Bridge via Camberwell;
76 : West Norwood - Blackfriars via Brixton & Elephant;
78 : West Norwood - Victoria Station via Brixton;
80 : West Norwood - Savoy Street via Camberwell & Westminster;
X 86 : Clapham Junction - Savoy Street via Battersea;
X 92 : Brixton Road - Blackfriars via Camberwell (rush hours only).

(Note: X - Routes 86 & 92 operate during rush hours only).

All-Night Services (unnumbered) operated thus:-

Tooting Broadway - Savoy Street via Clapham & Westminster;
Battersea (Prince's Head)- John Carpenter St, Blackfriars;
Water Lane, Brixton - John Carpenter Street, Blackfriars.

During some period between 1912 and 1914 Service 14 operated between Streatham Library and Latchmere Road, Battersea at certain hours of the day.

Service 10 was diverted via Marshalsea Road and Borough High Street (instead of Southwark Bridge Road) by February 1913, Service 6 being similarly diverted by April 1915.

One wet day, November 13th, 1913, a descending tramcar ran away on Mitcham Lane hill, Streatham. It failed to negotiate the curve into Southcroft Road, became derailed and crashed over on to its side by

Fallsbrook Road. As a result, a compulsory stop was instituted at Credenhill Street for descending cars, in addition to the existing stop before the corner.

Mr. Morant remembers that one evening, probably in 1914, when returning home from the office, the D Class tramcar in which he was travelling on Service 28 from Victoria jammed its plough at Vauxhall Cross (South Lambeth Road junction) during the rush hour. The damaged plough was pulled round the corner to a hatch and removed and the following No.54 car pushed the No.28 up Wandsworth Road till it was clear of the traffic and the spare plough could be inserted. One wonders what the folk on the No.54 thought of this sudden diversion!

One morning during the Summer of 1914, the Chancellor of the Exchequer, David Lloyd-George, and his friend Sir George Riddell, a newspaper proprietor, were being driven up to Westminster from Lloyd-George's house at Walton Heath when his motor car broke down at Streatham. An important Cabinet meeting had been arranged for 11 o'clock and, as no taxis were available, the two men boarded a No.16 tramcar for Westminster. But when the conductor came for their fares, they discovered that neither of them had a penny in their pockets! Fortunately, some other passengers came to their rescue and paid their fares and they reached their destination in good time, although the spectacle of the Chancellor of the Exchequer without a penny in his pockets may have seemed rather paradoxical to the folk on that No.16 tram!

THE 1914 - 1919 WAR

The following proposed tramway routes were among those never constructed, mainly because of the Great War:-

Wandsworth to Richmond, Kingston Hill and Wimbledon Hill; Nightingale Lane, Clapham via Burntwood Lane to Earlsfield; 'Plough', Clapham - Brixton Town Hall via Acre Lane; Cavendish Road, Balham - Streatham Place; Brixton Hill - Tulse Hill; Herne Hill Station - Goose Green, East Dulwich; and West Norwood - Crystal Palace.

Service 92 was withdrawn in April 1915 and this route number has never been used since. No.76 was altered to run to John Carpenter Street via Kennington & Westminster and No.80 direct to Blackfriars via Camberwell & Elephant. Service 14 was curtailed to work from the Hop Exchange to High Street, Wandsworth only, though extended to Earlsfield Station (L. & S.W.R.) at rush hours; it no longer ran on Sundays. On June 13th, 1915 Service 30 was withdrawn and Service 34 was extended to operate Chelsea - Clapham Junction - Cedars Road - Clapham Road - Waterloo Station; but this had to be curtailed to operate Chelsea - 'Plough', Clapham only from the Spring of 1918. No.86 was also withdrawn in 1915. It seems that Services 24 & 76 were temporarily withdrawn during the latter part of the War as an economy measure.

As at Woolwich, tramway development at Wandsworth had been delayed by narrow streets, but street widening in High Street, Wandsworth enabled the L.C.C. Harlesden - Hammersmith - Putney overhead trolley route to be connected with the lines in Garratt Lane. (The Hammersmith route - Service 82 - originally built to serve the White City Exhibition, had been opened in stages as follows:-

Hammersmith - Harrow Road on May 30th, 1908;
Hammersmith - Putney on January 23rd, 1909;
Putney - Wandsworth on January 30th, 1912).

A change pit was installed at the east end of Putney Bridge Road. No.82 was extended to operate from College Park junction (Scrubs Lane/Harrow Road), Harlesden - called "near Willesden Junction" by the L.C.C.T. - to Tooting Junction from July 16th, 1915, worked by trams from Hammersmith and Wandsworth Depots.

Croydon Corporation Tramways doubled a length of track on the Penge route by Selhurst Station in 1915 to serve the Crystal Palace Football Club, whose ground was then opposite the station; it moved later to Whitehorse Lane. 'Football Specials' were run to matches from Croydon and Penge by both the C.C.T. & S.M.E.T.; these were the only occasions when S.M.E.T. cars worked to Penge after 1907.

The S.M.E.T. had introduced extra short workings between the 'Robin Hood', Anerley and the Crystal Palace at the end of 1912, but now the C.C.T. found it necessary to curtail the Penge service at the 'Pawleyne Arms' for the duration of the War. Since 1908 both tramway systems had suffered extensive motor omnibus competition, especially the C.C.T. on its Purley route, but the War caused the withdrawal of many omnibus services and the tramcars carried the bulk of the wartime road passenger traffic. A munitions factory was opened on the south side of Stafford Road, Waddon on the S.M.E.T. Sutton route, by the Croydon boundary. A siding was laid into the factory yard about 1916 and special cars were operated from West Croydon for munition workers. A S.M.E.T. shuttle service from Tooting Junction to Mitcham Cricket Green, which had operated since 1906, was withdrawn during the War and no more passengers were carried until the L.C.C.T. took over the branch in 1926.

Tramcar lighting had to be dimmed to avoid detection by Zeppelins and German bombers at night. A L.C.C. all-night tramcar was blasted by a bomb at Streatham Hill, by the Station, and Conductor C. Boys and Motorman T. Gaymer of Telford Avenue Depot were fatally injured. This occurred during an early-morning Zeppelin raid on Monday, September 25th, 1916, which left a trail of damage among houses and shops on either side of the main road from Streatham through Brixton to Kennington and disrupted the L.B. & S.C.R. in the Streatham area. (For other notes on the L.C.C.T. during air raids see the S.E. London Section). Croydon Corporation fitted the headlights of their tramcars with blackout stencils lettered N for Norbury, P - Purley, RD - 'Red Deer' and TH for Thornton Heath.

Croydon Corporation began to employ women conductors on the tramcars in the Autumn of 1915 and the 'Southmet' followed suit. The S.M.E.T. provided canvas draught screens on the open platforms of its cars for the benefit of its women conductors. During the War a passenger tramway shelter was erected at Crystal Palace terminus.

The tramway staff had been dissatisfied with conditions and a serious strike for higher pay started on the S.M.E.T. on April 10th, 1916 and spread to the Croydon system next day, causing the C.C.T. to curtail the Penge service at Selby Road boundary; this strike lasted until June 9th. However, the C.C.T. was able to operate a daily average of between 20 - 50 tramcars out of a total of 75, the number increasing gradually during these two months as the weeks went by. The crews were awarded ½d. per hour increase, and fares on the joint C.C.T./S.M.E.T. route were increased. In March 1918 it was recommended that all transport workers in Britain should receive a wage increase, but Croydon Corporation rejecting this, all C.C.T. staff went on strike on August 18th. The bonus was eventually awarded in September 1918.

A southbound tramcar proceeding along North End, Croydon at speed branched off into George Street in error and knocked down Inspector J.W. Chandler, who unfortunately sustained fatal injuries, one of the very few victims of the Croydon trams (January 10th, 1917).

Turning again to the L.C.C.T., while home on a day's leave from the Royal Flying Corps about 1917, Mr. Morant was returning from Clapham Junction on a D Class car (26/28 route). At the 'Craven Arms' stop on Lavender Hill the tramcar was halted while the P.W. gang removed a rail, laid a new length and connected it up to enable the 'D' to drive slowly over. No night work on tracks was allowed at this time because of the German air raids.

A motor-bus ran away downhill between Streatham Common and Green Lane, Norbury and collided with a L.C.C. tramcar in August 1917. The tram driver was taken to the local cottage hospital and the woman conductor was also injured.

The L.C.C. withdrew transfer fares between London and Croydon from June 18th, 1918, but they were restored after the War.

Early in 1919 an up E/1 Class tramcar was disabled with a broken axle on the junction at St. Leonard's Church, Streatham. A single-decker works car towed the 'culprit' home to Telford Avenue Depot. On August 6th two tramcars collided in Clapham Road.

<u>A CLIPPIE's LIFE DURING THE GREAT WAR</u> by Mrs. E.M. TOLL of Streatham

I was the first conductress to learn at Clapham Depot. It was hard work pulling the levers at crossovers and, when I had passed, I taught other women the routine.

Then they sent me to Streatham and I was the first woman there and, I might say, not very welcome, as they said I was taking a man's job away. I was also the first conductress to marry, but by then I was treated well and they gave me a lovely wedding present. I was working on the double-deckers at first, but when the trailers came to Telford Avenue I had the first service on one, but I didn't like them; I was thrown down the stairs twice, so I went back on the big bogie cars.

We had to wear a thick grey uniform with leather bindings and long leggings and mackintosh hats. Our ticket holders used to have Workmen's 1d. single tickets and 2d. return for the whole journey, then after 8 o'clock we had to change the racks to put in single fares, returns, transfers and children's tickets. The money bags were heavy leather and when theywere full of coppers we had to pad our shoulders.

We worked six days a week and only one Sunday off in six. We were suspended if we sat down on the stairs or inside the lower saloon when not busy or feeling queer, and all for 38/- a week. What a difference now!

When crossing the Thames bridges we had to turn off the tram's lights in case of air attack and it was most difficult on the trailers when crowds were packed like sardines and there was only one switch; if this was in the front you couldn't get to it and so were reported and suspended.

The first Winter was terrible: we had so much snow that we were out till the early hours of the morning; either the plough got jammed or the salt stopped the electricity. People coming out of the Kennington Theatre and living locally either took us in for a hot drink or brought one out to us. There were large advertisement boards hanging on the front of the tramcars. The drivers used to take them off and use them as sledges to keep themselves warm and gave us girls some nice rides in the snow. We had fun and games even then. In the Summer two horse brakes took us for outings to Box Hill, near Dorking.

I joined the Union to keep it going for the men away at the Front. When the tram was blasted by a Zeppelin bomb at Streatham Hill near the

Station I was on weekend leave as my husband had leave from the Army, otherwise I would have been conducting that tram. The bomb actually fell on a big house used as a boys' school, but it was empty at the time; in those days there were big houses on the west side of Streatham Hill from the Station to Telford Avenue; now it's all shops.

The damaged tram was towed into the Depot and the Home Office people came down to inspect it. I was told that they found the dead driver still standing with his hand on the brake. There was a long funeral procession for the driver and conductor through the centre of Streatham on the following Friday and I marched with my colleagues through the rain, but I declined to carry one of the wreaths as I felt so upset and sorry for the victims and their families.

STREATHAM'S 'TRAVELLING CLOCK' by F.L. DIX

There is a Great War story about Streatham's 'travelling clock' - a bracket clock suspended above a jeweller's shop in the High Road between Sunnyhill Road and St. Leonard's Church. After a short stretch of single track south of Streatham Library the line became double again by the 'clock shop'.

The women conductors had difficulty in securing the trolley poles of the E/1 Class tramcars and in several cases the roof hook, securing the trolley when not in use, became bent. It is said that one such E/1 Class car was crossing the points from the single line on to the double track when the motion caused the insecure trolley pole to jerk upwards and crash through the clock face.

As the unwitting driver proceeded, the trolley pole wrenched the clock from its bracket and, whirling it around, flung it through a window on the upper deck of the tramcar! Fortunately nobody was harmed and the tram travelled some distance before the driver was made aware of the happening. The clock was recovered from the floor of the tram's upper deck and returned to its shop. Thus it was said for some years that Streatham was unique in possessing 'a clock which travelled by tram'.

There was a further stretch of single track down the hill from the junction at St. Leonard's Church to Gleneagle Road, by Streatham Station (L.B. & S.C.R.), where the change pit is situated. One day during Summer 1916 an E/1 Class tramcar on Service 16 proceeding downhill towards Norbury derailed on entering the single track and ran into 'The Chocolate Shop' (which also served Teas). Little damage was done and it was soon rerailed and worked into Telford Avenue Depot.

These two sections of single track in the High Road at Streatham were later doubled in 1931, but the two single-line sections in Mitcham Lane (by Fernwood Avenue and Thrale Road respectively) remain to this day.

POST-WAR L.C.C. DEVELOPMENTS

In November 1919, after new curves had been laid from High Street, Tooting into Mitcham Road, Service 6 became a daily service operating Tooting Junction - Southwark Bridge, while No.8 operated Tooting Junction - Victoria Station. To allow space for the outer curve, it became necessary to remove the outward curve into Garratt Lane, thus singling the 1905 extension from Totterdown. The inward curve was a new one from the double-track connection: Mitcham Road - Merton (once used by the No.10) to the up line of the 2/4 route.

For some years Services 2 & 4 had operated as a circular route, cars changing route numbers while running along Victoria Embankment (officially while passing Waterloo Bridge). Now from June 16th, 1921 Services 16 & 18, 22 & 24, 76 & 80 also became Embankment circulars.

At the same time Service 6 was diverted to Southcroft Road (instead of Tooting Junction) and worked as a circular route with No.10: Tooting & Streatham to Southwark Bridge on weekdays, (to St. George's Church, Borough, only on Saturday afternoons and evenings and Sundays); No.6 ran via Clapham and No.10 via Brixton.

Further street widening in Wandsworth allowed the final connection between East Hill and High Street to be completed, and on August 4th, 1921 Service 28 was extended from East Hill to Harrow Road and Service 26 to Putney Bridge; No.26 was further extended to Hammersmith Broadway on December 1st, 1921.

During 1921/1922 the roadway under the railway bridges at Clapham and Balham was again lowered, this time to allow the running of trolley-fitted cars. The new series of E/1 Class tramcars was now introduced (Nos. 1727-1851), fitted with two trolley poles. They were tried out in S.E. London, mainly on Routes 40 & 46, but have spent most of their working lives in S.W. London. At first, all were allocated to Clapham Depot, though Nos. 1727-1776 later went to Wandsworth and Streatham Depots. The E Class cars were moved from Clapham to Wandsworth and Hammersmith Depots to operate on the extended Routes 26 & 28 after being fitted with trolley poles for overhead working west of Wandsworth change pit.

Owing to the Coal Strike, Service 20 was temporarily withdrawn in May 1921, though it was subsequently restored from October 3rd, 1921 and diverted at Streatham down Mitcham Lane to Southcroft Road (extended to Tooting Broadway on Saturday afternoons and Sundays).

From September 3rd, 1921 a triangular junction was brought into use at the 'Latchmere', Battersea on Routes 12, 14, 34. The east curve was used by 'Football Specials' from Westminster to King's Road, Chelsea (for Chelsea Football Club) until about 1933.

Under an agreement with the L.U.T., tracks were connected at Hammersmith Broadway and Tooting (Merton) in 1922, and a change pit installed at Longley Road. At Hammersmith Service 26 was extended to Kew Bridge on May 2nd, 1922 (through fares from Hop Exchange: 8d. single; 1/2 return). On the same day Services 2 & 4 were extended from Longley Road to Wimbledon Hill, this section being sold to the L.C.C.T. The L.U.T. Service 71 cars now terminated at Wimbledon (Worple Road) by a loop near the Station. From May 22nd, 1926 L.C.C. Trams on Services 2 & 4 worked through from Wimbledon to Hampton Court over L.U.T. metals on Summer Saturday afternoons and evenings in 1926/1927, then from May 13th, 1928 annually at Summer weekends and public holidays (through fares from Victoria Embankment: 11d. single; return 1/5 Saturday afternoons, 1/8 Sundays; by 1930 the return fare had been reduced to 1/4).

During this period, in the summer months, the L.C.C.T. ran several special trams at a time, laden with schoolchildren from S.E. London, on day trips to Hampton Court, E/1 Class trams from Clapham Depot being used.

The opening of a new curve at the 'Swan', Stockwell on January 22nd, 1922 enabled Service 34 to be extended to operate from King's Road, Chelsea to Southwark Bridge via Clapham, Brixton & Camberwell. Service 74 was withdrawn by September, its route number being used for a new service in S.E. London. No.34 became unique in South London as a route consisting of two conduit sections separated by an overhead trolley section using two change pits en route. (There were two similar cases in North London - Routes 53 & 71).

The L.C.C. made several attempts in the 1920s to promote a tramway extension from West Norwood via Auckland Hill, Gipsy Road, Dulwich Wood Park and Farquhar Road to the Crystal Palace, but were again unsuccessful; such a route would have been well-patronised.

During 1923 a new depot was erected at the top of Brixton Hill near Christchurch Road; it was originally provided for trailer cars. The tram rails in this depot were not bonded and motor tramcars, stabled here since 1924, have to use both trolley poles on the double-wire overhead (as used on Routes 44 & 46). Among the first to do so were the 1727-1776 series of Class E/1 used on Route 10. Two change pits are provided outside the depot entrance.

In 1923 rush-hour short workings, numbered 2A & 4A, between Longley Road and Victoria Embankment were instituted.

The trailer cars had helped to move the wartime queues, but after the War it was considered that they caused traffic congestion so the L.C.C. decided to fit the older E/1 Class cars with more powerful motors - two 60 h.p. instead of two 42 h.p. motors - and build further motor tramcars, instead of using trailers. All the trailers were withdrawn by 1924.

When the Victoria Embankment services were finally paired up on November 12th, 1923, Nos. 2 & 4, 2A & 4A, 16 & 18, 22 & 24, 76 & 80 became circular services: 2, 2A, 16, 22, 76 in via Westminster, out via Blackfriars; 4, 4A, 18, 24, 80 in via Elephant & Blackfriars, out via Westminster. The Norwood services diverged at Herne Hill Station with the result that No.76 trams bound for London would pass other No.76 trams only between West Norwood and Herne Hill - a mere seven minutes of a 36-minute journey. (The same applied to No.80 trams travelling to London in the reverse direction).

About this time, one of the staff at Balham Hippodrome left a tin box containing £800 on a tramcar, which had to be thoroughly searched at Telford Avenue Depot to recover the money.

On June 2nd, 1924, in connection with the Wembley Exhibition, a new Service 30 (weekdays only) was extended to run from Sudbury in Middlesex over the Metropolitan Electric Tramways to Harlesden, then via Hammersmith, Putney and Wandsworth to Tooting Junction; this became a daily service in February 1925. After the Exhibition the normal Service 30 became Harlesden - Tooting Junction and Service 82 was withdrawn (this route number has not been used since). Until 1933 some trams on Service 30 operated to Wembley at rush hours, and at weekends and public holidays.

Services 6, 10, 34 (with 46, 52, 60) were extended over the new Southwark Bridge to the new City terminus (Queen Street) on July 14th, 1925.

THE ADDISCOMBE TRAMWAY IN THE TWENTIES by R.S. HUNT

(by kind permission of the 'Croydon Advertiser')

The Addiscombe trams were problem children ..... but we had a great affection for them. They came swaying, lurching and grinding along at about 10 m.p.h. The route ran from the Whitgift Hospital via George Street and Cherry Orchard Road, until abruptly terminated by the railway bridge at Bingham Road Halt, where the ceremony of reversing took place. These trams advanced by a series of loops at which they waited until the tram travelling in the opposite direction screeched over the automatic points.

Tired workers and laden women shoppers had, with great stoicism, decided that a long sit-down on the curved and perforated seats, which ran lengthways along each side, was less irksome than reaching home more quickly by walking! As children we found the trams a continual source of interest and excitement.

When possible we always travelled on the roofless upper deck, which had twin slatted seats each side of the gangway. A centrally-sited metal post supported the trolley pole which ended in a pulley wheel that swished endearingly along the overhead electric wire. Narrow twisting stairs at each end enabled penniless small boys to make a quick exit. In inclement weather the upper deck passengers sat under umbrellas and pulled a canvas covering over their knees.

How thrilling when the trolley pole suddenly shot skywards and, after bouncing around, finally came to rest looking like a rocket stick pointing irresponsibly towards heaven! The pulley wheel was finally coaxed on to the wire again by a patient conductor manipulating a long hooked bamboo pole or tattered piece of rope.

Actual derailment caused the biggest thrill. We sometimes placed ourselves in a strategic position at the Cherry Orchard Road corner which could always be relied on to produce the best derailments, and special jacks were kept permanently outside the 'Leslie Arms' for getting them back on the rails. In those days Cherry Orchard Road was narrower and the cottages had quite long front gardens.

Rerailment depended for its thrills upon how far the tram had run from the rails. Sometimes we blissfully watched a perspiring conductor and driver trying to complete the electrical circuit by using a long iron crowbar attached to the front of the tram which, owing to the one big headlamp in the middle of the dash made us think of the face of a Cyclops. If successful, the tram moved backwards amid a shower of sparks, making two neat grooves in the wooden road blocks. Sometimes another tram was used as a tow when, to our intense enjoyment, this procedure led to many complications and much jostling for position among the onlookers.

Two particular drivers were our heroes. There was a large rotund jolly one whose motto was 'slow but sure' and who navigated his tram without mishap from one end of the route to the other. Standing there in all weathers, clad from head to foot in shiny black oilskins, topped by an enormous sou'wester, his colossal mittened fists twirled the two brass handles, as though defying his tram to 'play him up' if it dared! The other, our favourite, was tall and thin and of a reckless disposition. I suspect that he very soon gravitated to the covered eight-wheelers which ran from London to Purley. He could be relied upon to derail his tram twice upon the journey and, if our luck was in, the overhead arm would come off too! He always made us feel we had full value for our pennyworth. We often forwent gum drops or liquorice cuttings in order to gain our sea legs on the top of an Addiscombe tram.

Getting to school presented a problem. By walking and running it was possible to leave home at nine o'clock and be in school for Assembly just as the prefect was closing the door. We were, however, sometimes hopeful in getting there more quickly by tram .... which was possible with the thin driver. If, however, the fat driver's tram hove into sight, our hearts sank and we resigned ourselves to the inevitable fifty lines for missing Assembly.

Our greatest achievement occurred one day in high summer. My brother and I had been inveigled into organising an exhibition of pets at school to help raise money for the purchase of a bird sanctuary at Selsdon.

We sallied forth with Chippy the white rat, so named because he had been donated to us by a leave-taking ship's carpenter whose girl-friend objected strongly to his presence. Chippy, whose character left much to be desired, had an endearing habit of leaving the warm space under my blazer, climbing out, walking up my lapel, round my collar and descending on the other side to the warmth and safety whence he came.

It happened that the thin driver's tram was crowded with bargain-hunting female shoppers who did their best to avoid overflowing into the central aisle. We, as usual, were in front, confidently hoping that at least the tram's trolley arm would come off the overhead wire, when suddenly Chippy decided on a circular tour.

A fat lady, hugging a huge shopping basket, spotted the rat, and letting forth a shriek like a steam siren, precipitated herself towards the rear door, followed by an undignified surge of terrified shoppers. The tram came to an abrupt halt as Chippy returned to his haven of warmth.

Our astonishment knew no bounds at these capers; what were they all doing and why this sudden exodus? "Yer can't bring rats on 'ere!" bawled the conductor as he advanced upon us and unceremoniously deposited us in gaping bewilderment upon the pavement, while the trembling passengers climbed aboard again.

Smarting under this injustice, we started to walk when 'oh justice!' there was the tram well and truly derailed at Hall's corner; our thin driver had not let us down. Triumphantly we held Chippy aloft as we walked past the row of frustrated angry faces. We dared not stop to watch the re-railing operations, as the lean driver appeared to bear us some animosity and we suspected that his long thin legs were capable of a hidden turn of speed.

The exhibition was also a great success. We raised several pounds .... and Selsdon duly got its bird sanctuary.

(The Croydon Corporation Tramways, in common with many tramway undertakings, had suffered badly from shortages of supplies and lack of maintenance during the Great War. Track had deteriorated badly and though a start was made as soon as practicable after the War to relay all the tram routes, Addiscombe was last on the list and at the time of Mr. Hunt's amusing anecdotes was served by the oldest cars in the fleet, built in 1901. Eventually the Council decided not to relay the tracks but to withdraw the tramcars and negotiate with a suitable operator to provide a motor omnibus service instead).

CROYDON IMPROVEMENTS

After the War, Croydon Corporation faced the problem of renewing the tram tracks, which had deteriorated during the war years. The main line was relaid entirely from Norbury to Purley (single-line working with temporary passing loops being used to maintain the tram service while the work was in progress) and the roadway was further lowered under Norbury railway bridge for covered-top tramcars to pass. Span-wire overhead replaced bracket-arm overhead between Thornton Heath Pond and Norbury and also along Brighton Road from South Croydon to Purley, and the overhead wires were realigned in the centre of the roadway over the tram tracks. Thornton Heath Depot was enlarged.

Wiser counsels had now prevailed and negotiations for a joint through service with the L.C.C.T. proved successful - another reason for relaying the main line. Single and interlaced track was gradually eliminated on the main line until only two single-line sections remained by 1933: outside the Whitgift Almshouses in North End, and near the 'Blue Anchor' in South End between Parker Road and Aberdeen Road. In June 1921 half fares for scholars were introduced, this facility being extended later to include all children at any hour.

After the main line, the Thornton Heath branch was entirely relaid, followed by the South Norwood route as far as the Selby Road boundary during 1924-1926. Additional loops having been laid in Wellesley Road, West Croydon, tramcars on the Penge service commenced using Wellesley Road and Station Road in both directions from January 1925; the Oakfield Road loop was then abandoned.

During 1925 the L.C.C. and Croydon tramways were connected at Hermitage Bridge, Norbury and on February 7th, 1926 through running between Victoria Embankment and Purley Fountain commenced, L.C.C. Services 16 & 18 being extended to Purley. Croydon Corporation had ordered 25 new trams, but they did not arrive until late 1927, so the L.C.C. hired twenty E/1 Class trams to Croydon to maintain the joint service. The through fare from London to Purley was 10d. single, 1/6 return. Croydon's No.2 service from Thornton Heath to Purley was curtailed to operate from High Street, Thornton Heath to the Davis Theatre, Croydon (destination blinds showed 'Greyhound'). Croydon Corporation closed its Addiscombe branch in 1927, having decided not to relay the tracks, which had deteriorated. The last Addiscombe tram ran on March 31st, but transfer fares were available between the replacing

General Motor-buses and the main Croydon tram route and still are today (1949). Sixty staff were transferred to the buses. The Addiscombe route had been the best paying of all the tram routes up till this time (though the slowest), but now the new joint service was proving a financial success.

The Croydon bogie trams delivered in 1927-1929 are similar to the L.C.C. E/1 Class trams and are equipped for both overhead and conduit operation. They seat 27 passengers inside and 42 upstairs. Unlike the E/1s, they carry large route number stencils similar to the E/3s. They were painted dark red and ivory when delivered. They were Croydon's first top-covered trams and have proved extremely popular with the travelling public, partly due to their comfortable moquette seats.

The Croydon livery was changed again about 1928 and finally became red and grey. By 1930 all the older bogie cars had been fitted with top covers, though the driving platforms and stairs were left open. The Croydon Corporation fleet now consisted of twenty four-wheel tramcars (Nos. 1-20) and ten bogie cars (Nos.21-30) all about twenty to thirty years old, together with the 25 new bogie tramcars (Nos.31-55), also an electric welding car (converted from a water car about 1917). When Mr. Goodyer retired in June 1928, he was succeeded as General Manager by Gordon Valentine Stanley Esq.

FINAL L.C.C. PROGRESS

The modernisation of the E/1 Class tramcars - the 'Pullman' programme - began in 1926 with No.1817 on the 2/4 Wimbledon route. Longitudinal seats in the lower saloon were mostly replaced by transverse seating on the 2-1 pattern except by the doors. Seats were upholstered in moquette downstairs and leather upstairs, where smoking was allowed. Broader side route boards were fitted. E/1 Class trams now seated 73 passengers (27 inside, 46 upstairs).

This was such a success that all the class were improved, beginning with the trams at Clapham Depot. The new dark red and pale yellow livery with the L.C.C. crest caused the 2/4 service to be nicknamed 'the All-Red Route'. Later, No.1814 was experimentally fitted with Hoffman roller bearings.

During the General Strike of 1926, Clapham Depot was so crowded with trams that three had to be parked in the entrance yard by Clapham Park Road. Volunteers drove several E Class trams from Hammersmith Depot, including No.448.

About 1926, during reconstruction at the 'Plough', Clapham (in connection with the building of the new Underground Station for the Morden Extension) preparations were made to remove the loop line on the up track. The roadway being excavated around the points at the southern end of the loop, a southbound tram derailed during the morning rush hour at the junction and tilted to a precarious angle blocking both tracks; but it had been removed by lunchtime. During reconstruction at Hammersmith Underground Station in 1932 the L.C.C. trams continued to cross the excavations quite unperturbed, while other road traffic had to be diverted.

At Tooting Junction the L.C.C. & S.M.E.T. tracks were connected in 1926, but the change pit was installed in London Road just south of Amen Corner, at Otterburn Street. Service 8 was extended to Mitcham Cricket Green on September 1st, thus restoring to use the disused S.M.E.T. spur from Fair Green, Mitcham. (The S.M.E.T. was not interested in through running, so the 'Southmet' cars now reversed at Fair Green, Mitcham instead of Tooting Junction. Several L.U.T. Class U covered-top cars were loaned to the S.M.E.T. and worked on this route across Mitcham Common and on the Sutton route).

L.C.C. Services 12 & 30 continued to terminate at Tooting Junction on conduit operation, so a lever had to be pulled at the change pit to divert into the pit the ploughs of trams for Mitcham on Service 8 (later No.6) which changed over to overhead trolley operation south of Amen Corner. At this time Service 20 was extended from the corner of Mitcham Lane and Southcroft Road to Tooting Broadway daily.

When Routes 16 & 18 were extended to Purley, extra rush-hour workings between Victoria Embankment and Norbury Station were numbered 16A & 18A. E/1 Class trams of the 1727-1776 series were used regularly on these runs. Other regular short workings to and from Angell Road, Brixton; Water Lane, Brixton; Telford Avenue; and Streatham Library, have always carried EX route stencils.

It was soon found that the 1727-1776 series were too slow for the fast Purley service, so many of these were sent to Wandsworth Depot, faster E/1s being transferred from Clapham to Streatham Depot to work Services 16 & 18.

The roadway under Queen's Road railway bridge at Battersea was lowered in 1927 enabling Service 32 to be extended to work Chelsea Bridge -'Plough', Clapham, using double-deck trams from Wandsworth and Clapham Depots. From 1927 a special service was operated on Bank Holidays between Camberwell Green and Kew Bridge via Routes 34 & 26, which was numbered 26EX.

On Whit Sunday 1928 E/1 Class Tram 1141 (Service 8 for Tooting) braked sharply to avoid a collision on Clapham Common just short of Nightingale Lane, left the rails, crossed the up track and came to rest in the tarmac on the west side of the road, blocking both tracks. After two trams and the breakdown tender were unable to tow it back on to the track, two power cables were connected to the conduit conductor rails from the tramcar and, with the breakdown tender towing, No.1141 was driven back on to the track. Meanwhile, up trams had been reversing at the crossover south of Nightingale Lane while down trams used the turning circle - a rare occurrence.

There was a reorganisation of several Tooting services on July 19th, 1928. Rush-hour workings 2A & 4A were diverted from Longley Road to Southcroft Road. Service 6 became the Mitcham service (instead of No.8) though still running through to City terminus. The L.C.C.T. discontinued the 6-10 circular service and No.10 reverted to its Tooting Broadway terminus in Defoe Road. Instead, Services 8 & 20 were combined to work a circular service thus:-
8: Victoria Station - Stockwell - Clapham - Tooting - Streatham - Brixton - Stockwell - Victoria Station; 20: vice-versa (in via Tooting & Clapham; out via Brixton & Streatham).

By 1930 the Brixton all-night service had been extended to Streatham and Tooting and combined with the Tooting all-night service to operate a circular route with Victoria Embankment.

About 1930 (with the advent of the HR/2s) Camberwell Depot sent its C Class tramcars to Wandsworth Depot together with some M Class, the other Ms going to Hammersmith Depot.

After the reopening of Kingsway Subway on January 15th, 1931, a new Service 31 was inaugurated between Wandsworth High Street and Hackney Station via Battersea & Shoreditch (Journey time: 72 minutes; through fare 8d. single, 1/- return) operated by Wandsworth and Hackney Depots. On Sundays this was extended to 'Baker's Arms', Leyton; on Summer Sundays certain trams worked through to Tooting Junction. A new Service 33 commenced to run between Highbury Station and Water Lane, Brixton at rush hours only, some trams working through to Streatham Library. The through return fare from London to Purley was reduced to 1/- by 1932; Croydon Corporation joined in the L.C.C.T. 'All-Day' and 'Evening Tourist' schemes from June 1st, 1932. With the advent of the E/3s all C and D Class tramcars were withdrawn from S.W. London and the M Class trams transferred to East London.

Also during 1931 the final connection between the L.C.C.T. and the L.U.T. was made when tracks were connected at Summerstown and a change pit installed at the boundary. L.C.C. Service 14, which had been projected from Earlsfield Station to Summerstown on January 15th, was now extended via Haydon's Road to Wimbledon Hill on April 16th. (The L.U.T. Service 81 was withdrawn). The London terminus of Route 14 was at the Hop Exchange, but on Sundays No.14 worked between Wimbledon Hill and Wandsworth High Street only.

In December 1930 Service 34 was curtailed to operate Chelsea - Brixton only, terminating first at Water Lane, Brixton Hill; then at Gresham Road; then at Stockwell Road. A new Service 48 (weekdays only) was introduced between Victoria Station and City terminus via Brixton & Camberwell. These arrangements caused traffic delays, so the L.C.C.T. had to formulate another scheme. From June 4th, 1931 Service 34 from Chelsea was extended to Camberwell Green on weekdays, working to the City on Sundays only. The new Service 48 now worked between Brixton Road and the City via Camberwell on weekdays only.

The southern terminus of Route 33 was diverted to St. Luke's Church, West Norwood on May 14th, 1931 and it became a daily service. The northern terminus became Manor House, Finsbury Park (via Essex Road & Green Lanes) on October 8th, 1931 (Journey time: 69 minutes; through fare 8d. single, 1/- return). In consequence, Service 76 was withdrawn and No.80 worked in both directions between West Norwood and John Carpenter Street, Blackfriars via Camberwell. In May 1933 E/1 Class Tram 1564 (Service 80 for Blackfriars) was derailed under Herne Hill railway bridge and crashed into the United Dairies. A motor car driven by Randolph Churchill (son of Winston Churchill M.P.) collided with a No.80 tram in Milkwood Road, Herne Hill on March 20th, 1933.

Certain trams on the Battersea all-night service were extended to Tooting Broadway from the Autumn of 1932.

A story of the early 1930s concerns an old motor-car chassis, which had to be taken from a Brixton Hill yard to Balham. The purchaser and his friend hailed a passing No.8 tram and hopefully asked the driver if he could oblige them; the driver stood the chassis on end behind him on the front platform for twopence. At the 'Swan', Stockwell the two friends changed trams. The second driver was just as helpful, so the chassis travelled at a total charge of fourpence, the price of two luggage tickets! This is an example of the fine service given by the trams as luggage carriers - anything reasonable being conveyed - and a luggage ticket still costs only twopence today!(1949).

Unfortunately, on September 2nd, 1931 the L.U.T. changed its Wimbledon - Hampton Court route over to trolleybus operation and that put an end to the weekend extension of L.C.C. Services 2 & 4 to Hampton Court. The trolleybuses were extended a short distance to Wimbledon Town Hall on December 15th, 1932, so the L.C.C.T. abandoned the Wimbledon Hill spur from that date, since when Tram Services 2 & 4 have terminated at Wimbledon Station (S.R.) by the Town Hall - also Service 14 until it was curtailed in 1934.

Reference has already been made (in the S.E. section) to the L.C.C.T's effort to attract off-peak passengers and the running of trams to a late hour at night to benefit the public. These are the times of the last trams Mondays to Fridays for this area (the last tram on Saturdays usually runs some minutes later):-

From Central London to:		L.C.C.T. 1927	L.C.C.T. 1932	L.P.T.B. 1949
Wandsworth	(via Battersea)	12.15 a.m.	12.15 a.m.	11.30 p.m.
Wimbledon	(via Clapham)	11.0 p.m.	11.6 p.m.	10.37 p.m.
Tooting	(via Clapham)	12.30 a.m.	12.30 a.m.	11.29 p.m.
Clapham		1.5 a.m.	1.5 a.m.	11.29 p.m.
Streatham		1.32 a.m.	1.32 a.m.	11.35 p.m.
Norbury		12.3 a.m.	12.43 a.m.	11.35 p.m.
Croydon		11.2 p.m.	11.51 (Sats)	11.35 p.m.
Purley		10.22 p.m.	11.51 (12.0)	10.0 p.m.
West Norwood		12.1 a.m.	12.5 a.m.	11.44 p.m.

These times do not include special late journeys, e.g. the 12.35 am tram from the Embankment to Croydon.

LONDON PASSENGER TRANSPORT BOARD

On July 1st, 1933 all the tramways in the London area, including those belonging to the L.C.C. and Croydon Corporation, were taken over by the new London Passenger Transport Board.

After the formation of the L.P.T.B., Service 34 was finally altered to operate from Chelsea to John Carpenter Street, Blackfriars via Clapham, Brixton & Camberwell from November 1st, 1933. At the same time, Service 80 was withdrawn and its place was taken by daily Service 48: West Norwood - City & Southwark via Camberwell. (The staff at Norwood Depot have always been proud of their trams and looked after all their equipment well and it is interesting to note that a stock of No.76 & No.80 stencils remained at this depot for many years after 1933, a few being still available this year! (1949).

The Croydon Corporation tramcars were gradually repainted in the L.P.T.B. livery of red and cream and renumbered Nos.345-399. From October 3rd, 1934 Service 2 to Thornton Heath was renumbered No.42.

On December 7th, 1933 L.C.C. Service 30 was combined with S.M.E.T. Service 6 to give a through service (No.30) from Harrow Road - "Near Willesden Junction" - to West Croydon Station, worked by E and E/1 Class trams based on Hammersmith and Thornton Heath Depots. The new service covered 14¾ route miles (through fare 9d. single, 1/3 return - 1/4 on public holidays). The connecting curve from Tamworth Road into London Road at West Croydon was now regularly used for depot workings to Thornton Heath Depot. (Aurelia Road Depot was only used for storage).

However, L.C.C. Service 6 was curtailed to Tooting Junction from December 6th, 1934 and the spur from Fair Green to Cricket Green, Mitcham was abandoned. On the same day the Penge route was closed by the L.P.T.B., as it was paralleled by motorbus services, but the frequency on the Crystal Palace tram route was increased. Some of the Croydon four-wheelers were withdrawn from service and No.349 was sent to Erith.

The Haydon's Road tram route at Wimbledon was replaced by a motorbus service on May 16th, 1934 and Tram No.14 curtailed to Wandsworth High Street again, working on weekdays only. The track in Wimbledon Road, Summerstown was retained and used by workmen's cars and 'dog track specials' to Wimbledon Stadium from Battersea and Streatham until January 1940, trams being supplied by Wandsworth, Clapham and Streatham Depots.

There were several slight improvements to the tram services during 1935. On May 6th, 1935 T.M. King George V and Queen Mary celebrated their Silver Jubilee and the trams carried crowds to the celebrations. The single track in South End, Croydon between Parker Road and Aberdeen Road was doubled during June 1935. This left only one section of single track on Routes 16 & 18 in the Borough of Croydon - that outside the Whitgift Almshouses in North End. In September 1935 Service 6 was extended from Tooting Junction to Fair Green, Mitcham.

About 1935 a T. & L.R.S. member was journeying southwards along Brighton Road in a friend's Baby Austin motor-car. Soon after passing the 'Royal Oak', the car's wheels dropped into the tramlines and the driver couldn't get out of them. Outside Purley Depot the spring points were set for the depot yard and the car branched off the main road into the depot, much to the surprise of the staff! They soon came to the rescue, however, and helped the two friends to get the car out of the rails and back on the main road.

On the evening of October 25th, 1935 a stationary four-wheel tramcar, whose driver and conductor had alighted, suddenly moved away from Crystal Palace terminus and, carrying eight passengers, quickly gathered speed and careered at 40 m.p.h. down steep Anerley Hill.

Possibly disaster was averted by the presence of mind shown by a passenger, Mr. Leonard Tofield of Elmer's End Road, Beckenham, who applied the handbrake with such force that he strained his wrist badly. He was successful in bringing the tram to a standstill after it had travelled about 400 yards downhill. Only one passenger was injured, when he leapt from the tram as it began its wild descent of Anerley Hill.

About 1936, the staff car from Telford Avenue Depot ran away down Mitcham Lane hill about 2 o'clock one morning and overturned at

London Tramways Company: Cable Tractor No. 18 coupled to Horse Car No. 232 outside Telford Avenue Depot, Streatham (July 1894).
(Photo: by courtesy of the LCC)

Cable tramcar No. 923 (Workmen's Car) at Brixton (c. 1900).
(Photo by courtesy of the LCC)

H.R.H. Prince of Wales opening the LCC electric tramway from Westminster Bridge Road to Tooting, May 15th, 1903. (A Class car, painted white, probably No. 95).
(Photo by courtesy of the LCC)

'The Royal Car': A Class (probably No. 95), painted white, in Clapham Depot.
(Photo by courtesy of the LCC)

Marius Road Depot, Balham (1903). A Class Nos. 22, 35, 10 and 9.
(Photo by courtesy of the LCC)

E Class No. 473 at the 'Plough', Clapham (c. 1910).
(Photo by Card House)

E Class No. 506 outside Telford Avenue Depot, Streatham (August 1907).
(Photo by courtesy of the LCC)

E/1 Class No. 1628 (Service 16 to Norbury) at Streatham Library (1913). Note route-number plate under canopy.
(Photo: Card House)

E/1 Class Nos. 1088 and 1080 at West Norwood terminus, (c. 1910).
(Photo: Commercial view, by courtesy of J.H. Price)

D Class Tramcar No. 342 (Service 14 to Battersea) at corner of Mitcham Lane and Southcroft Road, Streatham (November 1913).
(Photograph by courtesy of the LCC)

E/1 No. 1007 and trailer in Clapham Park Road (November 1913).
(Photo by courtesy of the LCC)

Trailer of T1-T8 series leaving Clapham Depot coupled to E/1 Class No. 1410 (December 1913).
(Photo by courtesy of the LCC)

Illuminated tramcar in Thornton Heath Depot (July 1908).
(Photo: C.H. Price, by courtesy of J.H. Price)

Croydon Corporation Tramways: Single-truck Car 45 and Bogie Car 48 in Brigstock Road, Thornton Heath (c. 1910).
(Commercial view, by courtesy of J.H. Price)

South Metropolitan Electric Tramways: Board of Trade Inspection, August 11th, 1906. Car No. 25 in Park Lane, Wallington.
(Photo: French & Co., Wallington, by courtesy of J.H. Price)

South Metropolitan Electric Tramways: First tram in Westmead Road, Sutton: October 27th, 1906.
(Photo: French & Co., Wallington, by courtesy of J.H. Price)

Crystal Palace Tram Terminus (c. 1920): S.M.E.T. Car No. 40 (Anerley Hill).
(Photo: C.H. Price, by courtesy of J.H. Price)

North End, West Croydon (c. 1913). C.C.T. Single-truck Car 73 (for Purley).
Note connecting line with Penge route.
(Photo: C.H. Price, by courtesy of J.H. Price)

Croydon Corporation Tramways: Single-truck Cars 22 and 64 at Hermitage Bridge, Norbury: Whit Monday, 1917. L.C.C. E/1 Class tramcar in background over boundary. Note wartime blackout stencils on trams and hoods on street lights.

(Photo: O.J. Morris)

Croydon Corporation Tramways: Single-truck car No. 26 (to Crown Hill) in Lower Addiscombe Road, by Ashburton Road, 1917.

(Photo: O.J. Morris)

Croydon Corporation Tramways: Single-truck Car 67 and Bogie Car 55 passing on temporary loop during track re-laying in London Road, Thornton Heath (1924).
(Photo: O.J. Morris)

Croydon Corporation Tramways: Bogie Car No. 55 at Broad Green (1924).
(Photo: F. Merton Atkins)

E/1 Nos. 1784 and 1788 in High Road, Balham (by S.R. Station) (c. 1927).
(Photo: Card House, by courtesy of J.H. Price)

E/1 No. 1741 at New Park Road, Brixton Hill (c. 1930).
(Photo by courtesy of O.J. Morris)

E/1 Class No. 1140 in High Street, Croydon (c. 1930). (Service 16)
(Commercial view, by courtesy of O.J. Morris)

'Silver Tram' E/1 No. 795, with aluminium panelling (February 1932).
(Photo by courtesy of the LCC)

E/1 Class No. 1100, HR/2 Class No. 110 at Victoria terminus (1932).
(Photo by courtesy of the LCC).

E Class No. 622 (Service 26); E/1 Class No. 836 (Service 72); E/1 Class No. 1032 (Service 36); at Victoria Embankment, Westminster.
(Photo by courtesy of the LCC)

The LCC Chairman reopening Kingsway Subway after reconstruction January 15th, 1931. E/3 No. 1931 (painted white) at the southern entrance.

(Photo by courtesy of the LCC)

Official inspection of the reconstructed Kingsway Subway: January 14th, 1931. Holborn Tramway Station: E/1 No. 1506; E/3 Nos. 1931 and 1979)

(Photo by courtesy of the LCC)

E/1 No. 1539 at Mitcham Road change pit, Tooting.
(Photo: K.H. Rudolph, by courtesy of W.A. Camwell)

E/1R No. 1577 at West Norwood terminus (1938).
(Photo: W.J. Haynes)

Thornton Heath Depot (1938): E/1s Nos. 1493, 1040, 1082; C.C.T. Nos. 378 and 393; old single-truck car in background.
(Photo: W.A. Camwell)

C.C.T. No. 390 terminating at the Davis Theatre, High Street, Croydon (1938).
(Photo: W.A. Camwell)

E/1 Class Trams 1600 (Service 34) and 1825 (Service 2) severely damaged by a H.E. bomb at Blackfriars Road railway bridge, October 25th, 1940.
(Photo: L.P.T.B., by courtesy of L.R.T.L.)

Snowplough 023 (converted from B Class No. 141) in Clapham Depot.
(Photo: W.J. Haynes)

E/1R Class No. 1762 at Hop Exchange terminus, Southwark Street.
(Photo: H.B. Priestley)

'Swan' junction, Stockwell: U.C.C. No. 2139 (Service 20), E/1 No. 1841 (Service 4), (Fare Stage No. 7).
(Photo: H.B. Priestley)

E/3 Class trams inside Jew's Row Depot, Wandsworth.
(Photo: H.B. Priestley)

E/3 Class No. 1925 and No. 203 at York Road, Wandsworth.
(Photo: H.B. Priestley)

Ex-Walthamstow Tram 2042 in Balham High Road.
(Photo: J.H. Meredith)

E/1 Nos. 1818 and 1849 at Longley Road change pit, Tooting. (Feeder No. 884).
(Photo: H.B. Priestley)

E/1 Class No. 1571 in High Street, Colliers' Wood.
(Photo: J.H. Meredith)

E/1 Class Nos. 1802 and 1571 at Wimbledon Station (S.R.) (Fare Stage No. 17).
(Photo: H.B. Priestley)

E/1 Class No. 1597 (rebuilt from E Class No. 420) at 'Latchmere' junction, Battersea. (Fare Stage No. 15).
(Photo: D.W.K. Jones)

E/1 Class No. 1395 in Coldharbour Lane, Loughborough Junction.
(Photo: W.J. Haynes)

E/3 Class No. 177 at Effra Road change pit, Brixton. (Feeder No. 826).
(Photo: R.J.S. Wiseman)

E/3 No. 1947 (to West Norwood) at Effra Road/Morval Road corner, Brixton.
(Photo: J.H. Price)

E/1R Class No. 1387 (down) and E/3 Class No. 1936 (up) at Herne Hill Station (S.R.): Norwood Road/Dulwich Road junction. (Feeder Y18 and telephone).

(Photo: J.H. Meredith)

(L to R): Snowbrooms 018, 022 and 028; Work Car 02; ex-Walthamstow Tram 2056; E/3 Class Nos. 2000 and 1990, Work Car 03 inside Norwood Depot.

(Photo: D.W.K. Jones)

U.C.C. (L.U.T.) No. 2143 leaving Brixton Hill Depot for Saturday midday rush hour.

Sand Carrier 015 at Streatham Hill, by Telford Avenue.
(Photo: A.D. Packer)

U.C.C. (M.E.T.) 'Feltham' Tramcar No. 2167 (Service 10) at Telford Avenue Depot, Streatham.
(Photo: D.W.K. Jones)

U.C.C. (L.U.T.) 'Feltham' Tram No. 2126 at Streatham Hill Theatre loading island.
(Photo: J.H. Meredith)

Ex-Walthamstow Tram 2057 and C.C.T. Tram 397 in Streatham High Road by Woodbourne Avenue loading island.
(Photo: J.H. Meredith)

U.C.C. (M.E.T.) 'Feltham' No. 2094 in Southcroft Road, Streatham on L.R.T.L. trip (May 1949).
(Photo by courtesy of W.J. Wyse)

U.C.C. (M.E.T.) 'Feltham' No. 2089 (Service 18) at St. Leonard's Church, Streatham (Fare Stage No. 12).

(Photo: W.A. Camwell)

C.C.T. No. 386 taking up the plough at Streatham change pit in the High Road at Gleneagle Road.

(Photo: R.F. Mack)

C.C.T. No. 390 leaving Whitehorse Road terminus, Thornton Heath.
(Photo: H.B. Priestley)

Thornton Heath Pond: No. 375 at Brigstock Road/London Road junction. Note line leading into depot in foreground.
(Photo: H.B. Priestley)

Rehabilitated Croydon Tram No. 379 reversing at Coombe Road crossover in South End, Croydon. U.C.C. (L.U.T.) 'Feltham' No. 2159 waiting to proceed to Purley.
(Photo: J.H. Meredith)

C.C.T. No. 381 in London Road, Broad Green, Croydon at St. James's Road.
(Photo: J.H. Meredith)

Ex-Walthamstow Tram 2054 at the 'Royal Oak' stop, Brighton Road, Purley. (Fare Stage No. 23)
(Photo: W.J. Haynes)

C.C.T. Tram No. 395 at Purley terminus (Brighton Road) Note Feeder Box 15 with telephone by overhead standard 480 on left. (Fare Stage No. 24)
(Photo: R.F. Mack)

Southcroft Road corner. E/1 Class Tram 1545 (Service 34) derailed at the 'Latchmere' junction, Battersea Park Road on May 21st, 1936.

About 10 o'clock on Friday evening, March 12th, 1937 three down trams were involved in a collision in Upper Tooting Road on the descent to Tooting Broadway. The middle tram, E/1 Class No.1597, was so badly damaged that it was withdrawn from service, but its bogie trucks and electrical equipment were transferred to E Class Tram No.420 which was renumbered 1597 and reclassified E/1 - this tram is still in service today (1949).

During 1935/1936 temporary track was in use while Blue House Bridge over the Southern Railway at Mitcham was being rebuilt. The terminus of Route 42 at Thornton Heath was extended round the corner from High Street to Whitehorse Road (Talbot Road corner) on November 17th, 1936. Ex-Croydon Corporation Trams 376, 379, 380 & 398 were 'rehabilitated' during 1936 with flush panel sides and inset route number and destination boxes, and glass windscreens.

There was a darker side to the picture. Service 26 was curtailed at Hammersmith Broadway from October 27th, 1935 because of trolleybuses replacing trams in the L.U.T. area. The Sutton and Crystal Palace tram services were replaced by trolleybuses on Route 654 on December 8th, 1935 and February 9th, 1936 respectively; with them disappeared the S.M.E.T. cars and the remaining Croydon four-wheel cars. The Crystal Palace did not long outlive its tram route, as it was destroyed by fire on the night of November 30th, 1936. About the time of the Crystal Palace fire the ten old Croydon bogie cars (Nos. 365-374) were withdrawn from Route 42 and more E/1 Class trams took their place at Thornton Heath Depot. It should be mentioned that Streatham Depot had been running 'Football Specials' to Thornton Heath for Crystal Palace F.C. home games since 1926, the trams having to reverse at the Pond. E/1 Class trams were used for this working until the War. Thornton Heath Depot provided trams for 'Football Specials' from Croydon.

As mentioned more fully in the S.E. London section, the trams rendered valuable service carrying huge crowds during Coronation Week 1937, while the motor-buses were on strike.

About this time a young man who lived at Holloway used to visit his fiancee at West Norwood several times a week, returning home on the last No.33 tram. One night he fell asleep on the tram and was woken by the sound of men shouting to see water pouring down the windows. At first he thought it was raining hard, but soon he discovered that it was only the tram being washed by hoses in Holloway Depot!

From September 8th,1937 Service 32 was replaced by motor-buses and the tracks from Chelsea Bridge to Lavender Hill were abandoned, though Service 34 continued to use Cedars Road. The next changeover was ill-conceived, as traffic flows of thirty years' standing were split and passengers had to change vehicles en route, while certain intermediate fares were increased. On September 12th, 1937 Service 30 was replaced by trolleybuses, which also covered Route 12 south of Wandsworth and Routes 26 & 28 west of Clapham Junction. The all-night tram services henceforth terminated at the 'Prince's Head', Battersea and Clapham Junction. Service 31 was curtailed at the 'Prince's Head', only Route 12 continuing along York Road to Wandsworth, where the crossover was moved some distance back, making the tram terminus a short walk from the corner of the High Street - an unnecessary nuisance especially to folk changing vehicles, though the No.612 trolleybus parallels the tram route as far as the 'Prince's Head', Battersea. Service 6 was further curtailed to Amen Corner, Tooting. The lines in Garratt Lane were maintained until January 1940 for special workings; in view of this, one wonders why the No.12 route was not left alone. This was destined to be the last trolleybus'conversion' south of the Thames, and it would have been better if it had not been effected.

In December 1936, 46 U.C.C. 'Feltham' type bogie trams built for the London United Tramways in 1930/1931, which had been fitted with plough carriers, were transferred from West London to Telford Avenue Depot, Streatham (Nos. 2120-2165). Another 55 U.C.C. 'Feltham' trams built for the Metropolitan Electric Tramways between 1929 and 1931, which had worked previously over the L.C.C. Northern system conduit lines, were transferred from North London to Streatham in two batches during March and May 1938 (Nos. 2066-2119, 2167).

These streamlined trams have front exit doors (now used for luggage only) in addition to the normal entrance doors, and an enclosed driving cabin with a seat, besides a vestibule for ten standing passengers, at each end. They seat 22 passengers downstairs and 42 upstairs and are fitted with half-drop windows and electric heating and concealed lighting. Direct straight stairs connect lower and upper saloons at each end, allowing the conductor to circulate. The maximum traction trucks are fitted with roller bearings, and three types of brakes - air, magnetic and manual - are provided. Since coming to South London they have had quick-release valves fitted to their air brakes. These fine trams are very speedy, comfortable and smooth running and their capabilities are best displayed on the fast section along Brighton Road between South Croydon and Purley terminus. Some 'Felthams' are housed in Brixton Hill Depot, but most are shedded at Telford Avenue Depot. They operate on Services 8, 10, 16, 18, 20, 22, & 24.

The L.C.C's famous "Bluebird" No.1, which first worked on the Kingsway Subway services, was transferred from Holloway Depot to Streatham Depot in March 1938; by that time it had been repainted red and cream. As it is fitted with special air brakes, only a limited group of drivers are allowed to handle this tram. Until the War Telford Avenue Depot used it mainly for special journeys and all-night services. No.1 was hired by the Light Railway Transport League for a special return journey from Waltham Cross in Hertfordshire to Purley in Surrey on May 15th, 1938.

Trolleybus substitutions in North London and East London during 1939 brought more trams to South London. E/3 Class Trams 1904-1921 were transferred from Hackney Depot to Thornton Heath Depot. In addition, twenty trams built for Walthamstow Corporation between 1927 and 1932 (Nos. 2042-2061), similar to the Croydon bogie cars, were transferred to Telford Avenue Depot, Streatham. These new additions together with the ex-Croydon Corporation trams Nos. 375-399, and ex-L.C.C. E/1, E/1R and E/3 Class trams have operated the Streatham and Croydon routes ever since.

During April/May 1938 a traffic roundabout was constructed at Vauxhall Cross, using the station yard and a new street - Parry Street - specially constructed. Now the trams and other traffic make a gyratory movement around Vauxhall Station (S.R.).

Between 1937 and 1939 Purley Depot was not in regular use and was used to store surplus trams. As it happened, this proved to be of great value during the war emergency.

During 1939/1940 ex-Croydon Trams Nos. 375, 377, 378, 381-397, & 399 were fitted with timber-framed windscreens.

From 1939 Service 6 was diverted at Tooting Broadway from Amen Corner to Wimbledon Station on Saturdays only after 3.30 p.m., but this working ceased during the War, about February 1943. Service 14 was withdrawn officially on August 1st, 1939, apart from some early morning journeys.

A head-on collision between two E/1 Rehabilitated trams occurred on the single line in Norwood Road, Herne Hill, by Trinity Rise, on March 22nd, 1939, when No.1652(Service 48) ran into No.1078(Service 78). Both trams were severely damaged and several passengers hurt.

From 1939 onwards, Norwood Depot sometimes used Rehabilitated E/1 Class trams on Service 33 to Manor House via Kingsway Subway. This occasional working was stopped in 1944, following a police complaint about their use through Kingsway Subway.

BOYHOOD REMINISCENCES

'Nanna' (my Grandmother) moved house from Lee to Purley in 1930, so Mother and I used to go to see her about once a fortnight. This meant a long journey on the No.75 Tilling motor-bus (which worked from Woolwich Free Ferry to Caterham Valley until the War), though occasionally I got rides on the Croydon and 'South Met' trams. Once, when I was about four, Mum put me on the 'bus at Purley and was just getting on herself when it suddenly started off without warning, dragging her several yards along Brighton Road before the conductor got it stopped; she became more friendly to trams after that!

After we left the No.58-62-74 tram route at Catford Hill, the No.75 'bus proceeded through the dreary (to me) tramless landscape of Sydenham, enlivened only by the Gas Works at Bell Green (sometimes little shunting tank engines could be glimpsed there, but I was always sure that the Works were on the point of blowing up, so strong was the smell of gas!) until we met the Croydon trams rounding the High Street corner at the 'Pawleyne Arms', Penge and the 'South Met' cars at the 'Robin Hood' junction, Anerley.

All these trams seemed to be four-wheel open-toppers with open platforms. A large hoop (to protect passengers from the trolley-pole) and a single lamp were fixed at each end of the upper deck. The trolley 'arm' was fixed to a mast in the middle of the top deck with the rope wound round the trolley pole. They were quite unlike the more modern L.C.C. trams which I knew so well, but somewhat similar to the seaside trams that ran from Margate through Broadstairs to Ramsgate.

The route was double track as far as Selby Road, then it was nearly all single track with passing loops all the way to West Croydon, though there was a short stretch of double track at Selhurst Station. Just before the 'Robin Hood' at Anerley a single track ran off part way down a hill and then curved into the depot on the left. The overhead standards supporting the span wires on the double-track sections and the posts with bracket arms on the single-line sections had ornamental scrollwork at the crossbars.

When I was about four, Nanna took us on the tram from the 'Robin Hood' up Anerley Hill to the Crystal Palace. There was double-track all the way and the trams had special track brakes worked by the hand-wheel. The Crystal Palace was a wonderful place to a small boy and I remember that the vast glass building seemed full of statues, potted palms and ferns, fountains, goldfish pools and miniature trains running everywhere on a multiplicity of tracks - it must have been a model railway exhibition. From the girders hung the flags of the nations and the pipes of a huge organ - 'the Handel Organ' - towered up towards the roof. Outside were terraces connected by flights of steps with beautiful gardens below, more pools, fountains and statues and strange prehistoric monsters (made of concrete) prowling around the lower lake.

I enjoyed every visit to the Crystal Palace and I missed it like an old friend when it was destroyed by fire on the night of November 30th, 1936 - it did not long outlive the Anerley trams. I did not see its death-throes as my parents did not wake me, as I had to go to school next morning. The first I knew of the disaster was when my Father woke me with the words: "The Crystal Palace was burnt down last night". At first I thought this was a poor sort of joke in very bad taste and could not believe it. To me the Crystal Palace was one of the Wonders of the World which would last for ever, like the Pyramids. The two towers remained like mournful sentinels until the War, when they were demolished by the Government so that they would not be landmarks for enemy bombers, as some people had said in the Great War.

At West Croydon Station, which was being rebuilt in the modern Southern Railway style, there was another 'South Met' terminus with tramcars for Sutton and Mitcham (later L.C.C. trams on Service 30 right through to 'Near WILLESDEN JUNCTION' via Putney). There was no direct connection across North End: a tramcar from the Penge routes had to join the 'main line' down track, reverse on to the up track, then branch off down a curve into Tamworth Road to gain the Sutton route, while the conductor had to swing the trolley pole with a long bamboo pole from one overhead wire to another: of course, this manoeuvre was only effected in the rare case of a special working. The 'South Met' tramcars in Tamworth Road actually waited on the connecting points at their terminus.

Bamboo poles were hung on the overhead standards at Penge, 'Robin Hood', Crystal Palace and both West Croydon termini for use in swinging the tram trolley-poles round. I travelled on the Sutton route only once, when we visited Croydon Airport to see the airliners taking off and landing.

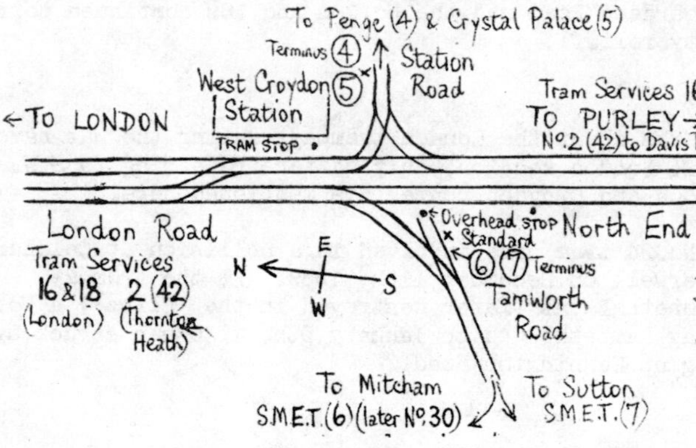

Diagram of Tramways at West Croydon Station 1930 – 1934

The new Croydon Corporation bogie tramcars on Routes 16 & 18 were, and still are, very comfortable, but I did not like their crude large number stencils, which were not so neat as the L.C.C. type on the E/3s. The old angular bogie cars with their outside staircases on the Thornton Heath route reminded me of huge moving castles, compared with the neat regular contours of the new Croydon bogie cars and the L.C.C. E/1 Class on the No.16/18 route.

One thing that stuck in my mind was the colourful names of certain public houses between Croydon and Purley, such as 'Greyhound', 'Green Dragon', 'Blue Anchor', 'Swan and Sugar Loaf', 'Red Deer', 'Windsor Castle' and 'Royal Oak', most being used as tram stops and several being shown as fare stages on the tram tickets.

Purley Depot was of great interest to me, particularly when the gates were shut and all I could see were the tops of trams standing in the yard peeping over the wall - most tantalising! The depot consists of two buildings side by side, a corrugated iron and wooden building on the north side with tracks numbered 1 to 4 and a brick building on the south side with tracks numbered 5 to 8. At that time there was a scissors crossover at Purley terminus by the Fountain. Sometimes we had tea in Williamson's Cafe and sat by the window to see the No.16 & 18 Trams coming and going outside. The Fountain stood in the middle of the road junction until about 1934, when it was removed to its present position at the S.E. corner of Godstone Road.

The Borough of Croydon has had electric lighting for many years, but the 'South Met' tram routes in the Borough of Penge were lit by gas. During the 1930s Croydon installed ornamental electric light standards with hexagonal lanterns giving a blue mercury-vapour glow at night.

Such a fuss was being made about trolleybuses replacing trams about 1935 that, when we were looking at road works near the 'Blue Anchor' at South Croydon one day, someone told Mum that the Purley trams were going to be replaced by trolleybuses soon. Fortunately this story proved false: it was only the permanent way men busy doubling the tram track in South End near Aberdeen Road and the No.16s and 18s continued to run to Purley, much to my relief!

THE 1939 - 1945 WAR

As general remarks about the London tramways during the War have been made in the S.E. London section, only matters referring to S.W. London and the Norwood and Croydon routes are mentioned here.

A No.48 and a No.34 tram were involved in a collision at Coldharbour Lane junction, Camberwell on December 11th, 1939. At the tramway crossing outside Lambeth Baths (later destroyed in the 'Blitz') a No.12 tram proceeding along Lambeth Road on January 9th, 1940 was struck by an E/1 Class car coming up Kennington Road.

As a result of the fare increases of July 1940 the 5d. maximum in the County of London was raised to 6d. single, another stage being added, while the through fare between London and Purley disappeared, the 9d. Return being available to Norbury Station only (though knowing passengers purchased 1/- Day Tickets instead until their withdrawal in October 1942). These 1/- Day Tickets were not available before 10.0 a.m. The 1/- through fare on Routes 31 & 33 was withdrawn.

The Sunday extension of Service 31 to Leyton was withdrawn from June 1939, and from January 10th, 1940 Route 31 was diverted at Holborn Hall to operate via Rosebery Avenue to Islington Green (instead of Hackney Station). Further trolleybus substitutions for trams in North and East London meant that the Kingsway Subway services (31, 33, 35) became the only tram routes operating in London north of Bloomsbury from July 1940. (Nine tram services were operating in North and East London at the outbreak of the Second World War but, in spite of the war effort, London Transport persisted in changing over six tram routes and diverted the No.31 The last trolleybus 'conversion' in London took place the weekend after the Dunkirk Evacuation - not a very patriotic move).

Air Raid Incidents :-

Friday, September 6th, 1940 : Store collapsed across Borough High Street: Tram Services 6, 10, 48 diverted via Southwark Bridge Road (route reopened September 16th).

Saturday, September 7th : Clapham Depot hit: several trams damaged.

Sunday, September 8th : High-explosive bomb fell in Ball's Pond Road Stoke Newington. Route 33 now terminates there. No alternative service to Manor House and the crater was not filled in until Christmas 1940.

H.E. in Brixton Road, by Angell Road, near the 'White Horse': next day Nos. 10, 16, 18, 33 via Stockwell, Vauxhall & Lambeth Road to 'Elephant', or via Stockwell to near Clapham Station (S.R.), reverse there and continue via Clapham Road to Kennington. (Brixton Road remained closed until October 7th).

E/1 Class Tram 1739 (which had been stored in Purley Depot) was seen passing Thornton Heath Pond en route for London.

Monday, September 9th : Southwark Bridge closed: trams diverted to Hop Exchange. Westminster Bridge closed (reopened at 6.0 p.m.).

Tuesday, September 10th : No service between St. Leonard's Church, Streatham and Norbury Station. Kennington Road blocked at 'Horns' - trams use Kennington Park Road. No. 2/4 working Elephant (terminus) - Clapham via Embankment & Vauxhall.

H.E. on Victoria Embankment at Charing Cross Station during night, blocking road, Another crater on Embankment at the Temple blocked tram track until September 18th.

Wednesday, September 11th : Victoria Embankment still blocked. Trams took half an hour to negotiate Vauxhall Cross during evening rush hour, because so many now routed this way.

Thursday, September 12th : Main cable from Greenwich Power Station damaged - all services suspended except No.34 Brixton - Camberwell and 16/18 Purley - New Park Road only (extended to Brixton Station evening). Emergency bus service: London - Streatham. E/1R Tram 1388 stranded in St. George's Road - later moved to Short Street, Elephant. Streatham Depot damaged.

Friday, September 13th : Track blocked at Clapham Common. 2/4 operating Wimbledon - Nightingale Lane only, also trams from the 'Plough' to Westminster (2) and Victoria (8). Clapham Road blocked north of Stockwell: 2 & 6 diverted via Vauxhall (reopened during following week). Rush-hour Services 2A & 4A, 22 & 24 (combined) working Hop Exchange - Lambeth Road - Albert Embankment - Vauxhall - Stockwell - Clapham - Tooting - Streatham - Brixton - Stockwell, etc. to Hop Exchange (and vice-versa) whenever practicable. (Present termini are 'Plough', Clapham, or Nightingale Lane via Streatham).

Milkwood Road, Herne Hill and Effra Road, Brixton closed, also Norwood Road, so Norwood Depot isolated. Milkwood Road reopened the following week; Norwood Depot thereby reconnected to main system.

Service 14 has reappeared, working 'Prince's Head', Battersea - Hop Exchange via Vauxhall & Westminster whenever practicable (at present it terminates at Westminster).

Saturday, September 14th : H.E. on Albert Embankment: no service between Hop Exchange and Vauxhall (line soon reopened). Clapham Depot and sub-station hit - many trams damaged.

Sunday, September 15th : (R.A.F. and A.A. guns shot down 185 German aircraft today). Borough Road blocked: No.12 restored to Hop Exchange about a week later. Clapham Depot hit again - severe damage - more trams damaged.

Tuesday, September 17th : Lavender Hill, Wandsworth Road and Cedars Road blocked: 26 & 28 diverted via Battersea Park Road. No.34 operating in two sections: Chelsea - Clapham Junction; Clapham Common - Camberwell.

Balham High Road roped off at Trinity Road; no trams south of Nightingale Lane. Some trams marooned at Tooting Broadway. Unexploded bomb between Tooting and Streatham - no service.

Vauxhall Bridge Road blocked: 8, 20, 28, 78 terminate at Vauxhall. 16/18 Purley - Ederline Avenue, Norbury only; also north from Water Lane, Brixton (Brixton Hill - Norbury section closed).

Wednesday, September 18th : Victoria Embankment: through running resumed, using temporary bridge over crater (for trams only) at Charing Cross Station. 16/18 operating in two parts: Purley - Norbury;

New Park Road - Embankment.

Herne Hill - Brixton and Herne Hill - West Norwood sections blocked. 33's southern terminus; Brixton Station.
48 working Herne Hill - Southwark Bridge only.

Thursday, September 19th : Up line in Kennington Road reopened, but trams return via Elephant. Brixton Hill - Norbury section reopened (afternoon), but Brixton - Kennington still closed. Emergency bus service: Blackfriars - Streatham via diversion routes, though trams still maintaining through 16/18 service via Vauxhall and Stockwell.

Friday, September 20th : Tooting - Streatham still closed - emergency bus service. Nos. 8/20 & 10 start at Streatham Library. 16/18 via Vauxhall.

Herne Hill - West Norwood reopened, but Herne Hill - Brixton still closed. No.33 from Westminster via Vauxhall, Stockwell, Brixton, Loughborough Junction, Herne Hill to West Norwood. 48 working normally.

Thursday, September 26th : 2 H.E.s at Kennington: (a) Brixton Road/ Camberwell New Road; (b) Clapham Road just south of Harleyford Road. Only services operating (no route numbers): Kennington - Elephant - Southwark Bridge; Kennington - Elephant - Blackfriars (both directions); Kennington Gate - Kennington Road - Embankment - Elephant - Kennington Park Road (one direction only - clockwise). Clapham Road closed north of 'Swan', Stockwell. Nos. 6 & 10 to Hop Exchange via Vauxhall, Victoria Embankment, Southwark Street.

Lavender Hill and Wandsworth Road reopened, but 26 & 28 split at Lavender Hill/Cedars Road junction - passengers change trams.

Friday, September 27th : Single-line working in Lambeth Road on down track (Service 12). Part of Southwark Bridge Road closed: 12 diverted via Borough Road, Borough High Street, Marshalsea Road.

Approx. 9.0 a.m. H.E. in front garden in South Lambeth Road a few feet behind U.C.C. No.2142 broke all windows, covered it with earth and blew a bush on to the roof. Tram services resumed after a short delay.

No tram service Tooting Broadway - Nightingale Lane, but trams working between Tooting and Wimbledon. Special bus services: Tooting - Victoria.

Saturday, September 28th : Open-fronted trams working Bloomsbury - Ball's Pond Road. Trams resumed working Wimbledon - Balham. Unexploded bomb at Holborn Hall affected Services 33 & 35; cleared within two days.

Tuesday, October 1st : Southwark Street closed: 26 terminates at Blackfriars. Brixton - Herne Hill reopened, though some 33s and 78s still working round Loughborough Junction.

By evening 8/20, 28, 78 running over Vauxhall Bridge to Grosvenor Road (emergency bus service to Victoria).

Wednesday, October 2nd : Emergency bus service for Route 10 via Stockwell to Kennington.

Thursday, October 3rd : Crater in London Road, Thornton Heath, near Dunheved Road: Track torn up; overhead wiring damaged. Motor traffic diverted. No trams south of the Pond. Emergency bus service: Thornton Heath - Purley. Stockwell - Kennington reopened, but Brixton services still via Vauxhall.

Saturday, October 5th : Southwark Street reopened for Service 26. Repairs being carried out in Brixton Road. 16/18 Route: Four trams which had been stored in Purley Depot for a year (E/1 Class Nos. 1484, 1741, 1765, 1776) commenced a shuttle service between Mayday Road and Purley terminus.

Monday, October 7th : Brixton Road reopened throughout to Kennington.

Wednesday, October 9th : No.34 now operating normally Chelsea - Blackfriars.

Friday, October 11th : Owing to track repairs at Tooting Broadway 8/20 circular service worked in two parts, trams reversing at each side of the junction.

Saturday, October 12th : Down track at Thornton Heath has been repaired (single-line working and overhead O.K.), though one standard down. Trams working between Norbury and Purley, also between Thornton Heath Pond and Embankment on Routes 16/18.

Monday, October 14th : Trams to Victoria again, but South Lambeth Road closed. No.8 (up) via Brixton Road to Kennington Church, reverse over up line into Camberwell New Road, reverse again and continue via Harleyford Road to Victoria; 20 (down) via Albert Embankment, Lambeth Road, Elephant, Kennington Park Road, Brixton Road.

Tuesday, October 15th: H.E. at Vauxhall roundabout near Gas Light and Coke Company. Wandsworth Road closed. Nos. 12, 26, 28 diverted via Cedars Road, Clapham, Stockwell, then 28 via South Lambeth Road; 12 & 26 via Kennington, Elephant to Hop Exchange.

H.E. had destroyed both tracks near Balham Station and a No.88 bus fell into the crater - no trams between there and Nightingale Lane. (Subsequently, crossovers were laid on the south side of Balham railway bridge and by Ramsden Road, trams reversing on either side of the obstruction until the crater was bridged for trams only. The crossover by Ramsden Road has been retained permanently).

Unexploded bomb at Angel, Islington: No.33 terminates at Bloomsbury. Holloway Depot damaged.

Wednesday, October 16th : Services 10, 16, 18, 33 via Stockwell this morning, but normal by evening via Brixton Road.

Thursday, October, 17th : Track blocked at Dulwich Road, Brockwell Park: Nos. 33 & 78 routed via Loughborough Junction.

Friday, October 18th : Down overhead wire damaged by explosion at Warwick Road, Thornton Heath - repaired by evening (trams used up wire in both directions in morning). Through 16/18 service restored between Victoria Embankment and Purley, but only single-line working between Thornton Heath Pond and Mayday Road.

Mitcham Lane closed: emergency bus service Streatham - Tooting. Unexploded bombs in Theobalds Road and at the Angel, Islington cut Routes 33 & 35 - roads cleared by November 2nd.

Sunday, October 20th : Double-track working resumed between Thornton Heath Pond and Mayday Road, but other traffic diverted until Christmas.

Monday, October 21st : Blackfriars Road blocked (soon reopened), also Southwark Bridge Road (reopened November 15th) and Vauxhall Cross (reopened October 26th). Nos. 4, 18, 34 terminate at Elephant; 12 St. George's Circus; 8/20, 28, 78 Vauxhall. Shuttle service: Vauxhall Bridge - Victoria.

Some trams operating down Effra Road (part way to Herne Hill), but 33 & 78 working via Loughborough Junction to West Norwood.

Friday, October 25th : H.E. scored direct hit on centre of five southbound trams waiting at the traffic lights at Blackfriars Road railway bridge during morning rush hour. E/1 Class Trams 1600 (Service 34) and 1825 (Service 2), both from Clapham Depot, damaged beyond repair. U.C.C. 'Feltham' tram on Service 16 had its windows smashed. Tram services restored by evening.

Saturday, October 26th : Services restored from Vauxhall right through to Victoria terminus again.

Walworth Road blocked: 34 & 48 diverted via Kennington & Elephant. U.C.C. 'Feltham' Tram No.2113 destroyed in Stockwell Road, Brixton.

Monday, October 28th : Large crater in Stockwell Road, Brixton outside Quin and Axten's store. 8/20 diverted via Kennington, reversing twice to negotiate the junction. No.34 operating in two sections: Chelsea - Stockwell; Brixton Road - Blackfriars. (Road closed until February 17th, 1941).

Tuesday, October 29th : Through service on Routes 8/20 discontinued. Trams on Services 8/20 from Tooting and Streatham terminate at Kennington Church. Skeleton service of 'Felthams' between Victoria and Camberwell New Road. Recent crater on Vauxhall roundabout near Gas Light and Coke Company now repaired.

No.48 operating West Norwood - Camberwell only.

Thursday, October 31st : Service 33 reopened from Bloomsbury to Ball's Pond Road. Slight damage near 'Horns', Kennington - restored by evening (morning down trams worked via Vauxhall and Kennington on 16/18 service).

Monday, November 4th : Unexploded bomb discovered on Brixton Hill during evening; consequently tram services ceased between Water Lane and New Park Road.

Tuesday/Wednesday, November 5th/6th : H.E. on tracks in Streatham High Road (opposite Streatham Common, South Side) during evening, approximately five yards north of crossover (overhead wires not damaged). Services 16 & 18 operated in three sections: Victoria Embankment - Water Lane, Brixton; New Park Road - Streatham change pit (emergency 'bus service to Streatham Common); from Streatham Common, South Side (where trams overhung the edge of the crater - only room for one tram at a time to reverse) to Purley terminus. Two 'Felthams' stranded between Streatham Common and Purley shedded each night at Thornton Heath Depot.

During the same night, H.E. fell in High Street, Thornton Heath near the Clock Tower. Crater covered north side of street and eastbound track, but overhead wires not damaged. Motor traffic diverted. Service 42 from Croydon reverses at the Clock Tower, one tram providing shuttle service on westbound track in High Street to Whitehorse Road.

Unexploded bombs in Wandsworth Road and Southwark Bridge Road - removed within a week. H.Es át Balham Hill (line reopened December 4th), Balham High Road (reopened November 20th) and Colliers' Wood (see note on November 17th about this incident).

Friday, November 8th : H.E. in Mitcham Road, Tooting (near Granada Cinema) - no trams between Tooting Broadway and Amen Corner.

Walworth Road blocked: Nos. 34 & 48 diverted via Camberwell New Road and Kennington Park Road (normal again in a few days).

Unexploded bomb on Brixton Hill removed: tram services resumed.

Monday, November 11th : During the evening a tram from Purley went a little too far at Streatham Common - the front wheels went over the edge of the crater, stopping the tram service for the rest of the day, other trams having to reverse at Hermitage Bridge, Norbury.

Wednesday, November 13th : Three H.Es just south of Streatham Hill Station destroyed both tracks. Emergency 'bus service: Telford Avenue - Streatham Common (diverted between the Station and Leigham Avenue). Service 10 operating between Streatham Library and Southcroft Road.

Eastbound track in High Street, Thornton Heath reopened to trams (other traffic permitted some days later).

Sunday, November 17th : Huge crater in both tram tracks in High Street, Colliers' Wood (just by Merton 'Bus Garage). E/1 Class Tram No.1549 marooned on down track with all its windows smashed. Shuttle service to Wimbledon by three stranded E/1 Class trams Nos. 1659, 1801 & 1844, but they could only use the up track for some distance at the

Colliers' Wood end. No trams between Colliers' Wood and Balham. Four 'Felthams' (Nos. 2078, 2121, 2130 & 2161) working a shuttle service between Tooting Broadway and Streatham Library.

A few days later, these four 'Felthams' were maintaining a shuttle service between Balham High Road and Colliers' Wood also, showing No.2A on their number indicators but blank destination blinds.

Tuesday/Wednesday, November 19th/20th : H.E. at south end of Kingsway Subway - hole through tunnel. Eight trams damaged by blast. Single-line working instituted on the up line next morning; service fully restored on December 18th.

Monday, November 25th : Down track at Streatham Hill Station reopened, allowing trams to leave Telford Avenue Depot for the south. Full service operating between Streatham Library and Tooting Broadway in the evening.

Wednesday, November 27th : Tram service past Streatham Common resumed. Down track temporarily laid on sleepers at extreme edge of crater (covered with tar macadam a few days later and southbound motor traffic restored). Single-line working past crater; new pair of left-hand points laid north of crater.

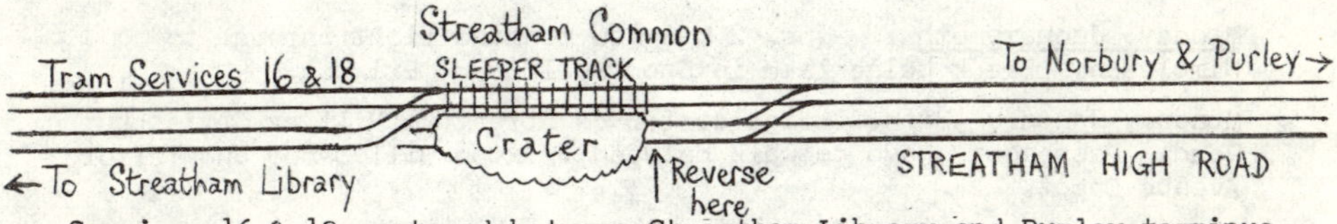

Services 16 & 18 restored between Streatham Library and Purley terminus.

Tuesday, December 3rd : Both tracks now open at Streatham Hill Station (other traffic still diverted). Services 10, 16, 18 now operating normally throughout.

Wednesday, December 4th : Trams to Longley Road, Tooting (via Clapham) again.

Monday, December 9th : No trams north of Kennington this morning. Terrific chaos by Kennington Oval. Service 48 running via Camberwell, Kennington, Vauxhall, Lambeth Road, Borough Road, Southwark Bridge Road. Several 78s seen at Kennington showing destination 'SAVOY ST STRAND'. During the evening No.10 returned from the City via Southwark Bridge Road to St. George's Circus, reverse there and proceed via Lancaster Street to the Elephant & Castle.

Clapham Road roped off between 'Swan', Stockwell and Stockwell Park Road because of bomb crater. Infrequent emergency bus service (not well patronised) for Services 2, 4 & 6 diverted up via South Lambeth Road and Lansdowne Road, down via Stockwell Park Road and Stockwell Road.

Friday, December 13th : Temporary crossovers being laid at the 'Horns', Kennington (in use on Christmas Eve).

Tuesday, December 17th : H.E. at corner of Walworth Road and New Kent Road. Nos. 34 & 48 used Short Street (Elephant) in both directions. Normal at Elephant on December 19th.

Sunday, December 22nd : No.42s not proceeding beyond the Clock Tower, Thornton Heath, owing to demolition work in the High Street. (Services restored next day).

Thursday, December 26th : Up line being relaid at Streatham Common (reopened on December 31st).

Monday, December 30th, 1940 : After the great fire raid on the City: Blackfriars Bridge and Victoria Embankment closed as far west as Somerset House because of firemen's hoses - reopened by evening.

Southwark Street closed: No.26 diverted via Route 12. Theobalds Road blocked (until January 5th, 1941).

Wednesday, January 1st, 1941 : Owing to dangerous buildings, very few trams between Kennington and Elephant, also Kennington and Westminster. No.16 via Kennington Road, Lambeth Road, St. George's Circus to Blackfriars (terminus). Normal services next day.

Sunday, January 5th : Theobalds Road reopened: E/3 Class Tram No.1937 (Service 33) first tram through at 11.50 a.m.

Monday, January 6th : Nos. 2 & 4 now running right through to Wimbledon. Track being laid in Stockwell Road, Brixton.

Monday, January 13th : Large crater on Streatham Hill by Christchurch Road. Passengers have to walk between Brixton Hill Depot and Telford Avenue Depot.

Tuesday, January 14th : Blackfriars Bridge closed (reopened next day), also Southwark Street blocked: No.26 diverted via Route 12 again.

Thursday, January 16th : No trams from Brixton to Victoria: H.Es in Stockwell Road and South Lambeth Road, on both sides of the 'Swan' junction.

In the morning there was some trouble from the cold weather and a tram smashed its plough on the points at Streatham.

Unexploded bomb by the 'Swan and Sugar Loaf' at South Croydon affected Routes 16 & 18 - cleared by January 24th.

Saturday, January 18th : 8/20 shuttle service working single line in South Lambeth Road past crater by Lansdowne Road (full services restored by January 22nd).

Wednesday, January 22nd : No.34 shuttle service working on down line in Stockwell Road between 'Swan' and Brixton: E/1 Class Tram 1007 used on 24th; No.1653 on 25th (full services restored by January 28th).

Friday, January 24th : Southwark Street reopened to Service 26.

In the evening single-line working on the up track commenced between Telford Avenue and New Park Road, a section box and telephone at both these points facilitating signalling.

Saturday, February 1st : Crater in road at West Norwood. Ordinary surface track laid round crater, giving through running. Road closed to other traffic.

Sunday, February 9th : No service between Telford Avenue and New Park Road as a crossover was being laid at Christchurch Road to reduce the length of single track in use.

Friday, February 14th : Service 33 now restored throughout between West Norwood and Manor House.

Monday, February 17th : Crater at Stockwell Road Junction, Brixton practically filled in. Tram services all normal since yesterday.

Unfortunately a tram inspector on duty was crushed to death between two trams at West Norwood terminus during February.

Saturday/Sunday, March 8th/9th : Bombs fell in Essex Road, stopping Service 33. E/3 Class Trams Nos. 1928, 1995 & 1996 stranded between Ball's Pond Road and Manor House. Remainder of 33s run to Highgate.

Another crater at Christchurch Road: emergency buses between Telford Avenue and Brixton Hill Depot using diversion route. Some trams diverted between Kennington and Streatham to run via Stockwell, Clapham, Balham, Tooting and Southcroft Road; U.C.C. 'Feltham' Tram 2138 (Service 18) routed this way on Tuesday (11th).

Wednesday, March 12th : Single-line working resumed at Christchurch Road, Brixton Hill - normal working resumed by March 23rd.

Monday, March 24th : Up line in Essex Road repaired: marooned trams able to reach Holloway Depot.

Monday, April 7th : Service 33 operating normally through to Manor House again.

After the Wednesday night raid of April 16th :-

H.E. in Rosebery Avenue. Single-line working started 6.0 p.m. Thursday.

Southwark Street closed - direct hit on railway bridge at west end and fires. No.26 working Clapham Junction - John Carpenter Street via Lambeth Road & Blackfriars Road.

Clapham sub-station destroyed and Clapham Depot damaged. Trams got their 'juice' from the Underground sub-station. Full service on Clapham routes within two days.

Incendiary bombs in Wandsworth Road (blocked by firemen's hoses).

Very large crater in Brixton Road immediately south of Stockwell Road; entire roadway and both tracks destroyed. U.C.C. 'Feltham' Tram No.2090 marooned at Brixton Station, No.2089 just north of Stockwell Road. Apparently track damage at Quin and Axten's (Stockwell Road). Emergency 'bus service worked by Croydon and Merton Garages from Embankment and City to Water Lane. (Small crater in down track just north of Water Lane). Trams working south of Water Lane.

C.C.T. No.389 seen at Kennington. One No.34 tram running shuttle service: Kennington - Elephant (Thursday morning, April 17th).

Coldharbour Lane closed, also Effra Road, Brixton: a No.33 tram marooned at change pit. Trams operating West Norwood - Herne Hill only. No signs of tram services between Brixton - Camberwell, Brixton - Herne Hill, Brixton - Stockwell, Herne Hill - Camberwell (Thursday evening).

Friday, April 18th : Clapham Road open as far south as Clapham Depot. 8/20 working Brixton - Victoria; 34 Brixton - Chelsea.

Clapham services normal on April 20th.

After the Saturday night raid of April 19th :-

Islington sub-station out of action - power failure north of Bloomsbury. Dangerous ruins in Theobalds Road. Service 31 working to Holborn Tram Station only, from the south.

No signs of tram services between Kennington - Vauxhall and Kennington - Westminster (crater at the 'Horns', Kennington).

Monday, April 21st : Double track now open at Streatham Hill.

Wednesday, April 23rd : Nos. 10, 16, 18 working between Angell Road, Brixton and Town.

Thursday, April 24th : No.31 reached the Angel, Islington again. No.34 working Chelsea - Loughborough Junction.

Friday, April 25th : Service 34 normal again. Track being laid across 'Horns' crater at Kennington.

Monday, April 28th : Service 48 now normal.

Tuesday, April 29th : Services 16 & 18 working between Purley and Brixton Station.

Sunday, May 4th : Double-line working at the 'Horns', Kennington again. No.33 working Angell Road, Brixton - Angel, Islington.

Tuesday, May 6th : No.33 working between Angell Road and Manor House.

Thursday, May 8th : Brixton - Herne Hill opened for trams only, using track round crater in Effra Road, during the evening.

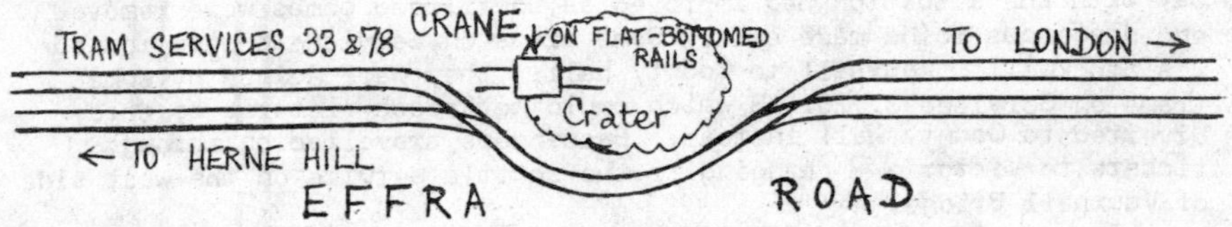

Friday, May 9th : Nos. 10, 16, 18, 33 normal between suburbs and Town.

Saturday/Sunday, May 10th/11th (the great fire raid) :-

C.C.T. Tram No.396 destroyed outside South Croydon Omnibus Garage, by the 'Red Deer': the tram conductor was killed. (The 'bus garage was badly damaged by incendiary fires).

Crater on Victoria curve at Vauxhall roundabout; unexploded bomb in Parry Street, Vauxhall: shuttle service to Victoria. UXB on Albert Embankment. Track damage in Lambeth Road and Southwark Street. Emergency 'bus service: Nine Elms - Hop Exchange. No. 12 & 26 Trams turn back at Nine Elms.

Southwark Bridge closed: trams terminate on south side of bridge. Newington Causeway blocked by debris near the railway bridge, also Borough High Street: trams diverted via Southwark Bridge Road. UXB in London Road, Southwark. Dangerous buildings blocked Blackfriars Road and Kennington Park Road. Huge fire at the Elephant & Castle, which developed into a conflagration.

Westminster Bridge Road blocked: 2 & 16 terminated at Christ Church, Lambeth. All other trams from Clapham and Brixton terminate at Kennington. Down line in Walworth Road/Camberwell Road damaged: 34 & 48 terminate at Camberwell.

UXB at Balham Grove: emergency 'bus service between Marius Road and Nightingale Lane using diversion. Trams operating south of Marius Road. From Nightingale Lane No.2 to Christ Church, Lambeth and 8 to Vauxhall only.

The roof of Norwood Depot was slightly damaged, also the overhead wires in Norwood Road were damaged but were quickly repaired.

Direct hit on southern entrance of Kingsway Subway. Dangerous ruins in Theobalds Road. Track damaged in Essex Road, Islington (near Cross Street) - soon repaired. Trams from Highgate to Holborn Hall only.

The tramways in the central area were badly affected by this raid - the Luftwaffe's final attempt to destroy London utterly - because no trams could approach the Central London termini. However, by Monday, May 12th the situation had improved as unexploded bombs were removed and dangerous ruins made safe. Some trams on Service 16 were routed via Stockwell & Vauxhall to County Hall; they were joined by some trams on Services 8, 20, 78 which could not reach Victoria so were diverted to County Hall instead. Passengers travelled on through tickets to Victoria - changing to the shuttle service on the west side of Vauxhall Bridge.

There were no trams on Victoria Embankment for some days, so Nos. 4 & 18 worked to Blackfriars only, 16 & 33 to Christ Church, Lambeth only. The Embankment was soon reopened, also Westminster Bridge Road on May 16th. By May 15th, Services 33 & 35 were working from North London to Aldwych Tram Station and on May 18th Kingsway Subway was reopened throughout (with a hole in the roof).

By May 14th Services 6, 10, 48 were working through to the south side of Southwark Bridge. 34 & 48 were diverted via Kennington Park Road and Camberwell New Road on down journeys (on up journeys Walworth Road could be used). No.12 was restored through Southwark by May 20th, but it had to terminate at the south side of Southwark Bridge until a crater at the Hop Exchange was filled in and the track relaid. A huge crater at the City end of Southwark Bridge had to be crossed by a girder bridge which has become a permanent feature. The tram terminus therefore had to be cut back about a hundred yards south and has remained there ever since.

This was the last major air raid of the 1940/1941 'Blitz' and all South London tramway services were back to normal by June 1941. The tramways in S.W. London escaped further damage until February 1944. Travel facilities were reduced from October 9th,1942 by the abolition of the 1/- Day Ticket and 6d. Evening Tourist ticket, and by a reduction in the availability of the 9d. Return fare.

Severe wintry weather during January and February 1942 meant that the snowplough trams were frequently in action. A sad accident occurred in Balham High Road on February 6th when a motor lorry and trailer skidded on the icy roadway and the trailer hit a passing tram, killing the tram driver.

At the beginning of the War No.1 had been withdrawn from service and surrounded by sandbags at Telford Avenue Depot, Streatham, but it was restored to service in June 1942.

From February 6th, 1943 Service 31 was curtailed to work between 'Prince's Head', Battersea and Westminster Station only, extended to Bloomsbury at rush hours. It thereby ceased to work through Kingsway Subway at normal hours. This was an awkward arrangement for the tram crews and involved reversing on busy trunk routes. No.6 was curtailed to work Tooting Broadway - City & Southwark and became a rush-hour service only. To supplement this withdrawal of service on Saturdays, extra trams were run between Wimbledon Station and Balham Station on the 2/4 route, showing 'MARIUS RD' destination when travelling to Balham.

There were some heavy air raids during the early months of 1944 - the last by piloted German aircraft on London - and on Sunday night, February 20th the up line (eastern track) in Falcon Road, Clapham Junction was blocked south of the railway bridge. Service 34 was maintained by single-line working on the staff principle between the crossovers at 'Prince's Head', Battersea and St. John's Hill, where reversal was necessary. Some days later, a temporary crossover was installed in Falcon Road, which considerably shortened the amount of single-line working necessary, though the junction westwards into St. John's Hill still had to be used until May 14th, when the up line was reopened and normal working resumed between Falcon Road and Lavender Hill.

A H.E. on Vauxhall roundabout at South Lambeth Road junction (Tuesday/Wednesday, March 21st/22nd) cut Services 8, 12, 20, 26, 28 31, 78 for some days, but Nos. 54, 58, 66 maintained through services, employing single-line working under the railway bridge in Kennington Lane.

Generally speaking, tram services were not greatly affected by Nazi flying bombs and rockets, but several incidents were recorded. During July 1944 there was superficial damage to Thornton Heath Depot, the glass roof being slightly damaged. The track at Newington Causeway/Borough Road junction was blocked in August and Services 6, 10, 48 were diverted via Southwark Bridge Road for some days. Another incident in Brigstock Road, Thornton Heath, by the Fire Station, affected Route 42 for a day or so.

V1 flying bombs destroyed three trams from Streatham Depot in August 1944: U.C.C. 'Feltham' No.2109 at Kennington Gate on Thursday, August 24th, and ex-Walthamstow Trams Nos. 2044 & 2051. The remains were towed late at night to Purley Depot, part of which was used as a store for damaged tramcars. Purley Depot was also providing a few trams on Services 16 & 18 and had others ready for use in an emergency.

Service 33 was affected by a German V2 rocket which fell in Green Lanes near Manor House on Monday, January 8th, 1945, damaging both tracks. Single-line working was instituted on January 18th and the tram service was working normally over double track by April 10th, one month before the War in Europe ended. Before this, however, Thornton Heath Depot had lost another tram, rehabilitated Croydon Tram No.376, which caught fire on Victoria Embankment during the evening rush hour on February 13th, 1945 and was completely burnt out.

AN EXHILARATING FREE LIFT - A Wartime Tale by S.P. HARRIS

One wartime January night, Mr. S.P. Harris, while a Serviceman, arrived at Waterloo Station with his lady friend, after an eight-hour journey from the West Country. They wished to go to Epsom, 16 miles away, and the last train had gone. The blacked-out streets were empty of public transport, taxis were far too expensive on a Serviceman's pay, and no other vehicles seemed to be headed in the right direction. They were not sure of the times of the all-night trams, so they started walking; it was then about one o'clock in the morning.

Then, somewhere along Clapham Road they heard the whine of tramcar motors and saw a single-deck tram approaching - it was a works car. The motorman, fat, red-faced and jovial, responded to the serviceman thumbing a lift; perhaps the lady's presence caused him to stop and offer a ride to them both.

They clambered on to the open-fronted platform alongside the driver and so began this extraordinary ride. The four-wheeler was soon swaying along the track at full speed; the cold wind howled around as the tram careered along beside Clapham Common, 'duff-duffing' over the rail joints as it literally bounced into Balham! The cacophonous drumming of the wheels and the vociferous complaint of the motors was flung back from the chasm of Upper Tooting Road. The probing silver fingers of searchlights in the black sky made the experience all the more bizarre. Suddenly an all-night tramcar on its way to Charing Cross flashed by with a roar, the two trams seeming almost to touch.

At Tooting the works car slowed down as the tubby driver made a jovial remark to a policeman pal, who waved them on with his gauntletted hand. The motorman was happily singing snatches of song: 'South of the Border' seemed to be his favourite! Mr. Harris was thoroughly enjoying this weird exhilarating journey down the 2/4 tram route, but the lady was not so enthusiastic!

At South Wimbledon Underground Station they alighted, where just round the corner the P.W. gang were busy working on the track in Merton Road. The Gang invited them into their canvas 'tent' to imbibe a well-sugared mug of hot tea brewed over an old L.C.C. brazier and that cup of 'char' fortified them for the long walk to Epsom along a tramless highway.

Mr. Harris frequently hitch-hiked, like most men in the Forces, during the War, but none of the other free lifts had the tang, the zest and the sheer sense of adventure that this zany four-wheeler provided on the 'All-Red Route' in the blackout.

WARTIME REMINISCENCES

At Purley in October 1940, during the 'Blitz', I remember seeing the trams on the shuttle service to Mayday Road.

When we left Caterham at the end of the Autumn Term 1940 for the Christmas Holidays, the School hired motor coaches to take some of the boarders to Waterloo, Paddington and the northern London railway termini in case the Caterham - London train service was cut by bombing that day. (There had been a bomb crater blocking both railway and road near Warlingham Station in September 1940).

Our coaches had to make several detours round back turnings in Thornton Heath, Norbury, Streatham, Brixton and Kennington, while the No.16 & 18 Trams continued unperturbed along the main road past signs reading: DIVERSION: TRAMS ONLY.

I wished that I could travel by tram instead, but my parents had paid the coach fare, then there was my luggage and it wasn't advisable to leap from a moving coach on the first day of the holidays, not even to board a tram! (This was the only time during the War that the School hired coaches for this purpose, as usually the Caterham trains ran normally at the end of successive wartime terms). I may say that our School was fortunate in that no bomb fell within a quarter of a mile (except a messy oil bomb in the school cabbage-patch); nevertheless Caterham was quite an exciting place and six or more Nazi bombers were shot down in the district. The school routine was little affected by the War, except that V1s (flying bombs) caused an 'ersatz' Speech Day without parents in July 1944 and that Summer Term ended early.

On several occasions during term time, when I was about 15 - 16, I was sent up to London for various messages; once to take a 'cello for repair, another time to fetch some photographic slides, and so on. The up journey was made by Southern Electric, but I always returned by a No.16 or 18 tram to Purley, then by train or 'bus to Caterham. I may say that I was fortunate never to be caught on a tram in an air raid, not even in the holidays, though regular travellers often preferred trams to any other vehicles in a raid because the tram's sound was friendly and reassuring; it obliterated the crash of bombs and the bark of A.A. guns.

In Spring 1945 the Sixth Form went to see a performance of William Shakespeare's play 'Hamlet' at the Guildhall School of Music and Drama at John Carpenter Street, Blackfriars. We travelled thither by Southern Railway to Charing Cross, thence along the Embankment in a No.2 tram. Some of my classmates had never been in a tram before, but everyone enjoyed the ride there and back, including our Headmaster. As we had some time before our train, several boys accompanied me on a return trip through Kingsway Subway. Perhaps Ken wasn't so mad after all and trams were certainly a lot of fun!

On VE2 Day in May 1945 I boarded a No.18 tram at Purley terminus and asked for a 1/- All Day Ticket, only to be told that they had been withdrawn during the War. As money was not too plentiful, I had to content myself with visits to Brockwell Park and Dulwich Park (via Brixton) using No.18, 33, 58 & 34 Trams, then a No.18 back to Purley. Still, I had a very enjoyable day celebrating Victory with the Trams!

1945 - 1949

Since the War several improvements have been made to the Clapham and Streatham routes. These include the provision of new loading islands for tram passengers at South Lambeth Road, 'Plough' Clapham, Nightingale Lane, Brixton Town Hall, Streatham Hill (near Downton Avenue) and Streatham High Road (near Woodbourne Avenue), and an additional island at Victoria terminus, also in Brixton Road at Gresham Road.

On April 1st, 1946 the Sunday service on Route 26 was extended from Savoy Street to John Carpenter Street, Blackfriars. At Croydon, commencing April 17th, 1946, Service 42 has been extended $\frac{1}{4}$ mile to Coombe Road crossover, to relieve congestion outside the Davis Theatre. The new terminal point is more acceptable to other traffic. Tram destination blinds have been amended to read 'COOMBE RD
CROYDON'

From June 26th, 1946 All-Night services have been numbered as follows:-

1. Tooting & Streatham - Victoria Embankment circular service.
3. Battersea (Prince's Head) - Blackfriars (John Carpenter Street).
26. Clapham Junction - Hop Exchange via Westminster.

The diversion of trams via Vauxhall during the 'Blitz' proving so successful may account for the alterations to rush-hour Services 22 & 24. Instead of travelling via Kennington then circular round Victoria Embankment, 22 & 24 now travel via Stockwell, Vauxhall, Albert Embankment and Westminster to Savoy Street, Strand, where they terminate. On the journey to the suburbs they part at 'Swan', Stockwell and work a circular service to Tooting and Streatham comparable to the 8/20 circular service: 8 & 22 down via Clapham & Tooting, up via Streatham & Brixton; 20 & 24 down via Brixton & Streatham, up via Tooting & Clapham. (Incidentally, rush-hour Services 2A & 4A were withdrawn as superfluous). To compensate for the loss of the 22/24 service via Brixton Road, extra trams run short workings on the 16/18 route (L.C.C. trams carry an EX stencil; 'Feltham' trams show 16X or 18X). The new 22/24 service gives 'a short cut' to Westminster from Brixton.

An up No.20 tram was struck by a No.54 to Victoria at Grosvenor Road, Vauxhall Bridge on December 12th, 1945 - there was a slight delay to traffic. The following morning, trams at Victoria terminus were held up during the rush-hour when a No.20 blocked the points.

A No.34 tram collided with a lorry and trailer on Battersea Bridge on December 21st, 1945. Traffic was delayed for an hour and meantime trams reversed at Parkgate Road crossover. The next day a cyclist skidded and fell under a No.42 tram in Brigstock Road, Thornton Heath but was saved by the lifeguard. He was released after ten minutes and taken to Mayday Hospital for treatment.

On the evening of July 3rd, 1946 E/1 Class Tram 1780 (Service 34 for Chelsea) ran away down Cedars Road Hill, derailed at Lavender Hill junction, hit the kerb at the corner of Beaufoy Road and overturned in Queen's Road. The roof was torn off and 33 people injured. There had been complaints of 'speeding' trams 'doing 50 m.p.h.' in Cedars Road; as mentioned in the S.E. section, some younger drivers were inclined to disregard the strict L.C.C. speed restrictions at this time.

A down No.26 tram and an up 'Feltham' on Service 16 collided on the points at County Hall junction on December 6th, 1946, both drivers and three passengers being injured. A down No.16 and a No.54 collided at Kennington Church on September 25th, 1947.

Snowstorms caused many delays to trams, besides other traffic, on January 31st, 1947, and Croydon Corporation Tram 394 on the 16-18 service diverted via Clapham became derailed there.

A new fare increase came into operation on February 9th, 1947. The 2d. fare became 2½d, single fares from 3d. to 10d. were increased by a penny; the 9d. Return became 11d. Return in the County of London. 2½d., 4d. & 6d. Workmen's Returns became 3d., 5d. & 7d. Workmen's Returns respectively. The 3d. Cheap Midday Fare rose to 4d. after four stages, though the 3d. Cheap Midday Fare is still available for shorter journeys. The single fare between London and Purley became 11d; on all other routes the maximum fare is now 7d. single, 11d. Return - still quite cheap.

On November 12th, 1947 Service 31 was restored to operate between Wandsworth High Street and Islington Green daily (though since November 14th, 1948 it has worked on Sundays from Wandsworth to Westminster only).

Since January 3rd, 1948 Services 2 & 4 have been augmented on Saturday afternoons between Balham and Stockwell and also Service 34 between Chelsea and Camberwell Green on Saturday afternoons.

Richard Attenborough, starring in the film 'London Belongs to Me' rode to and fro for two hours or so in the lower saloon of an E/1 Class tramcar between Clapham and Balham during filming on March 13th, 1948.

Three E/1 Class trams collided at Longley Road change pit, Tooting on January 6th, 1948. The conductor of the leading tram was crushed by the second tram as he was raising the trolley pole on the down journey.

A No.24 tram and a horse box collided in South Lambeth Road at Miles Street on March 3rd. On May 10th 'Feltham' Tram No.2097 (Service 20) collided with a lorry loaded with flour in South Lambeth Road at Lansdowne Road. The tram was derailed and ran into the front garden of a house. E/1 Class Tram 1611 (Service 28) was badly damaged when it ran into the back of E/1R Class Tram 1353 (Service 78) at Bridgefoot, Vauxhall on August 27th, 1948.

E/1 Class 1597 (Service 34) was damaged by fire after a collision on Battersea Bridge (March 26th, 1949), but was soon repaired and returned to service. E/1 No.1598 (Service 28) and a motor van collided in Vauxhall Bridge Road at Grosvenor Road on April 20th, while U.C.C. 'Feltham' Tram 2108 (Service 22) hit a No.16 tram outside Brixton Town Hall during the evening rush-hour on May 24th.

A No.34 tram and a No.16 tram were among five trams involved in a tail-to-tail collision at London Road, Elephant and Castle on November 26th, 1949. Thirteen passengers were taken to hospital for treatment. A motor lorry struck Special E/1 Class Tram 1103 (Service 34) in Coldharbour Lane on December 30th, 1949.

During March 1947 most of the trams stored at Hampstead Depot were moved to Purley Depot, joining the trams already stored there. However, on September 7th, 1948 the stored trams were moved to Wandsworth Depot, folding doors were fitted to Purley Depot and it has been used since as a repair depot carrying out routine tramcar maintenance. Preparations have been made recently to use it as a running depot again from January 1st, 1950.

Tram No.1 has been working quite regularly on rush-hour and all-night services since the War and on October 3rd, 1948 it was used for a special L.R.T.L. tour. On this occasion No.1 traversed the following route: Victoria - Wimbledon - Southcroft Road - Purley - Brixton - Camberwell - Dulwich - Catford - Greenwich - Abbey Wood - Woolwich - Westhorne Avenue - Lee - Lewisham - Westminster.

During January 1949 a water main burst in Balham High Road at Marius Road under the down track. The paving was excavated and a section of conduit T-rail had to be removed and trams coasted over the gap until repairs were completed in February. Another water main burst in Newington Butts in March and trams had to be diverted via Walworth Road for some hours.

Since 1948, permanent way repairs have been carried out in many places, including Victoria Embankment, Westminster Bridge Road, Borough Road, Lambeth Bridge junction, Kennington Road, Victoria terminus, Parry Street (Vauxhall), Clapham Road, Clapham High Street, Cedars Road, Lavender Hill, Clapham Common (South Side), Upper Tooting Road, Brixton Road, Gresham Road junction, Loughborough Junction, Brixton Hill, by Green Lane, Norbury and around Thornton Heath Pond. Track relaying in

North End and High Street, Croydon was carried out during 1946, and a further $1\frac{1}{2}$ track miles in the Borough of Croydon were renewed in 1948.

Mention should be made of the tramway track in the Borough of Croydon which is laid in tar macadam and is the best-laid section of Routes 16 & 18. Recently skid-type trolley heads have been fitted to the trolley poles of three ex-Croydon Corporation trams, notably Nos. 378, 382 & 387. These are less prone to dewirement and give smoother running on the overhead wires.

LOCAL SERVICES, 1949

The following tram services are now operating in South-West London, the Herne Hill district and in the Borough of Croydon (1949):-

Route No.		Journey Time
C 2 & 4	Wimbledon Station -- Victoria Embankment via Tooting & Clapham (Daily Services): (2 up via Westminster, down via Blackfriars; 4 up via Elephant & Blackfriars, down via Westminster).	(58 mins)
C 6	Tooting Broadway -- City & Southwark via Clapham (Rush Hours only).	(38 mins)
C/S 8 & 20	Tooting & Streatham -- Victoria Station via South Lambeth Road(Daily Services): (8 via Brixton (up), down via Clapham; 20 up via Clapham, down via Brixton).	(38 mins via Clapham; (46 mins. via Streatham to Tooting)
N/S 10	Tooting Broadway -- City & Southwark via Streatham & Brixton (Daily Service); (after 3.0 p.m. Saturdays works to St. George's Church, Borough only).	(51 mins)
W 12	Wandsworth High Street -- Hop Exchange,Borough via Battersea & Lambeth Road (Daily Service).	(39 mins)
N/S/T/P 16 & 18	Purley Fountain -- Victoria Embankment via Croydon, Streatham & Brixton (Daily Services): (16 up via Westminster; down via Blackfriars; 18 up via Elephant & Blackfriars, down via Westminster).	(75-78 mins)
C/S 22 & 24	Tooting & Streatham -- Savoy Street,Strand via Stockwell & Albert Embankment(Rush Hours only) (22 up via Brixton, down via Clapham; 24 up via Clapham, down via Brixton).	(38 mins via Clapham; (53 mins to Tooting via Streatham).

C/W	26	Clapham Junction -- Hop Exchange, Borough via Victoria Embankment & Southwark Street(Weekdays); Clapham Junction -- Blackfriars(John Carpenter St.) (Sundays).	(41 mins)
C	28	Clapham Junction -- Victoria Station via Wandsworth Road (Daily Service)	(25 mins)
H/W	31	Wandsworth High Street -- Islington Green via Battersea & Kingsway Subway (Weekdays); Wandsworth High Street -- Westminster Station(UD)(Sundays).	(53 mins)
H/N	33	West Norwood(St. Luke's Church)-- Manor House,Finsbury Park via Brixton, Westminster, Kingsway Subway & Essex Road (Daily Service).	(68 mins)
C/L	34	Chelsea (King's Road) -- Blackfriars(John Carpenter Street) via Battersea, Clapham, Brixton & Camberwell (Daily Service). (certain trams work to Camberwell Green only during slack hours).	(60 mins)
T/P	42	Thornton Heath (Whitehorse Road) -- South End, Croydon (Coombe Road) via Brigstock Road (Daily Service).	(20 mins)
N	48	West Norwood -- City & Southwark via Camberwell & Elephant (Weekdays); (after 3.0 p.m. Saturdays works to St. George's Church, Borough only); West Norwood -- St. George's Church, Borough (Sundays).	(38 mins)
N	78	West Norwood -- Victoria Station via Brixton & Stockwell (Weekdays only).	(33 mins)

All-Night Services 1, 3 & 26 operate as in 1946, when they were numbered.

The code letters shown above refer to the tram depots which operate these services, thus:-

C - Clapham; H - Holloway; L - Camberwell; N - Norwood; P - Purley; T - Thornton Heath; S - Brixton Hill and Telford Avenue, Streatham; W - Wandsworth Depot.
(These code letters are my own reference and are not carried on the trams, which show a duty number plate only).

Destination blinds used on trams in South West London and on the Norwood and Croydon tram routes (1949):-

CLAPHAM DEPOT

S P E C I A L

WESTMINSTER

ELEPHANT & CASTLE

ST GEORGES CH

BLACKFRIARS

via Streatham
TOOTING BDWY
via Clapham

M A R I U S R D

CLAPHAM SOUTH STN

STOCKWELL STN

KENNINGTON

B R I X T O N

STREATHAM

SOUTHCROFT RD

W I M B L E D O N
via Tooting
M E R T O N

via Kennington & Westr
E M B A N K M E N T
via Elephant & Blackfrs

W O R K M A N

Depot
C L A P H A M
Common Stn

(Continued.....)

STREATHAM TOOTING
via Brixton
TOOTING STREATHAM
via Clapham
V I C T O R I A
via Streatham
TOOTING Amen Cr
via Clapham
CITY & SOUTHWARK

B R I X T O N R D

B L A C K F R I A R S
via Camberwell
KINGS RD CHELSEA
via Clapham
CAMBERWELL GRN
via Walworth Rd

L A T C H M E R E
Battersea Pk Rd

GROSVENOR RD

C L A P H A M
Junction

via Stockwell & Vauxhall
SAVOY ST STRAND

V A U X H A L L
Station

V I C T O R I A

QUEENSTOWN RD
Lavender Hill

STREATHAM DEPOT

S P E C I A L
PLOUGH CLAPHAM
SWAN STOCKWELL
KENNINGTON
ANGELL RD BRIXTON
BRIXTON STN
Water Lane
BRIXTON HILL
Depot
TELFORD AVENUE
STREATHAM LIBRY
N O R B U R Y
THORNTON HTH POND
C R O Y D O N
CROYDON & PURLEY
via Elephant & Blckfrs
E M B A N K M E N T
via Kennington & Westr
W O R K M A N
TOOTING STREATHAM
via Clapham
STREATHAM TOOTING
via Brixton
TOOTING BDWY
CITY & SOUTHWARK
via Brixton
ST GEORGES CH
via Brixton
SOUTHCROFT RD

(Continued......)

V I C T O R I A
WESTMINSTER
SAVOY ST STRAND
ELEPHANT & CASTLE
VAUXHALL STN
M A R I U S R D
via Stockwell & Vauxhall
SAVOY ST STRAND
NORWOOD DEPOT

(Note: The lettering shown in lower case in these lists above and to the left and on Pages 98-100, 157 & 159 actually appears in SMALL BLOCK LETTERS on the tramcar blinds; the LETTERING shown in CAPITALS IN these lists appears in LARGE BLOCK LETTERS on the tramcar blinds.)

(The L.C.C.T. used lower case to show routing - Via......... for some years from 1919, but soon reverted to SMALL CAPITALS as used on trams today).

NORWOOD DEPOT (Continued......)

SPECIAL
VAUXHALL STN
SWAN STOCKWELL
KENNINGTON
BRIXTON STN
VICTORIA
via Brixton
WEST NORWOOD
via Camberwell
WEST NORWOOD
via Westr & Brixton
MANOR HOUSE
via Westr & Essex Rd
WORKMAN
WESTMINSTER
CITY & SOUTHWARK
via Camberwell
ST GEORGES CH
SAVOY ST STRAND
via Kennington & Westr
BLOOMSBURY
NORWOOD DEPOT
HERNE HILL
CAMBERWELL GRN
ELEPHANT & CASTLE
Angel
ISLINGTON
Green
ALBION ROAD
BALLS POND RD

THORNTON HEATH DEPOT

SPECIAL
WESTMINSTER
BLACKFRIARS
SAVOY ST
STRAND
ELEPHANT
& CASTLE
KENNINGTON
ANGELL
ROAD
WATER LANE
BRIXTON
STATION
STREATHAM
LIBRARY
WORKMAN
via Elephant & Blckfrs
EMBANKMENT
via Kennington & Westr
COOMBE RD
CROYDON
& PURLEY
NORBURY
STATION
CROYDON
THORNTON
HEATH
RED DEER
THORNTON
HEATH POND
PURLEY DEPOT

This completes the story of the tramways of South London and Croydon up to December 1949. I wish to thank the London County Council, the Light Railway Transport League and the Tramway and Light Railway Society for making available certain information and photographs used in this survey, also the Local History Department of the Manor House Library, Lee, for their kind help.

POSTCRIPT (1954)

The passing of London's trams from its streets has not improved the passenger's lot. Cheap fares disappeared with the trams. 'Buses are unable to cope with rush-hour crowds and many tram passengers now use Southern Electric or cycle instead. Trams kept road traffic in order, but main roads have now become speedways for motor vehicles (which carry no lifeguards, unlike trams) and death-traps for pedestrians.

As a result, road accidents have increased and 'buses congest roads, drawing in and out of stopping places, endangering the lives of pedal cyclists. An eminent radiologist at Bristol has stated that soot coated with unburnt oil fuel emitted from diesel exhausts is a contributory cause of lung cancer, and today trunk routes are polluted with fumes.

All progress in passenger road travel in London during the 20th Century has vanished. People who want new transport routes are unlikely to get them for years. Tramcar design is far in advance of omnibus design. Blackpool's trams are far superior to any London 'bus; their latest streamline trams are silent, speedy and comfortable - fitted with fluorescent lighting and free from dirt, noise and smell.

It is ironical that Great Britain is one of the largest builders of electric tramcars, but most of these are for export. (This was true in 1954, but unfortunately no longer; in 1965 Germany, Czechoslovakia, Switzerland and Russia lead the tramway world). Political wrangling and vested interest have ousted the citizen's car - the electric tram - "the stately lighted galleon" of the Edwardian municipal planners - from many British streets. Yet the modern tram, designed to harmonise with urban traffic flow, is the only practical vehicle for road passenger trunk routes. The only hope of South London and Croydon (as far as transport is concerned) is the Southern Railway, unless the London County Council regain control of municipal transport, and, together with Croydon Corporation restore their tramways to their former glory.

K.G. Harvie,
Lee, Kent.